W9-BKS-800

The Making of the 20th Century

This series of specially commissioned titles focuses attention on significant and often controversial events and themes of world history in the present century. Each book provides sufficient narrative and explanation for the newcomer to the subject while offering, for more advanced study, detailed source-references and bibliographies, together with interpretation and reassessment in the light of recent scholarship.

In the choice of subjects there is a balance between breadth in some spheres and detail in others; between the essentially political and matters economic or social. The series cannot be a comprehensive account of everything that has happened in the twentieth century, but it provides a guide to recent research and explains something of the times of extraordinary change and complexity in which we live. It is directed in the main to students of contemporary history and international relations, but includes titles which are of direct relevance to courses in economics, sociology, politics and geography.

The Making of the 20th Century

Series Editor: GEOFFREY WARNER

Already published

David Armstrong, *The Rise of the International Organisation:
A Short History*
V. R. Berghahn, *Germany and the Approach of War in 1914*
Brian J. L. Berry, *Comparative Urbanisation: Divergent Paths
in the Twentieth Century*
Richard Bosworth, *Italy and the Approach of the First World War*
Peter Calvert, *Latin America: Internal Conflict and International Peace*
Anthony Harrison, *The Framework of Economic Activity: The International
Economy and the Rise of the State*
Desmond King-Hele, *The End of the Twentieth Century?*
Peter Mansfield, *The Ottoman Empire and its Successors*
Sally Marks, *The Illusion of Peace: International Relations in Europe
1918–1933*
A. J. Nicholls, *Weimar and the Rise of Hitler*
B. N. Pandey, *The Break-up of British India*
B. N. Pandey, *South and South-east Asia 1945–1979: Problems and Policies*
David Rees, *The Age of Containment: The Cold War*
Esmonde M. Robertson, *Mussolini as Empire-Builder*
Zara Steiner, *Britain and the Origins of the First World War*
Richard Storry, *Japan and the Decline of the West in Asia 1894–1942*
Christopher Thorne, *The Approach of War 1938–1939*
Hugh Tinker, *Race, Conflict and the International Order*
Wang Gungwu, *China and the World since 1949*
Ann Williams, *Britain and France in the Middle East and North Africa*
Elizabeth Wiskemann, *Fascism in Italy: Its Development and Influence*
R. T. Thomas, *Britain and Vichy: The Dilemma of Anglo-French
Relations 1940–1942*

Titles in preparation include

John Darwin, *Britain and Decolonisation 1945–1965*
John Fox, *Nazi Germany, The Great Powers and European Jewry
1933–1945*
Zdenek Kavan, *Soviet Policy in Eastern Europe since 1944*
Dominic Lieven, *Russia and the Origins of the First World War*
John Kieger, *France and the Origins of the First World War*

Italy and the Approach of the First World War

Richard Bosworth

St. Martin's Press   New York

All rights reserved. For information, write:
St. Martin's Press, Inc., 175 Fifth Avenue, New York, NY 10010
Printed in Hong Kong
First published in the United States of America in 1983

ISBN 0-312-43924-5

Library of Congress Cataloging in Publication Data

Bosworth, R. J. B.
    Italy and the approach of the First World War.
    (Making of the Twentieth Century Series)
    Bibliography: p.
    1. Italy—Politics and government—1870–1915.
2. Italy—Foreign relations—1870–1915. 3. World War, 1914–
1918—Italy. 4. World War, 1914–1918—Causes. I. Title. II.
Series: Making of the twentieth century.
DG568.5.B66   1983   945.08   82-16841
ISBN 0-312-43924-5

Contents

FOR EDMUND

Preface

An Italian immigrant recently arrived in Australia commented: 'For the first time, we had a taste of Australia – beach, fried chicken and flies, flies swarming all around us, we had to be careful not to eat them.'[1] An Australian demographer who was a key adviser to governments on an immigration programme after the Second World War wrote in 1948 that earlier Italian immigrants had found a place on the Queensland sugar fields: 'Here they were tolerated and even welcomed so long as they did not compete with white labour and white owners.'[2]

When I walk around the corner from my house near the University of Sydney, the shop-fronts tell me 'Macelleria', 'Pasticceria', 'Farmacia' and the rest. Australia is now the host to perhaps 500,000, perhaps 1,000,000 who are Italian or of Italian descent. But Italian emigration to Australia has not necessarily brought profound understanding between our two countries, as the two introductory quotations indicate.

Cliché and prejudice are also not unknown among scholars. When my earlier book, *Italy, the Least of the Great Powers* (Cambridge, 1979), was assessed in Italy, one reviewer found it necessary to define me as a 'kangaroo' of scholarship. For another, conservative historian, worried that I traduce Liberal Italy's 'always honourable and advantageous' foreign policy, it was important and significant that I was one of the 'democratic sons' of 'Botany Bay'.[3] Among my Anglo-Saxon friends, on the other hand, I am often regarded as a curious and recalcitrant lover of Italy.

In this context, my book has a triple purpose. First, my task has been to follow the pattern in this Macmillan series so well established by Z. S. Steiner and V. R. Berghahn. What does modern scholarship say about Italy's part in the causation of the First World War? To what extent can a 'primacy of internal politics' or a 'primacy of external politics' be located in the diplomacy of Liberal Italy?

There are other, more diffuse tasks as well. Often in the European history courses of Anglo-Saxon universities and in the English language historiography, Italy has been accorded a minor role. Some acknowledgement of Garibaldi, Cavour and Mazzini, a few bad jokes about Mussolini; and that has been enough. As an object of history modern Italy has been as far down the list of importance as Italians used to be lowly placed on the hierarchy of race.

But Italian history deserves fuller consideration. In modern times, so many -isms, nationalism, liberalism, fascism, Eurocommunism or Christian Democracy, have flowered first in Italy or have provided there the most stark examples of gaps between theory and practice, intent and achievement. Italy is also the 'nation' of so many obdurate regionalisms; its history is not that of Italy but of the Italies. In providing a relatively general analysis of the relatively ignored period before 1915, I hope to stimulate some of my English-language readers into discovering more of this story of contradiction and failure, survival and humanity, which is the history of Italy since the Risorgimento.

With regard to my Italian readers, I have a final task. I write as an outsider, inevitably ignorant, and inevitably without the passion and the plotting of politics which continues so to influence Italian historiography. At the same time, I can offer some knowledge of the wider context in which Italy was and is placed abroad, and some understanding of the international structure to which Italy has contributed.

A preface is a place in which to preach, and in which to offer thanks – thanks to my publishers for their courtesy and efficiency (and to Sarah Mahaffy for lunch in a London pub), to my family for their patience (though they do get to participate in trips to Italy), to my friends, and to that Italy in which this book was researched and written (and which even digested the fact of an Australian, temporarily lost for words, and his son playing cricket in a Venetian park).

RICHARD BOSWORTH
Venice and Sydney

1 Liberal Italy: Myths and Reality

The year 1911 was an important one in Italy. Fifty years had passed since the Risorgimento, and, throughout the length and breadth of the country, officials and politicians busied themselves in praise of the achievements of the Liberal regime. In March, Giovanni Giolitti, the representative statesman of the Liberal system, returned to become Prime Minister for the fourth time. His government offered radical domestic change, the nationalisation of Italy's largely foreign-owned insurance companies, and, great symbol of modernity, an electoral reform which would carry Italy a long way towards universal manhood suffrage. Italian liberalism, the Italian parliamentary system, it seemed, was acknowledging or accepting that the twentieth century was to be the age of the masses.

In September, Giolitti's government took another, different, step towards modernity. Italy invaded the Turkish territories of Tripoli and Cyrenaica, and began what would be her first victorious colonial war. She would now have what enthusiastic publicists nominated as her 'fourth shore'. Italy would no longer be curtailed by the Mediterranean. Instead it would be Italy which, from her 'four shores', embraced the Mediterranean, the sea which politicians, learned in the classics, already liked to call 'mare nostrum'. In attacking Libya, Italy had crossed the Rubicon on an 'Italian road to imperialism'.[1]

The circumstances of 1911 set the parameters within which historians have debated the character of Liberal Italy. On the one side stood domestic reform, liberalism of a variety which was all the more far-reaching politically given Italy's evident social poverty and backwardness. On the other side lay imperialism, war, foreign adventure, the classic policies by which ruling classes in some other European states had sought and were seeking to divert 'the terrible masses', to exploit nationalism in order to prevent socialism.

But a debate about Liberal Italy, and certainly about her foreign policy, can never operate merely by reference to Italian affairs. Italy was too weak and vulnerable a Great Power not to be constantly influenced by international events and developments. Again, the year 1911 provided examples of the problems and advantages which confronted Liberal Italy. Symbolic of these were two books with reference to Italy published that year by foreigners. One was an historical work, G. M. Trevelyan's *Garibaldi and the Making of Italy*. The other was Thomas Mann's great novel *Death in Venice*.

Trevelyan, most distinguished of English Whig historians, had begun to publish a trilogy on the Risorgimento in 1907. *Garibaldi and the Making of Italy* was the final volume, neatly timed for a market stimulated by Italy's fiftieth anniversary celebrations.[2] The trilogy's message was plain, if sentimental. The Risorgimento had been a 'good thing', or, as Trevelyan preferred to put it, a major advance on 'man's long march to civilisation'.[3] There was Garibaldi, the Hero, 'the rover of great spaces of land and sea, the fighter against desperate odds, the champion of the oppressed, the patriot, the humane and generous man all in one'.[4] But it was not only Garibaldi who moved Trevelyan's pen in fealty. There was also Italy, almost the Christ among nations: 'not dead but risen, . . . not the home of ghosts, but the land which the living share with their immortal ancestors'.[5]

The Italy of *Death in Venice* was not so much Christ as Barabbas, or rather some more menial and less robust thief. The Italians of Venice, who formed the backdrop for Aeschenbach's tortured exploration of his soul and sensuality, were cheats, rogues and liars, aiming to defraud more noble and sensitive tourists of their money and contentment, fawning when challenged, but always corrupting, and nurturing cholera, disease, the Evil which would cut down Aeschenbach.[6]

Italy of Beauty, Sunshine, Romantic Heroism, the Glorious Past; Italy of Poverty, Disease, Scandalous Corruption, and a feeble present; these were the common, and conflicting, images of tourists, visitors, 'lovers of Italy'. The young Adolf Hitler remarked that the Roman Empire was 'incomparable', and went on dreaming of constructing Nazi architecture to match that of Rome.[7] An English diplomat confessed in his memoirs that he had known no greater pleasure than visiting Paestum.[8] Bernhard von Bülow, with just a hint of the sinister or the naive, recalled that, for him, Venice was the best of all cities in which to relax.[9] An English tourist guide of 1905 advised its readers: 'It is . . . the sun that redeems modern Italy from a sort of vulgarity or the suspicion of a kind of hideous squalor'.[10] Russian revolutionaries in Capri and homosexuals resident there or

travelling further south agreed that Italians were so 'natural'.[11] One
lady visitor of independent means put it plainly enough: 'Civilisation, cleanliness and comfort are excellent things, but they are sworn
enemies to the picturesque'.[12]

There was thus an equivocation in the tourists' joy. Goethe knew
that he had reached Italy when he found a people who led 'the
careless life of a fool's paradise'. In Venice he pondered the need for
the urgent application of more stringent sanitary regulations. In
Rome his religiosity was offended by 'a sensual people'.[13] More
directly political comments were similarly condescending. The
correspondent of the London *Times*, Henry Wickham Steed, found
Rome a city of 'bedraggled untidiness' where 'public affairs seemed
to be managed and the game of politics to be played according to
other rules than those to which I had been accustomed'.[14] Even
G. M. Trevelyan confessed his belief that 'the comic element is never
long absent in Italy', and that the Italy of Iago (sic), St Francis and
Garibaldi was a place where 'materialism and idealism' were 'in
sharper contrast' than in England.[15]

Sometimes, tourist musings hardened into racial theoretics.
German *volkish* intellectuals foresaw for the German race a 'Latin'
enemy which encompassed not only France, but also the whole
inferior south.[16] Max Weber had discerned that Protestantism,
Capitalism and Progress lay on one side of the balance, and
Catholicism, Feudalism and Regression on the other. 'As every
employer knows', Weber reported, Italy's workers lacked conscien-
tiousness 'compared with Germany'. It was not so much that 'the *auri
sacra fames* of a Neapolitan cab-driver or *barcaiuolo*, and certainly of
Asiatic representatives of similar trades, as well as of craftsmen of
Southern European or Asiatic countries is, as anyone can find out for
himself, very much more intense, and especially more unscrupulous
than that of, say, an Englishman in similar circumstances'. It was
rather that something in the character of Italian, Southern European
and Asiatic societies which acts as 'one of the principal obstacles to
their capitalistic development'.[17] Maurice Barrès learned from his
journey there that Italy was 'a country full of magnificent aesthetic
attractions' but one 'designed for dilettantes who were a bit weak,
elegant and incapable of all effort', a place which condemned people
to 'sterility while leaving them the voluptuous pleasures'.[18] Hilaire
Belloc, himself a convert to Catholicism, put it more briefly and more
wittily:

Behold my child
The Nordic Man
And be as like
him as you can.
His legs are long;
his mind is slow
His hair is lank and made of tow.

And here we have the Alpine race
Oh! What a broad and foolish face!
His skin is of a dirty yellow
He is a most unpleasant fellow.

The most degraded of them all
Mediterranean we call.
His hair is crisp, and even curls,
And he is saucy with the girls.[19]

More testily Karl Marx on occasion exhibited a proper German sense of superiority in dismissing the pretensions of Italy's intellectualising socialists as 'lawyers without clients, doctors without knowledge or patients, billiard-playing students, commercial travellers and various more or less unsavoury journalists of the gutter press'.[20]

These popular racial stereotypes were in turn absorbed and repeated by politicians. Bismarck thought Italy a country with 'a large appetite and very poor teeth'.[21] Salisbury, with a more English knowledge of the operation of poor laws and vagabonds, declared Italy to be a nation of 'sturdy beggars'.[22] Even Captain Alfred Mahan, greatest of naval strategists, decided that Italy, naturally powerful by reason of geography and the proper mistress of Malta, Corsica and the Adriatic, was unlikely to be dominant in the Mediterranean during the forseeable future given her troubled history and 'other matters', by which he meant the quality which he discerned in her leadership and people.[23]

Most indicative of all was the way in which foreigners (and even Italians), in describing Italy, had recourse to metaphors of sexuality or of childhood and adolescence. The most famous example was Bülow's comment in January 1902 that the Triple Alliance could be prolonged harmoniously since

in a happy marriage the husband must not get violent if his wife ventures to dance an innocent *extratour* with another. The main thing is that she doesn't run away from him, and she won't do that as long as she is better off with him than with anyone else.[24]

Others reinforced this unflattering image. A blunt British ambassador, Sir Francis Bertie (whose nickname in London was 'the Bull'), noted peremptorily: 'Italy was like a woman with two lovers whose jealousy of each other she utilised for her own profit'.[25] An Italian politician seeking to justify Libyan ambitions in the summer of 1911 saw Italy as 'a young girl who at the moment of first love has made a vow of chastity; but this vow cannot last forever'.[26]

The metaphors of childhood were also readily coined. Salisbury thought 'quite small sugar plums' could keep Italy in England's camp;[27] the French were habituated to fraternal admonitions for their small Latin sister, and the excitation of the Nationalist Association was ascribed by many ambassadors as due to the 'growing pains' or 'hypersensitivity' of 'adolescence'. 'Young Italy' vied with the 'Third Rome' as a title of the Liberal state.

Such comments do not deserve to be dismissed with derision as mere period pieces. Foreigners continued to say much the same things about the Italy of Mussolini. *The Times* graciously forgave or understood the Matteotti murder on the grounds that 'homicide' was 'commoner' in Italy than in most other civilised states.[28] Even after the Second World War, the popularity abroad of the cynicism of Luigi Barzini junior owed something to traditional Anglo-Saxon convictions about Italian inferiority.[29]

Nor were Italians themselves immune from such theorising. The Milan newspaper, *Corriere della Sera*, reviewing *Manon*, the first major operatic success by Giacomo Puccini, declared that Puccini was 'worthy' since his 'genius is truly Italian. His song is the song of our paganism, of our artistic sensualism'.[30] Antonio Gramsci located an 'extreme egoism' among Italians 'from twenty to fifty years old'.[31] Many Italians self-consciously regretted that they were 'not an *orderly* and *organising* people but a disorderly and disorganising race'.[32]

These clichés and prejudices within Italy were usually wedded to regionalism and to the 'southern problem'. 'Africa', said 'northern' Italians, began at Bologna, Rome, Naples or Calabria depending on the birth-place of the speaker. A migrant to Australia from Udine, accused in a provincial Queensland town of belonging to the Black Hand, anxiously confided in his piously patriotic memoirs: 'I am not a Sicilian, and, as far as I knew, there were no Sicilians in Gympie'.[33] In the United States there was the story of northern Italian migrants who had refused to work with southern, saying: 'We don't want no Dago here'.[34]

In Italian universities, racial theorists bolstered popular beliefs with their research and reputations. The great criminologist, Cesare Lombroso, judged that, in southern Italy, there were more crimes of violence, whereas in the north crimes were directed against property, and that this difference had something to do with race. Indeed, so common and widespread was this northern racism, that southern experts like the Sicilians, Napoleone Colajanni and Gaetano Mosca, adduced their own proof that it was 'a very rash hypothesis to ascribe a superior morality to the peoples of the north as compared with the peoples of the south'.[35]

For the Italians of Liberal Italy, tourism and racism, both popular and learned, intermingled and influenced each other. The profits from tourism and the remittances of emigrants were Italy's major source of invisible earnings, and the reason why she avoided bankruptcy despite her continued balance-of-trade deficits. In 1910, tourism was estimated to bring into Italy about 450 million lire each year, from an estimated 900,000 visitors. Italian hotels, it was then confidently predicted, would keep improving and therefore the exchequer could probably look forward to a steady increase in the number of tourists and in the amount which they spent.[36]

Italy thus began to experience earlier and more completely than any other European nation what would become one of the great factors of the twentieth century, mass tourism. It was true that the visitors to Italy before the First World War were mainly genteel and were often temporary residents for extended periods, rather than practitioners of the package holiday or denizens of the holiday camp, but their insouciance or contempt for contemporary Italians, their ignorance and parochialism, were no less galling for all that. As a British publicist, in receipt of funds from the Italian government to reflect favourably on Italy, admitted baldly: 'To find an English resident in Italy who is not perpetually in a state of only semi-suppressed irritation with the Italians is a thing so rare as to be remarkable. "They are like children" is the stock criticism . . . '[37]

Italy's lowliness and humiliation were made public by foreign visitors in many fields. One was the familiar matter of language. Before 1800, Italian had been one of the great international languages, the language of opera and of all musical expression, the language of art criticism, and, on the shores of the Mediterranean, often the language of strategy and commerce, medicine and engineering.[38] When Australia's troops reached Cairo during the First World War, they found Italian the natural European language of local street hawkers.[39] The bureaucracy of the Roman Catholic Church, spread throughout the world, also conducted much of its business in Italian. Denis Mack Smith has written that Italian as a language in 1860 was out-distanced by French in Turin, Spanish in Naples, Sicily and Sardinia, and Latin in Rome;[40] but it is equally and ironically true that, before the nineteenth century, Italian was probably more widely and better known outside Italy than within.

As the nineteenth century progressed and Italy became, politically, a nation, the Italian language lost ground on an international level. By 1914 a foreign statesman who could comprehend any Italian was a *rara avis* indeed, and Italians like King Victor Emmanuel III, Sonnino or Mussolini who could speak a foreign language passably earned themselves an immediate and usually undeserved reputation abroad for sagacity, honesty and intellectual penetration. Asquith was delighted by Victor Emmanuel's English when they met,[41] and G. M. Trevelyan, from the King's command of English, drew the comforting conclusion that he was 'quiet and shy', with an 'English' manner which has 'oddly distinguished several of the makers of modern Italy'.[42]

This effortless foreign superiority, drawn from the 'knowledge' of tourism or the 'science' of race, produced in Italy an inevitable reaction. Indeed, a psychologist might want to call it 'reaction formation', that is, a rejection of the criticism which in turn took on the characteristics of the criticism. Edoardo Scarfoglio, the Neapolitan publicist, during the First World War, in a toast to Asquith, developed his venomous attack on the English as the people of 'five meals a day', who constantly exploited 'natives', be they in Italy or in the Empire.[43] Filippo Tommaso Marinetti, spokesman of the intellectual movement known as Futurism, declared that the best thing that could happen to 'beautiful' tourist Italy, to cities like Venice or Florence, to museums and art galleries, was that they should be razed by bombing or modern machines; and only then would Italy be able to live and to modernise.[44] Enrico Corradini, the first major philosopher of the Nationalist Association, developed the anti-racist, racist theory that Italy was a 'proletarian nation'. Rather than wasting her seed on a domestic class struggle, what Italy needed to plan and eventually to practise was war against the plutocratic and exploiting foreigners. Italy must learn to combat Austria and France, and even Germany and England.[45]

What is most ironical about these conflicting but interlocking images and prejudices is that they contained more than a grain of truth. Italy was a poor country. Italy was also the country where reputation and ambition coexisted most uneasily with military power and social reality.

Statistics confirmed the common prejudice that modern Italy was scarcely a Great Power. In population Italy was the least numerous of the major states; in 1910 having only some 35 million against Germany's 65 and Austria's 50. France, with an almost static population after 1860 (she had then 37.4 million to Italy's 25) was not surpassed until after the First World War. One reason why Italy's population remained the least among the Great Powers was the wastage, or 'haemorrhage' as some patriots liked to call it,[46] of emigration. Especially in the decade after 1900, Italian society went through the great emigrant phase which had already occurred in many other European societies. By 1914 the number of emigrants per annum was threatening to reach one million.[47] There were some limiting factors. Many emigrants did not leave Europe, but went merely to find work in more prosperous parts of the continent. Mussolini, for a time, lived in Switzerland and Rinaldo Rigola, the great trade union leader, spent some years working in France.[48] The United States became the most favoured destination for Italians after 1900, but even emigrants who dared to venture to such distant climes often left wives and children at home in their *paesi* and many times eventually returned, older and perhaps richer. The total population loss caused by emigration is thus highly debatable, and probably was no more than 4 or 5 million in the 50 years before 1914. Even assuming that birth-rates would not have been affected had the emigrants stayed at home and thus not propped up the Italian economy with their remittances, Italy in 1914 would have been still only the equal of France in population, and much less numerous than Germany or Great Britain.

Contrary to the belief held in some circles that Italians 'breed like rabbits', Italy had not proved an especially prolific nation. In a way, there is an odd parallel between Italy's failure to take-off industrially before 1914 (and before 1950), and her failure to achieve the population growth rates which had already occurred in Great Britain and Germany, and which were being attained in Russia.

Internal population growth occurred as unevenly within Italy as did emigration. The population of Turin, the city which in 1861 was mainly an administrative centre but which was becoming that of heavy industry, more than doubled from 205,000 (1861) to 427,000 (1911).[49] Milan, the city of smaller industry and banking, had a similar growth from 321,000 (1881) to 602,000 (1911).[50] Growing even faster was Rome, a city with almost no industry, the city of bureaucrats and government, which was, in 1870, little more than a provincial town of 226,000 (171,000 in 1850) but, by 1911, had grown to 617,000.[51] And, in that year of patriotic celebrations, still easily the largest Italian city was Naples, with a population of 709,000. Given that, despite certain governmental initiatives in the preceding decade, Naples was almost entirely a pre-industrial city, a city of cholera epidemics, saints and lotteries,[52] it should not be assumed too readily that Italian history in 1911 is a story of Fiat and industry, big banks and modern class struggle. Indeed, Italy's next largest city after the big four was Palermo, city of aristocracy, middle-men and the Mafia, where many ancient patterns had merely adapted themselves to the 'efficiency' of Piedmontese or Italian rule. In that city down to the twentieth century, one sentimental memoirist has recalled, street urchins could buy happiness from a *caramellaro*. He sold a big oval-shaped toffee and, for a *centesimo*, a boy could suck it until he was told to stop, whereupon another took his place.[53] Presumably this small survival of early modern society also did something to keep up the tuberculosis and hepatitis rates in Palermo.

On a more directly political level, Italy was very different from the other European states, in that its capital, Rome, did not have the industry, size, and historical dominance possessed by Paris or London or Vienna. Although there were some similarities to the court-created, bureaucratic cities of Berlin, Madrid or St Petersburg, Rome's relative importance within Italy was at a lower level than that of the other capitals. But once again, as so often in modern Italian history, this reality was paralleled by a myth. The myth of the Eternal City, the Rome of the empires of Caesar and Christ, was at times more significant and thus more real than what actually existed, a city for officials, middle-men and tourists, which was plagued by malaria from the undrained Pontine Marshes, growing uncertainly through the boom and bust of building speculation.[54] Italians, until 1945, were never able to shake off the myth of Rome.

If the very capital of Italy indicated a certain artificiality in the

Liberal regime, so too did the state of the Italian language. Literacy levels remained depressingly low. Despite considerable spending on education in the Giolittian decade, the official illiteracy rate in 1911 was 37.6 per cent. In the south the figures were much higher, for example in the poverty-stricken province of the Basilicata in 1907, 75 per cent of the population was admitted to be illiterate.[55] Throughout the peninsula, female illiteracy levels were extreme and in some regions and classes almost total.

But the struggle against illiteracy was only part of the problem. Many a literate who could sign his name and, after his training as a conscript soldier, understood military commands in Italian, remained not so much an Italian as a member of his *paese* and spoke for comfort and communication its dialect. Even Fascism's allegedly totalitarian centralisation of language did little to extirpate local dialects. An English anthropologist working in the Basilicata in the 1960s reported that villagers thought his English might be a *patois* with a similar relationship to 'Florentine' (i.e. Italian) as theirs.[56] In the 1950s another anthropologist analysed the life of villagers in Lucania, who, self-contained in their *paesi*, had continued to speak *grico*, a dialect of Byzantine Greek which they had brought across the Adriatic seven or eight centuries before.[57] Earlier, Cavour himself had made the ironical boast, 'Je suis italien avant tout', in French.[58]

As, after 1860, Liberal Italy imposed a centralising administrative system on an intensely regionalised country, the problem of contact between government officials and *paesani* was often one of mutual incomprehension in the most literal sense. Even when the language or dialect was known, the local culture might not be mastered. Franchetti and Sonnino, in their famous investigation into conditions in Sicily (1876), remarked that *carabinieri* not only usually could not understand Sicilian dialects but were totally at a loss to discern what a Sicilian could convey by glance or gesture.[59]

Italy was still in 1914 very much an agricultural country. In 1911 agriculture provided 55 per cent of the gross national product.[60] Many of the cities and large towns of Italy were agricultural or traditional urban centres. Much of the south was dotted with large towns, such as the famous Canicatti, the place which northerners liked to mention when they wanted the proverbial reference expressed by English as Timbuctoo. Southerners lived in this or other agro-towns not because there was industry there, but because a modicum of personal safety was provided in the urban womb away from the perils of the Mafia or bandits, the landowner's bully boys or the *carabinieri*.[61]

Agricultural conditions in Italy rarely allowed much cause for enthusiasm or romance. Peasants struggled to survive and to be productive against numerous obstacles. Except in the Po Valley in the north, Italy was ruggedly mountainous and barren. The total land area available for productive agriculture was about a quarter that of France. Rain fell sporadically or was concentrated in the one season. The short streams of southern Italy were called 'torrenti' and torrents they were when it rained, though they were stonily dry when it did not. The Italian peninsula was also a prey to natural disasters. Etna, Stromboli and Vesuvius were Europe's only non-dormant volcanoes. However picturesque for tourists, and however much, in the short term, Vesuvius enriched the plain around Naples and Etna the plain around Catania, the volcanoes were also fearfully destructive. Catania was almost razed in 1693, and smaller eruptions continued to encourage peasants to believe the obvious – that mortality was a brief and fragile span. More terrifying than volcanoes were earthquakes, called by publicists the 'scourge of the peninsula', and afflicting parts of Italy continually. Messina, for example, suffered serious earthquake damage 21 times in 125 years[62] before the great earthquake of 28 December 1908 which tumbled the city to the ground: 100,000 people died. Croce, Salvemini and Silone, three of Italy's major intellectuals in the twentieth century, had all lost members of their family in natural disasters. Government officials did take notice when there was a major calamity, but property damage or the death of five or ten people in a *paese* was regarded as one of the hazards of life for the poor in the south, and was recorded as a statistic as were deaths from pellagra or dysentery. The resentment of *paesani* against the city, its government and officials was well, if horrifically, evidenced in the days after the Messina earthquake. Then, it seems, mountain men from the hinterland, their own villages ruined, came down to the stricken city, without government services or police, in order to pillage it. Northern reporters claimed that these 'Italians' were willing to slice off a still-living hand in order to carry off a gold wedding ring, even when the hand was trying to scrabble free from the debris or despairingly to summon help.[63]

Man-made disasters included the Mafia in western Sicily and banditry in Calabria and Sardinia. The Mafia grew and flourished as a sort of anarcho-feudalist alternate system of government in the area around Palermo, nearer to the people (and the landowners) in language and culture, and perhaps sometimes less corrupt, than were government officials. Eric Hobsbawm has romanticised bandits as heroic peasant-revolutionaries,[64] but the reality was more simple, more equivocal and more sordid. The most notorious bandit in the pre-1914 period was the Calabrian, Musolino. From January 1899 to October 1901, he survived brutal and inept government attempts at capture and earned a local reputation as 'a mixture of a Scottish Bardo and a Robin Hood'.[65] Musolino maintained that he never murdered, but merely killed spies and stool-pigeons, and that he was 'a man of honour'. The debate on his character was carried into intellectual circles by Lombroso who declared that Musolino was an example of the racial inferiority of Calabrians, and was in turn attacked by Colajanni, who saw Musolino as persecuted and misunderstood, almost as a noble savage.[66] The most recent student of the Musolino affair, the socialist, Cingari, does not share the sentimentality of Colajanni and Hobsbawm, and notes that Musolino only forebore to oppress the poor because of *omertà*, that unspoken understanding which existed between a bandit and the landowners' armed guards, who wanted the pillaging of the poor to remain their own preserve. The nicest tale of the whole affair is of an inn-keeper from Aspromonte who thought that, all in all, the pursuit of Musolino had been a good thing: 'With him, we got the telegraph'.[67]

In these circumstances, human and natural, it is not surprising that Italian agricultural productivity was low, nearer the figures for Russia or Spain than for Germany or England. It was also erratic, and vulnerable to events. After the bad season of 1897, for example, the Italian harvest was 32.67 per cent less than it had been the year before. England, afflicted by bad climatic conditions at the same time but with a much more organised and modernised agricultural structure, suffered a reduction of only 3.5 per cent.[68] In 1914 Italy also had a poor harvest, 10 per cent down on the year before, and this was a major discouragement to a too precipitous Italian entry into the First World War. In some parts of Italy that autumn, only a few weeks, grain supplies survived. Even though Riccardo Bachi, Italy's most zealous contemporary economic analyst, had claimed in 1913 that agriculture was 'the most serious and vital among the varieties of economic activity in Italy',[69] none the less agricultural production did not allow Italy to feed herself. Instead she too, in ironical parallel to the much more industrialised Great Britain, was dependent on imports of food, notably from Russia and Argentina.

Italian agriculture was poor overall, but it was also varied. The characteristic worker on the land was the *bracciante*, the landless labourer who could be found both in the Po Valley around Ferrara and Reggio Emilia and also in the *latifondi*, the great estates of the South and Sicily. He had lived an almost biblical life, standing in the square of his *paese* waiting for his hire and, even in the relatively prosperous Romagna, able to expect employment for only about 180 days per year.[70] After 1900, especially in the north, this life-style began to change a little as *braccianti* joined the great socialist peasant union, Federterra. Its membership rapidly surpassed 250,000, although a tendency to split always existed between the *braccianti* and other types of peasants.[71] A socialist peasant union had also been immediately countered by landowner groups. In 1901 the Lega fra i possidenti ferraresi was founded,[72] and in 1911 regional groups united into the National Confederation of Agriculture, although this body too preserved an uneasy unity.[73]

The problem was that agrarian Italy was certainly not divided neatly into rival classes of landowners and landless peasants. Pied-montese agriculture, much cherished by Giolitti himself, flourished in the decades after the 1880s when small specialist landowners developed the wine industry, for example around Asti.[74] In Tuscany, the ancient system of share-cropping was common, and was praised by conservatives such as Sonnino as the ideal way in which to construct a sound modern age, a sort of yeoman Italy.[75] Even the addition of these two further categories schematises Italian agriculture far too tidily. Ownership and productivity, political sophistication and interest, varied regionally and within regions. A detailed study of agriculture in the Bari province around 1900 has drawn a picture of great diversity. In the Capitanata in 1904 it was reported: 'Here the soil is scratched with a plough Adam would have known, sown and [then] one puts one's trust in Providence'. Yet, in other parts of the province, there were some modern attempts at semi-capitalist wine production, although these suffered from competition and disease, and increased the devastation of the region by encouraging further deforestation. Most of 49,000 hectares of forest in the Bari province in 1870 had been cut down and not replaced by 1913.[76]

Moreover peasants themselves stubbornly defied neat sociological categorisation. Many were *braccianti* and small landowners at the same time, possessors of a tiny, arid plot, or pieces of tiny, arid plots (*minifundi*) in the hinterland of their *paese*. Anthropological work on inheritance practices has indicated just how extraordinarily complex, and how extraordinarily woven together, pre-capitalist agriculture, ownership and production were.[77]

In spite of these complexities, is it possible to locate an agrarian interest heavily influencing the politics of Liberal Italy? Sometimes it is assumed that the politics of Giolittian Italy were, at root, a *connubio* between northern industrialists and southern landowners. The tax on grain and the special trading arrangements reached with Germany, Switzerland and Austria after 1900 to be the markets for Italian wines and fruits are cited as examples of this pro-agrarian policy.[78] Similarly significant is the failure of reform efforts, such as the Zanardelli investigation into the Basilicata, to grasp the nettle and dispossess inefficient landowners instead of merely exhorting them to abandon their *spagnolismo* and continuing to allow government 'public works' monies to fall into their pockets.[79] Yet, often the evidence for a coherent policy, let alone a conspiracy, is doubtful or forced, and the differences between the various landed interests remain as important as their similarities.

It is wise not to forget, however, that Liberal Italy was an agricultural country, and especially in the south, a country of great poverty. It was still a country of wooden ploughs, of disease, of a pre-modern world where in Sicily, in 1876, Franchetti and Sonnino prepared, with secrecy and an armed escort, to undertake what they called 'a journey into the interior', almost as if they were penetrating the Zambesi or the Juba.[80] Italy was still the country where, in the whole region of the Basilicata in 1907, there were only three unions with 242 members;[81] the country where, in prosperous and relatively developed Ferrara, in 1914 the average factory employed seven workers.[82]

Despite this, much of the debate about Giolittian Italy and the approach of war centres around the role of industry and big business in Italian politics and society. One major discussion is linked to the Romeo–Gramsci dispute on the character and effect of the Risorgimento.[83] In a series of articles from 1956, collected under the title *Risorgimento e capitalismo*,[84] Romeo attacked what was becoming the prevailing Marxist or Gramscian orthodoxy that the Risorgimento had been a *rivoluzione mancata*, a political but not a social change, bringing no benefit to ordinary Italians. Instead,

Romeo argued, an agrarian revolution in the Italy of the 1850s was either impossible or would have been regressive and hindered Italy's chances of industrialising, and thus of achieving major economic growth.

But Romeo's own work was in turn challenged by the research of Alexander Gerschenkron and others, who looked in detail at the figures of the Italian 'spurt forward' after 1897 to point out that pre-1914 Italy, although achieving some development, did not 'take-off' as might have been predicted in the classic model of an industrial revolution.[85] Italian iron and steel production figures, from 1896 to 1913 for example, actually fell relative to the results achieved by the other Great Powers except Great Britain.[86]

Recently, the American historian, Richard Webster, has added a new dimension to the economic debate which has linked it directly to foreign affairs. Webster has argued that, after the bad year of 1907, Italian industrial production fell steadily into crisis. The victim of unscrupulous competition, notably from German dumping, Italian industry underwent rapid concentration and thereupon reacted to crisis following the classic imperialist model. At home, industrialists campaigned for greater repression of socialists and unions, and sought to sweeten the pill politically, and to gain commercial advantages for themselves, by linking domestic law and order to an expansionist foreign policy. Thus, Giolittian Italy, according to Webster, possessed a 'military-industrial complex' which drove Italy along a course to imperialism and war, similar to the one followed by Imperial Germany.[87] But Webster pushes his evidence further than can be justified.

What then was the character of Italian industry in the Giolittian years from 1900 to 1915? In general terms there can be no doubt that it was a period of growth greater than that achieved by modern Italy at any period prior to the foundation of the Republic. There were major advances in very modern sectors. For example, Italy became one of the pioneers in developing hydro-electricity, and her total production of electric energy rose from 100 million kilowatt hours in 1900 to 3000 million in 1914.[88] In Turin, and especially in the Fiat concern of Giovanni Agnelli, the automobile and its associated industries began to prosper. By 1911, 6500 workers were employed in the car industry of Turin, and in 1914 Fiat alone produced 3236 units.[89] Export competition was severe both within Europe and especially from the United States, but Agnelli had been across the

Atlantic and had understood the challenge. After 1912 he preached
the principles of Taylorism both within his own factories and to the
other industrialists of Turin.[90] The industrial growth also brought
some benefit to workers employed in industry. There is dispute about
the reliability of the figures, but real wages rose perhaps 25 per cent in
the decade before 1913.[91] Similarly, in the more enlightened
municipalities, notably in Turin under the mayor, Senator Frola, a
friend and associate of Giolitti, there was a marked expansion of
municipal works, public transport and sanitation. Municipal
expenditure in Turin doubled from 1899 to 1909.[92] The state itself
took over the running of the national railway system in 1905[93] and the
insurance industry, which had been half foreign-owned, in 1912.

Italian banking had also become more sound and enterprising after
the disasters of the Banca Romana scandal in 1893–4. Then,
corruption, incompetence and traditionalism had threatened Italy
with bankruptcy, but in the years which followed, advised especially
by German expertise, the Italian banking system was reconstructed
on modern investment lines. Under its director Otto Joel, a German
Jew but naturalised Italian, and his cousin Giuseppe Toeplitz, the
Banca Commerciale became the smoothly efficient financial engine of
the Giolittian system. Other banks, the Credito Italiano, the state-
financed Banca d'Italia which was founded in 1893, and the Banco di
Roma, repository of much of the Vatican's money and sometimes
prone to unwise speculation, established themselves, and nurtured
their commercial investments both within Italy and, increasingly,
abroad.

The soundness and modernity of Italy's financial system should
not be exaggerated. Scarred by the crisis of the 1890s, most investors
were cautious, and preferred to lend their money to the developing
system of co-operatives and of Catholic rural and regional banks,[94] or
simply to purchase low-yielding state bonds. In 1913 over three-
quarters of all private Italian deposits were held by small local banks
and co-operatives.[95] Italian capitalists continued to bewail the reluct-
ance of their fellow citizens to risk investment capital. Italian business
thus was perennially open to foreign investment, especially from
France and Belgium, although such foreign 'aid' sometimes caused
resentment and exacerbated the patriotic inferiority complex.[96]

Nor was the history of Italian industrial development in 1900–14
one of unbroken success. The year 1907 was particularly bad.
Twenty-seven car-makers failed in Turin, and Fiat itself was only

saved from disaster by the government-fostered tardiness of the legal system to investigate deficiencies in the company's books.[97] After 1907 there was a return to growth, but it was inconsistent, and in 1914 there were new signs of crisis in an economy which was exhibiting a major inability to adjust to the economic effects of the end of the Libyan war. Riccardo Bacchi's report for that year was most pessimistic about the future prospects of Italian prosperity.[98]

Despite its successes, Italian industrial growth was predicated on unsafe ground. At the very base Italy, despite her achievements in hydro-electricity, was unable to supply her own energy needs. The Italian peninsula was weak in the sinews of industry as it was barren for the seeds of agriculture. Of coal resources Italy had virtually none, being dependent on imports especially from Great Britain. In 1910 Italy drew 87.6 per cent of her energy needs from coal, against 3.4 per cent from hydro-electricity and 2.3 per cent from oil.[99] Italy was notably backward in showing an interest in the new technology of oil. Her own production at home was, on a world table, ahead only of New Zealand,[100] and oil was certainly not a motive for Italy's interest in Asia Minor or Libya. Over 30 years of colonial ownership were not to lead Italy into developing Libya's oil resources, even though some part of them was known to Italian experts.[101] At the end of the Fascist period, the major mineral resource being exploited in Libya was salt.

Italy did possess some iron, especially on the island of Elba. There, after 1899, was built the Ilva plant which encouraged an increase in steel production from an annual average of 88,000 tons in 1896–1900 to 796,000 (1909–13).[102] But, overall, Italy remained a tardy developer of what minerals she did possess.[103] The Elba site in its exposed position off the coast, and dependent on the tiny port of Porto Ferraio, was unsafe strategically. A reliance on coal imports and the vulnerability of the Elba concern (as well as rival factories similarly placed on the coast at Piombino and Bagnoli) to naval power were excellent reasons why very few Italian politicians ever dreamed of breaking the 'traditional friendship' with Great Britain. In 1915 food and clothing products took up 60 per cent of Italy's manufacturing output.[104] The organiser of the Italian war effort after 1915 would complain bitterly that the entire national steel industry was 'fictitious'.[105]

Unlike Germany, Italy had not accepted that industrialisation must be linked to technical and commercial education. It is characteristic that Italy, before 1914, failed to innovate or develop far in the new chemical industries. (Marconi was an inventor of fame and achievement, but he enjoyed quick and cherished financial success and had few pupils or emulators within Italy.)[106] Italy's triumphs in hydro-electricity relied, to a marked degree, on German and Swiss expertise.[107] The education system of Liberal Italy trained lawyers and state officials, the characteristic university degree being in *giurisprudenza*.[108] The ability to quote Dante with feeling and aptness was regarded by most as more important than mastery of mathematics or physics. Italian libraries were very poor. Regional sensibilities required four 'National' libraries in Turin, Florence, Rome and Naples. In 1909 the Biblioteca Nazionale Vittorio Emanuele in Rome was reported to be in chaos: its holdings were uncatalogued, it had no settled acquisitions policy and its books were being stolen. There had been some improvements in local lending libraries. In Milan in 1908 over 200,000 volumes were lent out, mainly to workers seeking self-education, but as always there were tremendous regional variations. The University of Sassari library was reported to possess not even good dictionaries.[109] Although Italian socialism was almost painfully earnest in its invocation of self-education, and achieved much in that field, Catholicism had never surrendered its hegemonic influence over the education of the young and of women. The formal anticlericalism of the Italian state had made only the most half-hearted efforts to build lay education.

If education did little to mobilise men's minds for industrial growth, Italy's transport system imposed additional constraints: it blocked an easy exchange of goods, and hindered construction of a rapid and modern structure of military defence. Mussolini's later boast that Fascism made the trains run on time owed something to the devastation wreaked by the war. But the railways of Giolittian Italy were also not altogether satisfactory. In the south, they were often absent altogether. A 'massive' railway building scheme in the Basilicata under Giolitti managed to increase the total kilometrage in the region from 337 (1902) to 353km (1914).[110] Southern railways were almost all single-track, and with lines that ran capriciously across the countryside, passing stations set still more capriciously in open fields, far from the towns which they professed to serve.[111] In the 1960s an anthropologist found inhabitants of a southern *paese* who had never gone sufficiently far afield to visit their town railway station.[112] In the north the lines were better, although there too they were often single-track, and electrification had begun only on a few lines around Milan.[113] Strategically the railways were highly vulnerable, running down the very edge of the Tyrrhenian and Adriatic coasts, and constituted a sitting target for any superior navy.

Italy's ports were neither safe nor well-modernised. The most productive and important was Genoa, but there was located the very efficient and combative Seamen's Union, the Gente del Mare. In the decade after 1900 Giolitti spent much time ensuring the peaceful operation of the port of Genoa,[114] but, late in 1914, it was characteristic and predictable that food, badly needed because of harvest failure, and coal, acquired with difficulty in the dislocation of war, stock-piled on Genoese wharves because of strikes and inefficiency at the port, and because of the malfunctioning of the railway system leading north to Milan and Turin.[115]

The most noteworthy political step taken by Italian industrialists in the decade before 1914 was the foundation of a national employers' organisation, Confindustria, in 1910. The idea of a united employer group had gradually developed from the pattern of events both abroad (especially in Germany) and within Italy itself. In 1901 the ship-building and other heavy industries around Genoa grouped themselves into the Consorzio Industriale Ligure. In 1902 there was established the Federazione fra gli industriali di Monza. A more direct impulse came from the automobile and other new machine industries in Turin. There, in 1906, a Lega Industriale was founded which was widened into Confindustria in 1910. Leading members among Turin industrialists were Agnelli; Gino Olivetti, who acted as its enthusiastic secretary; Luigi Bonnefon Craponne, a French citizen who had interests in Piedmontese silk and banking concerns; and Dante Ferraris, prominent in many of the industries of Turin (he was deputy director of Fiat) and a patron of the Nationalist Association.[116]

The full influence of the world of commerce and finance on the making of Italian foreign policy will be discussed throughout this book, but it is important initially to warn that there were many limitations to Confindustria's strength and unanimity. Despite its efforts to attract small industrialists, Confindustria was basically the mouthpiece of the newer and large-scale industries. Regionally its power was centred in Turin and, to a lesser extent, in Lombardy and Liguria. Limited politically by a dislike of socialists, at least extreme ones, strikes, and Romans (Agnelli damned the last as 'courtiers, professors and public functionaries') who interfered in the ordered process and profits of business and blocked the achievement of productive elements in society,[117] Confindustria's unity hid many different shades of political and social opinion.

If, in Confindustria, there were currents moving towards Fascism, there were other streams which still ran directly from older traditions. One example was the textile industry of Lanerossi around Vicenza. There, in the Catholic Veneto, had occurred the success of Alessandro Rossi (1819–98). A part of Rossi's social ideology prefigured the Catholic corporatism of the 1920s, but he also preserved the concepts of paternal charity, and of small factories with boss and workforce remaining close to the soil, to the region and to the *paese*.[118] Elsewhere in Italy it did not take a capitalist's ideology to create this situation, since most Italian 'industry' was essentially that of the artisan and the family.

There was one more factor *sui generis* in the character and role of Italian business before 1914. Despite the adjective 'Liberal', Italian entrepreneurs (since the time of Cavour) had often worked in close association with the state, and expected protection, feather-bedding and subsidies from it. If some of Italian industry carried the seeds of Fascism, other elements of it, both Catholic and lay, bore promise of that curious variety of state capitalism which was differentiated the Italian economy from others since 1945.[119] Before 1914 what this meant, in the shipping industry for example, especially the Società di Navigazione Generale Italiana, or in the iron and steel works of Elba and the inland centre of Terni,[120] was a combination of 'corruption', the financial interpenetration of business and politics, and of caution, a hostility towards unnecessary speculation when safe profits could be expected from the state. In a way, this element of Italian business was the equivalent of the reluctant small investor who preferred a meagre but certain dividend to capitalist gain, and perhaps loss. Historians who find an industrialist-propelled Italian imperialism before 1914 stretch the evidence. More characteristic of Liberal Italy was the complaint made by Antonino Di San Giuliano, the aristocratic, Sicilian landowner who was Italy's Foreign Minister in 1910–14, that Big Business, which ought to be the 'secular arm'[121] of an expansionist foreign policy, was feeble in its own efforts, and needed more blood and finance to flow from the heart of the government before it would be an effective champion of the Third Italy. Indeed politicians of many persuasions in Liberal Italy were more 'modern' than were businessmen in their insistence, both in foreign and domestic affairs, that 'finance is *the* question of our times'.[122]

What was the character of this political world, of the institutions of Liberal Italy before 1914? Once again, the answer is very much *sui generis* that Italy was a parochial country, with its own systems and nature, very different from its neighbours, although influenced by them. Legally, Italy was a monarchy. Article 5 of the constitution gave the King formal control over foreign affairs and all military matters. However, the practice of kingship since the Risorgimento had curtailed the open power exercised by a monarch. After the assassination of Umberto I in 1900, King Victor Emmanuel was a much more constitutional ruler than were, for example, Francis Joseph in Austria–Hungary, or the Popes in their temporal or spiritual kingdom. Mainly, this was a matter of temperament. Victor Emmanuel was the very antithesis of an exuberant, superficially emotional southerner. He found any requisite psychological satisfaction in his coin collection, and in his bourgeois family life. His wife was loved by publicists for her charitable works and by her husband for her home-made blackberry jam.[123] A tiny man, who did not 'look a king', Victor Emmanuel had been married, in 1897, to the tall and strapping Elena of Montenegro 'for the good of the dynasty'. His strongest political feelings, if they may be called such, were his hatred of his handsome cousin, the Duke of Aosta, his dislike of his reactionary mother, Margherita (who had been particularly disgusted when Elena chose herself to nurse her infant son),[124] and his detestation of the Church. Victor Emmanuel was proud to be called a *mangiapreti*, and rarely went to mass. He let it be known that he ate meat on Fridays and when, finally, in 1939, he was persuaded to visit the Vatican, refused to kneel or kiss the papal ring.[125] Similarly the King was cynical and sarcastic towards soldiers and diplomats and must have been delighted by San Giuliano's comment in the last stage of the planning of the Libyan war that September was a good moment to act since the ambassadors were still out of town and it was easy to gull 'a simple *chargé d'affaire*'.[126] The Queen Mother was known to be derisive of parliamentary institutions and to think that the best socialists were dead ones. But Victor Emmanuel himself usually only gave advice, not altogether unintelligently, when asked, and confined his politics to pedantry (he liked to record errors in newspapers) and to malice.[127]

If monarchical tradition was to be looked for in Italy, then it was really to be found *in pectore*, in the great opposition court to the

Liberal state, that of the Vatican, the Roman Catholic Church. Italy had been united against the will of the Church, and had seized the temporal territories ruled by the papal monarchy. Until the First World War, both the Church and Italy remained uncertain that the lay victory had been a lasting one. In 1897 Pope Leo XIII still referred to 'some countries of Italy'.[128] The Italian government, in 1899, worked hard to prevent the Vatican being recognised as a legitimate member of the Hague Peace Conference, and in 1914–15 remained most anxious that the Vatican be excluded from any possible peace conference, lest the Church push irredentist pretensions to Rome.[129] Had the Central Powers won the First World War, it is conceivable that they would have restored the losses of the Church, at least those of 1870. Domestically, for a time, there was a serious contest between clericalism and anti-clericalism in Liberal Italy. As late as 1911, the Church was still anathemising as an evil 'son of Shem' Ernesto Nathan, the Jew, Free Mason and Giolittian, who was mayor of Rome.[130] In the repression of 1898, the Army was almost as inclined to shoot Catholic 'subversives' as it was socialist ones.[131]

Yet, there were many other indications of a *ralliement* between Liberal state and Church in pre-1914 Italy. These appeared first abroad. From the 1880s Catholic missionaries and state officials collaborated in defending what Giovanni Battista Scalabrini, the Bishop of Piacenza, described neatly as 'religione e patria'. The Africanism of the 1890s found favour with at least some churchmen. One Italian missionary in Eritrea was described as being 'ferociously intransigent towards Protestant missions and similarly of not very Christian sentiments towards those of French Catholics . . . with a long beard, [dressed] in a white but not sparklingly clean robe, with a crucifix in one hand and a Virginia cigar in the other, ready for any risk'.[132] In the 1900s, especially while the clerical Tommaso Tittoni was Foreign Minister, a marriage of interest flourished in the field of economic imperialism in Libya, Ethiopia and Asia Minor. *Osservatore Romano* began to say that there was nothing regrettable in the idea that Italy should mimic the Roman Empire,[133] and many churchmen applauded the sentiments of the Italian Foreign Minister who stated: 'When Italian interests abroad are involved the only permissible -ism is patriotism'.[134] At home, too, the grounds for collaboration grew. The Church was involved in finance, both national and regional; the Church was also involved in the social question. By 1912 there were 817,034 organised workers in Italy, and 104,614 of them were

enrolled in 'white' Catholic unions, both industrial and agrarian.[135]
Giolitti, cool and sceptical, remained loyal to Cavour's concept of a
'free Church in a free State', the two being 'parallels which would not
meet'. But he was also realistic enough to accept and favour increased
Catholic participation in politics, culminating in the Gentiloni pact of
1913 whereby Catholic votes were to be swung behind non-socialist
candidates in the elections being held under the new suffrage. A
certain equivocation in the Church's relationship with liberalism was
evident in that Catholic votes aided most the candidates of the
Nationalists and of conservatives critical of Giolittian compromises
rather than orthodox Giolittians.[136]

Any analysis of the structures of Liberal Italy must end with the
characteristic institution of liberalism, that is Parliament. There have
been many sophisticated studies seeking to unravel the web of power
in Liberal Italy. Some have detected monopoly capital at the centre of
the system. Others have concentrated instead on the personality of
Giovanni Giolitti, and remembered either the contemporary statement that he was 'a dictator', or the later statement that he played
'John the Baptist' for the Mussolini 'Christ'.[137] Others have
underlined the power or potential of the Army, or the bureaucracy,
or the Free Masons,[138] or the landowners. Almost all historians have
remarked on the gap between 'legal' Italy, the political world, and
'real' Italy, society at large. Within the limitations created by that
gap, there can be little doubt that Giolittian Italy was governed by
parliamentary institutions, even if again they were institutions *sui
generis*. Big Business, the Army, the Church, the Monarchy, the Free
Masons and landowners, and even the bureaucracy, acknowledged
this fact. In looking at comparisons with foreign systems, Italians
usually admitted that Italy was more akin to France or to Britain than
it was to Germany or Austria or Russia. Optimists decided that Italy
was in a golden age of parliamentarism; pessimists bewailed that
Italian institutions were sinking from the high standards attained by
Cavour or Gladstone.[139] D'Annunzio scorned the Chamber of
Deputies as a 'third-rate club',[140] but not so much because of its
powerlessness as its failure to savour the full bloom of his prose style.
Luigi Barzini senior, visiting Tsarist Russia by car during the famous
Peking-to-Paris car race in 1907, at once noted that Russia was
autocratic, a country of emperor and priests, soldiers and prisons,
which did not know the freedoms of the Liberal parliamentary
system.[141]

But what was this Parliament, how did it have any relationship with Italian society, and how did it exercise power? Italy had a bicameral system. By far the weaker of the two houses was the Senate, a body formally nominated by the King, but, in practice, consisting of distinguished intellectuals, retired diplomats and generals, and politicians whose careers had taken a turn for the worse. The Senate had no limit on the number of its membership, but most senators rarely attended. An attempt at reform in 1910–11, which discussed making the Senate elective, was aborted, and the upper house continued to lack either the political significance of the French Senate or the traditional prestige of the British House of Lords.

The real centre of power was the Chamber of Deputies.[142] Not that it followed the rules of an Anglo-Saxon party system. Only the socialists were anything like a party in the Anglo-Saxon sense, and even they were split into factions. The Nationalists before 1914 dreamed of becoming some sort of new conservative movement, but in the 1913 elections they only won five seats. Instead, deputies grouped themselves around important political figures or could change their position, be 'transformed', according to local interest, despite their formal allegiances as republicans, radicals, liberals or conservative liberals. In reporting elections, the press often simplified matters sensibly by describing candidates as being for the government, for the 'constitutional opposition', or 'extremists'.

To become a deputy a candidate, who was likely to be a lawyer or journalist, very unlikely to be a businessman or worker and certain not to be a peasant, needed usually to be well-regarded by the local bureaucracy – prefect, *questore* and *maresciallo* of the *carabinieri*. Under the very restricted suffrage existing before 1912, when only some 7 per cent of the population were eligible to vote, governments seldom lost elections. A local political power base was built on family and business relationships and on an interest in the local press, Italy being a country of many small and intensely parochial local newspapers. The example of the career of Marcello Soleri, one of Giolitti's bright young men, will suffice. Soleri, from respectable middle-class stock in Cuneo, took a law degree at Turin before returning home to work in the local administration. In that capacity he met Giolitti, whom he impressed, married a general's daughter, and, in 1911, launched a 'democratic liberal' paper, *Corriere subalpino*, polemicising against the existing liberal paper, *Sentinella delle Alpi*. That publication was owned by Tancredi Galimberti, the current representative of Cuneo in the

Chamber of Deputies, and a man who had begun to flirt with clerical and other opponents of Giolitti. Soleri became the *sindaco* (mayor) of Cuneo in 1912, fought hard to get his city a new railway station further up the hillside, and, in 1913, with Giolitti's staunch intervention in his favour, was elected to the Chamber.[143]

Usually, then, political success flowed from governmental sympathy. But this was not always true. If a politician had a firm local power base, then governmental intervention could do little. The most notorious example of such a case occurred in the career of Nunzio Nasi, deputy for Trapani in Sicily, and the only Cabinet member in the Liberal period to be gaoled for corruption (he was alleged to have embezzled state monies while Minister of Education). Nasi worked up a passionate local campaign, claiming that he and his city were being victimised. The electors of Trapani were convinced or rewarded enough to re-elect Nasi 14 times despite efforts to refill his seat, and relented only in 1914 when Nasi, released from prison, was again permitted to be their representative.[144] During the affair Nasi had compared Trapani's lot to that of Troy, and it was rumoured that a cable had been despatched to the French government stating: 'Trapani has proclaimed itself a Republic; send fleet!'[145]

A politician thus had his politics woven from a complex of local issues and requirements, and the needs and ambitions of more prominent deputies, especially those of the Prime Minister or Minister of the Interior. It was characteristic that Giolitti was always both Prime Minister and Minister of the Interior, and controlled formal power and practical patronage.

Ministries were made in a style which was again *sui generis*, although their composition bore some similarity to the practice in Third Republican France. A Prime Minister assembled his Cabinet from all over the Chamber, and there was very little sense of ministerial responsibility. Individual ministers were either in office fleetingly or were more loyal to their bureaucrats than to their fellow Cabinet members. One of the reasons why, in 1914, the Army did not know the terms of the Triple Alliance was that the Ministry of Foreign Affairs did not consider the Ministries of War or the Navy adroit, subtle or experienced enough to be informed. Giolitti, as Prime Minister, rarely held serious Cabinet discussions, dealt with his Ministers as individuals, and strongly discouraged ministerial exchanges which did not pass through his own office.

With regard to foreign policy, it has sometimes been argued that it was crucial that the Italian Chamber was deliberately kept from meeting both in the months in 1911 when Italy was deciding to go to war with Turkey over Libya, and again from June to December 1914. Yet, debate in the Chamber never openly decided foreign policy on the basis of party division. That simply was not the way in which the Italian parliamentary system worked. Individual deputies, on the other hand, had a major influence on policy in 1911, and in 1914, whether or not Parliament was meeting.

Giolittian parliamentarism has a relatively unhappy reputation both because it does not follow the Anglo-Saxon model, and because the liberal rhetoric of debates in the Chamber, or of articles in the press, was so blatantly detached from the real social conditions of ordinary Italians. Here lies the significance of the terms 'legal' and 'real' Italy – an Italian Parliament which passed laws in the 1880s legalising strikes but which, in their immediate aftermath, allowed its bureaucrats and police to be more savagely repressive than ever of worker unions;[146] an Italian Chamber which enthused over Dante and passed reforms for compulsory education, when social conditions in the south made it absolutely certain that peasant children would not attend school; an Italian Chamber which boasted of the level of freedom, yet left Italy with the most backward and anachronistic labour laws. In defence of Giolittian liberalism it might be argued that this division between theory and practice, city and country, can be found in other ideologies, and in other contemporary European societies. But, moralising aside, it simply has to be recognised that a Giolittian deputy could see no inconsistency in proclaiming his noble love of self-sacrifice and freedom, his superiority over the citizens of the autocracies to the north, and in writing passionately about reform and liberty, yet in practice, at home in the provinces, being repressive to peasants, women, children and sometimes to other groups, workers and his political opponents. That essential, if sometimes unrecognised, inconsistency, added to so many of the other divorces between myth and reality in the Liberal system, explains why in so many aspects Giolittian Italy drifted towards crisis around 1910.

The historian must react with scepticism to the discovery of a hidden crisis before an open one, to the idea that the augurs of Giolittian Italy already foretold the story of war, *dopoguerra* and Fascism. Yet there is much evidence that many comfortable Liberal assumptions were being questioned from 1911 to 1914. The economy turned down in 1907, and never regained its earlier buoyancy. The international situation became more stressful, marked for Italy by the great crises of Bosnia–Herzegovina, the Libyan campaign and the Balkan wars. Domestically, extremists advanced. The Nationalist Association, symbol of the discontent of bourgeois intellectuals, was founded in 1910. From 1912 extremists among the socialists outdistanced reformists, and shouted their challenge to the whole Giolittian system. Even FreeMasonry, that once great unifying force behind the post-Risorgimento structure, was under bitter and widely successful attack in 1913–14. For Italy, the approach of the First World War coincided with a major crisis. Any discussion on the problem of whether Italy provides an example of the primacy of internal or the primacy of external politics must admit that the numerous and always perilous gaps between myth and reality in the Liberal state and society were more obvious and more foreboding then than they had ever been before.

2 The Making of Foreign Policy

Historiography outside Italy has rarely taken very seriously Italy's role in the coming of the First World War. Comment has varied from total omission, a tacit acknowledgement that Italy was not a Great Power,[1] to the opinion parallel to that held about the domestic character of Liberal Italy, that Italian diplomacy was on a lower level morally than all the rest. A. J. P. Taylor has implied that Italian foreign policy was essentially dishonest; S. B. Fay declared briefly that the Italians were 'fickle'; and Koni Zilliacus, employing a characteristic metaphor, observed that, in their foreign policy, the Italians displayed a 'bland unscrupulousness remarkable even in power politics. Italy was like an all-in wrestler who attracts attention even among his fellow brethren for fighting foul'.[2] No doubt, these words exhibit some of the colour of the politics of the 1940s and a sound leftist abhorrence for Mussolini's Italy, but even after the Second World War Norman Kogan, an American political scientist, could readily draw the conclusion that Italian foreign policy was different from the rest in that it sprang from the 'amoral familism' which lay at the root of Italian society.[3]

There were occasional specialised studies defending Italy,[4] but much more influential was the work of the Austrian professor, A. F. Pribram. Pribram, the teacher of A. J. P. Taylor,[5] wrote conventional and patriotic diplomatic history, justifying the cause of Austria–Hungary. He dismissed the Triple Alliance as an arrangement which brought gain to Italy and loss to Austria, and argued that Austria was always the likely victim before Italy's boundless and unjustified ambition.[6]

In Italian historiography there was little overt recognition of this lowly and hostile assessment granted to Italian foreign policy. The writing and study of diplomatic history was often bound to the state in a way which had some parallels to the situation in Germany before the Fritz Fischer affair.[7] Even very recently Italy's leading conservative historian, Rosario Romeo, has briefly defined the First

World War as 'the greatest triumph of our history'.[8] Indeed, it was
Giolitti himself who, in 1912, enunciated an archives policy which
would have been applauded in a totalitarian state. Refusing to release
some documents on the Risorgimento, Giolitti declared drily that the
period was too recent to be assessed without 'bias', and that 'it would
not be right to have beautiful legends discredited by historical
criticism'.[9] Under Fascism, this attitude was entrenched, being
symbolised by the appointment of the fiercely mustachioed Cesare De
Vecchi di Val Cismon as head of the Directorate of Historical
Research. De Vecchi, a Piedmontese and a monarchist, had been one
of the quadrumvirs in the march on Rome.

Nor did the links between state and history-writing disappear after
the fall of Fascism. Both because of the degree of pluralism in fact
tolerated in intellectual circles under Fascism, and because of the
complete absence in Italy from 1943 to 1947 of a major purge of the
bureaucracy responsible for archives or the university and teaching
professions, many a research career continued with small hindrance
through Fascism into the Republic. The classic examples are those of
Augusto Torre and Mario Toscano. The former was the most zealous
analyst of the detail of pre-1914 Italian diplomacy and editor of some
of the *Documenti diplomatici italiani*. He had begun his teaching career
in 1913 and pursued it without major interruption until his recent
death. The latter became the doyen of the Italian diplomatic
historians, a figure known and respected even outside Italy.[10]
Interested and expert in international law, Toscano acted as legal
adviser to a series of Italian governments, preparing briefs for
example, on the vexed question of Italy's borders in the Alto Adige,
or South Tyrol, with Austria. At the same time, Toscano wrote the
history of the Alto Adige question, not surprisingly from a patriotic
and legalist viewpoint.[11] But Toscano had begun his career under
Fascism. His first major works on the Treaty of London and the Pact
of St Jean de Maurienne at least paid lip-service to Fascist ideals,
claiming that the Treaty of London was the first independent
diplomatic action taken by Italy since the Risorgimento, and being
certain that Italian aims were purely defensive.[12] As a Jew, Toscano
fell out of favour in the last years of Fascism; he then could participate
in the 'Resistance' and afterwards resume his academic career. But
these experiences did little to affect the character of his history-
writing. He taught two generations of diplomatic historians, and
some are still loyal to his memory, methods and conclusions.[13]

These attitudes to diplomatic history arise more from the structures of the Italian university system than from individual idiosyncracies. Until the 1960s there were no chairs in contemporary history in Italy and, as in other European countries, study of the recent past was dismissed as an area of hopeless and regrettable political bias. International history, on the other hand, was usually taught in law faculties in courses which were part of the *giurisprudenza* degree. The relationship with law meant an inevitable emphasis on the terms of treaties, on legalism, and on the fact that *giurisprudenza* was still the essential training course for politicians and bureaucrats. It also re-emphasised the contacts between diplomacy and the state, and made it unlikely that patriotic interpretations of historical events would be much challenged. Outside such orthodox courses, the hegemony of the ideology of Marxism and the politics of the PCI, with their fixation either on Fascism or on the domestic story of Italian socialism, meant that there was little interest in a critical history of Italian foreign policy. Even in the world of archives there was discouragement for diplomatic historians. The official *Documenti diplomatici italiani*, although thorough and well-presented, have appeared very slowly and, apart from those of the Fascist period, seem now almost to have stopped appearing at all. Whereas students of domestic history could find in the Archivio Centrale dello Stato an archive and library in one, which was well up to world standards of efficiency and courtesy, students of diplomatic history were banished to a sub-section of the Ministry of Foreign Affairs. The Foreign Affairs archives, housed rather appropriately in the Farnesina, a building erected to be the Fascist Party headquarters, are difficult of access, and are sometimes as useful in understanding the mal-functioning or non-functioning of the bureaucracy of Christian Democratic Italy as they are for a study of Liberal or Fascist foreign policy.

All of this is similar to the situation in West Germany before the Fischer controversy and, for that matter, only another example of the special relationship which long existed in most countries between international history and the state. Yet, in Italy, there have been currents running in the other direction. One, for example, is the brilliant work done by Federico Chabod. His *Storia della politica estera italiana dal 1870 al 1896*, first published in 1951, confronts the problems both of the relationship of foreign and domestic affairs, and of the unspoken assumptions of ideologies, developed and popular, in a way which is well ahead of its time. Yet Chabod, an anti-Fascist, began his work in 1936, the Year of the Empire for Italy, and was backed by the Istituto per gli Studi di Politica Internazionale,[14] a body headed by Alberto Pirelli and Gioacchino Volpe, which usually published, with certain conservative bias, predictably pro-Fascist works. Another anti-Fascist, Luigi Salvatorelli, who also remained in Italy after 1922, survived by writing mutedly patriotic diplomatic history, one example being his study of the Triple Alliance.[15]

More well-known abroad, if a case *sui generis*, is Luigi Albertini. Albertini's three volume *History of the War of 1914* has been saluted especially in the Anglo-Saxon world as the most magisterial study of the origins of the war, before the new work sparked off by Fritz Fischer. By a strict analysis of the published documents, Albertini argued that the nations did not 'slither into war'; instead, if any nation was responsible for war, that nation was Germany. Albertini, naturally, spent more time than other historians of the war's origins in analysing Italian foreign policy. There, he was severely critical of the Giolittian 'achievement', and especially of the policies of San Giuliano from 1910 to 1914. San Giuliano, he asserted, followed, before the July crisis, a line of 'utter, unreserved surrender to the Central Powers'. His amorality meant that Italy entered the war 'down the back streets' instead of by 'the high road'. This forfeiting of 'every shred of dignity by seeking rewards without fighting for them' was largely responsible for the disasters to come at the Treaty of Versailles and under Fascism.[16]

But Albertini's conclusions must be seen in relation to his own politics. An anti-Fascist, he was dismissed in 1925 from the post of *direttore* of the Milan newspaper, *Corriere della Sera*, after Fascist intervention.[17] It was then that he turned his mind to history. However, Albertini's career had already been a long and distinguished one. He became the major figure at *Corriere della Sera* in 1900, and both increased the circulation of the paper and underlined its political authority.[18] For Giolitti, the press was a most important aspect of his political structure, being not only the route to power but also one of the most important ties which bound together politics and society, the ruling class in Rome and the ruling class in the provinces.[19] But after 1905 the crisis coming to the Giolittian system was foreshadowed in a rising tide of press criticism of Giolitti. In this movement, *Corriere della Sera*'s was the most prestigious and authoritative part, and, indeed, in the decade before 1914, Albertini was arguably the conservative leader of the opposition against *giolittismo*. In 1906, appalled by Giolitti's *laissez-faire* policy towards urban strikes, *Corriere della Sera* commented sorrowfully: 'parliamentarism is at such a level of decadence, the practice of government is sunk so low, so deep is the discontent, so many are the causes of disorder, revolt and anarchy spreading through the country' that, but for 'the best men' (that is the conservatives around Sonnino), the paper could only preach a message of total despair.[20] Albertini also picked up the phrase 'a parliamentary dictatorship' with which to define the Giolittian administration, and then recalled this idea under Fascism with the obvious message that Giolitti begat Mussolini.[21] Apart from domestic affairs, *Corriere della Sera* had a distinctive line on foreign policy, especially in the *intervento*, 1914–15. Albertini, who had received early training on *The Times*, was an Anglophile, and he rapidly advocated intervention in the war on the Triple Entente side. Despite the solidity of Albertini's documentary study in *The Origins of the War of 1914*, his conclusions on Germany, on Giolitti and on Italy's role among the Powers, do not differ from the politically-based conclusions which he had already reached before 1915. His ideas remained those of an upright Milanese conservative who did not well understand the rest of Italy and who, with not unusual Italian parochialism, sadly over-estimated the opportunities for independence and 'morality' open to an Italian diplomat.

What of more recent Italian writing on foreign policy, writing which has occurred in the aftermath of the publication of *Griff nach der Weltmacht* in 1961 and the subsequent emphasis by Fischer, Geiss, Joll, A. J. Mayer and others on the connection between domestic affairs and foreign policy? Marxists have occasionally asserted that Liberal Italy did enter the imperialist phase, and that, even if Italian industry was relatively weak, it was also relatively monopolised.[22] But major studies there have not been, with the exception of the American historian, Richard Webster's *Italian Industrial Imperialism*, already noted in chapter 1. Webster's book contains some brilliant insights, but it is repetitive and inconsistent, and ultimately wrong-headed in its conclusion, paralleling Liberal Italy to Wilhelmine Germany.

Certainly, of the Great Powers, Italy affords, in some incidents, unusually clear and direct examples of the way in which decisions about foreign policy are made. Doubts may still arise about the level of clarity and planning in the German or British decisions for war,[23]

but it is quite plain that an Italian government, with deliberate
process, decided not to enter the war in August 1914 and decided to
enter it in May 1915. There can be no defence for a case that Italy
'slithered into war'.

Of course the real question, and the major task of this book, is to
explain how and why the different decisions of 1914 and 1915 were
made. Did they spring from domestic conspiracy, a fear among the
ruling classes of the pressure of approaching democracy, a desperate
attempt to divert socialism by nationalism and war? Or was Italy's
policy a classic example of traditional, almost dynastic, eighteenth
century diplomacy, where borders were to be expanded as the
occasion arose, a continuation of the ideas of Cavour for an
'artichoke' policy, a 'leaf by leaf' expansion of Italian power? Was
Italy always a fearful state, whose policy was decided for her by the
Greater Powers? Or does Italian diplomacy reflect, in its formulation
and execution, the primacy of internal or the primacy of external
politics?

A simple answer to the last question is not easy to give. Once again
the Italian case turns out to be *sui generis*; the mainspring of her
diplomacy does not fall neatly into either category. There were
domestic pressures on Italian foreign policy as the crisis of the
Giolittian system deepened. Yet the extent and very character of
Italian business interventions, for example, rarely provide proof of a
direct connection between domestic needs and particular diplomatic
decisions. The making of foreign policy usually lay in the hands of the
Foreign Minister and his diplomats, or, on profoundly serious
occasions, in the hands of Giolitti himself. Indeed, there is more
evidence of Italian diplomatists bewailing the timidity and
backwardness of the business sector's interest in imperialism, than of
industrialists conspiring to push a reluctant government into
profitable adventures. Yet, on a more vague and less coherent level,
among what Joll has called the unspoken assumptions,[24] there were
links in Italy, as in other European countries, between domestic and
foreign affairs. There was an Italian publicist who gained fame with a
book on the shape of wars to come;[25] there were Italian intellectuals
who thought war was hygienic, and indeed necessary for the
development of civilisation;[26] there were Italian politicians who
eagerly used the metaphors of Social Darwinism and believed in a
coming 'struggle of the peoples' (though they sensibly placed the date
for this Armageddon safely in a future when militarily feeble Italy

might at last be 'ready'). On the other hand, despite the rhetorical flourishes of politicians and publicists, while general peace survived, no Italian statesman ever seriously contemplated launching in the immediate present a preventive war among the Great Powers.

However, the major relationship between domestic and foreign affairs in Italy was a more subtle and obscure one, and characteristically one largely sprung from myth. The Liberal state had been founded during the Risorgimento on the concept, the false concept, that Italy was a serious Great Power. After 1860, this concept was merged into the whole *raison d'être* of the Liberal state, of the Savoyard dynasty, and even of *giolittismo*. To a very significant extent, Italy, ironically rather like Austria–Hungary,[27] existed in order to have a foreign policy, in order to be a Great Power. This was the ultimate reason why Italian foreign policy was so tenacious in requesting a recognition of Italy's status, why Italy attended every Great Power conference, why a (tiny) Italian brigade helped to suppress the Boxer rebellion, why Italy expected to be included in police duties on Crete or in Macedonia. In the final analysis, Italy entered the First World War quite deliberately because not to do so would have been to admit that her pretensions to being a Great Power were false, and therefore, by implication, that her pretensions to liberalism, parliamentarism and a constitutional centralised monarchy were equally false. Italy thus provides a sort of upside-down example of the primacy of foreign affairs. Italy did not so much have her foreign policy decided by domestic affairs, as her domestic affairs decided by the fact that it was unimaginable that she would not have a foreign policy.

In the day-to-day management of Italian diplomacy, much responsibility fell into the hands of the Minister of Foreign Affairs. The more able or politically adroit of such Ministers could expect a fair tenure of office, even amid falling governments. All Ministers were *persona grata* at court, and all were likely to be politically conservative, but, that said, it is not easy to typify the major figures from 1896 to 1915. After the humiliating defeat of Italian arms by the Ethiopians at Adowa in March 1896, a defeat which also indicated Italy's complete lack of worthwhile friends and patrons among the Great Powers, Italian diplomacy in July passed into the hands of the Marchese Emilio di Visconti Venosta. Visconti Venosta, born in 1829, had been personally involved in the Risorgimento, first with Mazzini, and later as Cavour's contact with Garibaldi. An aristocrat, he was the lineal heir of Cavour and had been four times Foreign Minister in early Italian governments in 1863–4, 1866–7 and 1869–76. After 1876 he remained out of office, thus exhibiting his contempt for the corruption and mediocrity of the Left, and acquiring a reputation as a diplomatic Coriolanus. In office, Visconti Venosta steered Italy back towards friendly relations with France, while he served as Foreign Minister in 1896–8 and 1899–1901. On the other hand, he had no time for what he regarded as cheap irredentism. His watchword remained what he had declared it to be in 1863: Italy must be 'independent always, isolated never'.[28] Though very old, Visconti Venosta was recalled in a moment of difficulty in 1906, and sent off to head the Italian delegation at the Algeciras conference. In 1914, just before his death, he blessed the decision to opt for neutrality at the start of the First World War.

Very different was Giulio Prinetti, Foreign Minister in 1901–3 and architect of the rather frenetic policies of that period. Prinetti, a Lombard bicycle manufacturer and a *nouveau riche*, irascible, with a penchant for authoritarian solutions at home, was the most uncourtly of Italian Foreign Ministers. At formal dinners, it was rumoured, Prinetti was so maladroit that he ate fish off his knife.[29] While he seemed, on the surface, to exemplify the new diplomacy and the connections between industry and foreign policy, Prinetti was attracted to adventures abroad, but more from temperament than financial interest, and notably by the mechanisms of diplomatic manoeuvre and not those of commerce.

From November 1903 to 1905, and from 1906 to 1909, the Foreign Minister was the much more equivocal figure of Tommaso Tittoni. Trained in the prefectural service and having ingratiated himself with politicians, criminals[30] and the king,[31] Tittoni was made Foreign Minister because of his other contacts with the Vatican and political clericalism.[32] Tittoni was a Roman of the Romans. His father, a rich merchant of the Agro Romano, had been, in 1870, one of the delegation from Rome to the Italian government in Florence, which worked out the formula for the plebiscite which was to set the seal on Rome's annexation to Italy. Tommaso's brother, Romolo, who was nominated a Senator in 1913, was a major official in the Vatican-financed Banco di Roma, and very prominent in the Rome Chamber of Commerce, which had, for example, a special role in the selection of the Italian delegate to the Ottoman Public Debt. Tittoni, then, as Foreign Minister, seemed to represent not so much the realm of

industry or Milan, as finance and Rome, and then the finance of the
Vatican, not that of the Italian state. A feline, if rather superficial,
figure, Tittoni greatly enjoyed political plotting for its own sake.
After 1909 he intrigued to return to the Foreign Ministry and perhaps
to become conservative Prime Minister. He finally achieved the first
ambition, briefly and unhappily, in the Nitti government from June
to November 1919. After 1922, he enjoyed a reputation as an elder
statesman under Facism.

The most able of Foreign Ministers in the period was Antonino Di
San Giuliano, who held office briefly in 1905–6, and then from 1910
until his death in October 1914. A Sicilian aristocrat of Norman
descent, San Giuliano had turned to foreign policy after failing in his
ambition to become a major figure in internal politics. By origin a
large landowner, San Giuliano succeeded neither in doing well in his
own finances nor in blocking the ascent of the middle classes to
political power at his expense in his city of Catania. Wickedly cynical
(he complained publicly that his ill health was the result of his mother
being an honest woman[33]) San Giuliano was also the most expert
Italian Foreign Minister since Visconti Venosta, and was rather more
hard-working and penetrating than that elder statesman. San
Giuliano had served in the Eritrean Commission of 1891,
participated in the colonialist debates of Crispi's period, travelled
widely in the Adriatic and Mediterranean and even to the United
States, and was a member of a series of public bodies interested in
foreign affairs. He was one of the major spokesmen in the Italian
Chamber on emigration, and, after 1906, was ambassador in London
and, briefly, Paris. Though, in office, he was at first rather timid and
fearful of the worst, San Giuliano gradually grew more confident,
especially after the Libyan war. By 1913–14 he was perhaps the most
masterful, and certainly the most subtle, of the Foreign Ministers of
the Great Powers, even though his numerous stratagems, always
being rooted in the essential unreality of Italy's claims to being a
Great Power, often look more brittle the more closely they are
examined.[34]

During the crucial months of Italy's decision for war or peace after
November 1914, the Foreign Minister was Sidney Sonnino, a figure
from the political world. Indeed Sonnino was the major opponent of
Giolitti in the Chamber of Deputies, and had been Prime Minister in
1906 and 1909–10. In Anglo-Saxon historiography, Sonnino often
has an extraordinarily high reputation, for extraordinarily little

reason. A landowner, with a Jewish and international background, Sonnino defined himself as an intelligent conservative. As a belle-lettrist, he had detected that Dante was a prophet of the monarchy, united Italy and the returning glory of Rome.[35] But his political prestige was rooted in the alleged clarity with which he offered a moral alternative to Giolitti. In practice, certainly as a diplomatist, clarity was the one quality which constantly eluded Sonnino. Instead, his combination of rigidity and fussiness, and a general inability either to work out priorities or to set Italian foreign policy in any other than parochial terms, made him the most unsuccessful of Italy's Foreign Ministers.

Although Foreign Ministers carried major responsibility for the management of ordinary, peacetime diplomacy, the 'expertise', in the sense of international knowledge, of Visconti Venosta and especially of San Giuliano, was more the exception than the rule in the history of Italian foreign policy. It is also true that all Foreign Ministers had to admit the ultimate superiority of the Prime Minister. Often when the course of international relations was smooth or obvious, this did not involve much supervision. Zanardelli, for example, when criticised for appointing Prinetti said: 'But ... I have only given him the Ministry of Foreign Affairs,[36] Giolitti, too, for a long time, kept foreign policy very low on the list of priorities for his governments.[37] He probably made Tittoni Foreign Minister because of the domestic, political more than financial, advantages of the appointment. However, when the international situation did become tense, in the Bosnia–Herzegovina, Libyan or Scutari crises, Giolitti openly took the reins of diplomacy into his own hands. The only exception was during the July crisis and its immediate aftermath; but then there was the most unusual circumstance of a Prime Minister, Salandra, with a weak power-base in the Chamber, who was heavily involved in domestic affairs, and a Foreign Minister, San Giuliano, able and independent, in the Ministry as much by the wish of Giolitti and the King, as of Salandra.

The relations of Ministers of Foreign Affairs to their diplomatic staff in the Foreign Ministry, the Consulta, and abroad in embassies and consulates are also not easily typified. In the Ministry, the most important post was that of Secretary-General,[38] the equivalent of the Permanent Under-Secretary in the British Foreign Office. From 1896 to 1907 this office was held by Giacomo Malvano, a Piedmontese, who was also most unusual in international diplomatic circles in being a Jew. He was a severe but grey figure, known as a 'walking archive', and the object of respect and incomprehension as the only major diplomatist willing to remain in Rome during the summer.[39] Malvano was succeeded by Riccardo Bollati, another parochial Piedmontese, who was renowned for his love of peace, quiet and home. On a one-year assignment in Athens, he managed to spend only 15 days at his post, and, in another posting at Cetinje, he complained to an adventurous English lady: 'Nothing bites you, everything bites me. Your method of seeing lands [by constant travel] is undoubtedly the best, but I am satisfied with what I can see from the windows of the best hotel'.[40] Only in 1913–14 was the Secretary-General, Giacomo De Martino, a more authoritative figure, but he was very much the personal choice of San Giuliano, and acted as the loyal second to his policy. On the other hand, when it became obvious that San Giuliano was dying, De Martino, a Neapolitan, showed all the political skills of a southern bureaucrat in sufficiently detaching himself from his old master to be kept on in the post until 1920 by Sonnino, who was no admirer of San Giuliano.

The Italian diplomatic and consular services were, naturally enough, drawn from the ruling elite of Liberal Italy. Among the older staff, the traditions of Piedmont and the Savoy monarchy were very strong indeed, but, in the service as a whole, a marked process of 'southernisation', a take-over by southerners from poor noble or bureaucratic families, had begun. This same process can be seen in other areas of the Italian bureaucracy, and it remains unchanged today. In the pre-1914 period, therefore, Italian ambassadors and consuls were likely to come from the most traditional parts of Italy. An example is Avarna, the ambassador in Vienna, a Sicilian aristocrat who, to 1915, rather than purchasing a Fiat or some other patriotic symbol of modernity and industrialisation, had himself taken to the Ballhausplatz each day in a coach and four.[41] Financial expertise was also very rare in the Italian foreign service. The Neapolitan aristocrat, Guglielmo Imperiali, who was almost naively courtly in his manners and garrulous as well, had a most difficult and unrewarding time from 1904 to 1910 as ambassador to Constantinople where his rival was the French ambassador, that most skilled, up-to-date and bourgeois political and financial operator, Ernest Constans.[42] Italian diplomats usually were more capable of writing light, lyrical essays on Dante or matters of local colour, than they were of comprehending economic processes. Italian diplomats, too, sometimes lacked the secure financial base held by the rest of the international circuit. One memoirist alleged that a hard-pressed colleague briefly attained liquidity by selling his dress uniform to an opera company.[43]

Italy was seldom progressive or rich enough to indulge in modern technology. Memoirs recount tales of embassies without typewriters, secretarial assistance or trained translators. The archives in Rome were not easily accessible. It was characteristic that San Giuliano conducted much Foreign Ministry business in pencil, in an execrable longhand, made worse by his combination of gout and arthritic deterioration. It was also characteristic that Italy was very slow to see any significance in the world outside Europe. Despite the volume of emigration across the Atlantic, the United States was not granted an Italian legation until 1881, nor an Embassy until 1893. In those two decades the successive posts were occupied by an ex-Bourbon official, Saverio Fava. Despite major events encouraging greater contact, such as the infamous lynching of 11 Italian immigrants at New Orleans in 1891, Fava, who was despised in Rome both for his politics and because he lived 'like a miser in an ordinary boarding-house where only barbers lived', and who was a diplomat sufficiently insouciant to stay away from his post for ten months in a row in 1897–8, was none the less allowed to remain in tenure. His successors, notably Vincenzo Macchi di Cellere,[44] ambassador in 1913–19, were more expert in that they had had a training in the Americas, but this variety of expertise helped to isolate them from colleagues more knowledgeable about Europe. Italian diplomacy believed that the world was centred in the *mare nostrum*, and that the United States was not a serious player on the world stage. Olivetti and Agnelli may have understood the meaning of Taylorism and Fordism, but the Consulta did not.

Nor did foreign diplomats in Rome do much to raise the confidence of Italian diplomacy. Rome was a relatively minor posting, a place for the gracious spending of the last years of a distinguished career, or a diversion briefly to be endured before a more important assignment. One British ambassadorial couple were described as 'not born to be diplomats. After dinner they presented their dogs to the company'.[45] The exception to this rule was Camille Barrère, the French ambassador from 1898 to 1923, and an ex-communard and ex-journalist who knew much about the modern world.[46] The Roman summer was too hot and too unhealthy for all but the most zealous or most junior staff. British ambassadors retreated for months to Posillipo on the Bay of Naples, to a palace granted to them by Lord Rosebery. In July–August 1914, San Giuliano spent much of his time pumping information out of the neurotic German ambassador, Hans von Flotow, with whom he was sharing the same hotel at Fiuggi, a spa in the hills south of Rome. Foreign ambassadors, too, were often attracted by the delights of 'bella Italia'. Sir James Rennell Rodd, the British ambassador, 1908–19, was slow to realise the seriousness of the July crisis because, as a prelude to his summer holidays, he was then touring the towns of Tuscany in search of art treasures.[47]

To end with an image only of incompetence and traditionalism is not quite fair. However disorganised, the Italian diplomatic service worked for a country which had experienced the Risorgimento. It was not as totally aristocratic and courtly as was that of Austria–Hungary, Germany, Russia and perhaps Britain. It was also not so much of a closed shop. There were contacts and interchanges between the consular and diplomatic services. There was also contact with the political and wider bureaucratic worlds. A deputy as father or uncle was excellent recommendation for a candidate seeking to pass the entry exams into the Consulta. There could also be interchanges at a higher level. San Giuliano was an ambassador in 1906–10, and Tittoni was sent as ambassador to France in 1910. In 1911 Giolitti himself intervened to choose Camillo Garroni as ambassador to Turkey. Garroni, from the prefectural service, a renowned negotiator and intimate acquaintance of both Giolitti and Genoese shipping and industrial circles, was, at least on the surface, admirably qualified to do business in Constantinople more effectively than were his aristocratic predecessors.

A study of the bureaucrats of Italian foreign policy and of their influence on diplomacy is thus replete with paradoxes. A foreign service of some ability was countered by the jealousy of the Foreign Ministers who regarded ambassadors as mere bagmen and nothing else. A diplomatic staff of some modernity and competence after the Risorgimento was being weakened and made more traditional by the process of southernisation. The Giolittian Italy of the beginning of industrialisation and of an approach to universal manhood suffrage was being represented abroad more and more by landowners or intellectuals. In its diplomatic staffing as in its policy, the Italian approach to war was an Italian one, and not the same as that of any other state.

The most uncharted area of Italian foreign policy-making lay where it met the exigencies of defence, that is where the game or art of diplomacy was threatened by the reality of war. The Army Officer Corps occupied a curious place in Italian domestic affairs,[48] and an even more curious one in Italy's relations with foreign states. *Prima facie*, despite the names of Pelloux and Badoglio, the Army has played an extraordinarily minor part in Italian history since the Risorgimento. The comparison with Spain, for example, is striking if paradoxical. Though the two states had, in the nineteenth century, a somewhat similar socioeconomic structure and a markedly similar centralising system of political 'liberalism', their military have played remarkably different roles in civil affairs. Spain had its *pronunciamientos*, and then the dictatorships of General Primo De Rivera and General Franco; Italy, apart from rumours around General De Lorenzo in the 1960s, has never experienced an attempt at a military *coup d'état*. Pelloux and Badoglio did head governments, but they were very much political generals and, in any case, were being used by political figures rather than seeking power for their own sake or that of the Army. Spain provides the most graphic contrast but also, compared with those of the other Great Powers, the Italian Army has been of little political significance. There have been no Italian Hindenburgs or Ludendorffs, no Pétains or De Gaulles.

Why is this so? Partly because military history in Italy is one of defeat: the Risorgimento battles were fought out between French and Austrians; in the nineteenth century, the most famous and publicised contests involving Italian arms were the fiasco of the naval defeat at Lissa in 1866 and the still greater humiliation of the rout of Italian forces at Adowa in 1896 by the Ethiopians. Military 'heroes' have been hard to find among Italian generals or admirals.

But mere failure cannot be a complete answer. After all, the record of the Spanish Army in combat was scarcely a glorious one. The exclusion of the Italian Army from overt influence in politics is evidence again of the complex and ambiguous nature of the Risorgimento, its combination of short-term modernising aspects and a long-term failure of modernisation. The political heroes or victors of the Risorgimento were liberals – businessmen, lawyers, journalists, 'intellectuals' – men who scorned the military career. Giolitti, for example, cautiously stayed at home to safeguard his family interests during the battles of the Risorgimento. Though rarely witty as a politician, he could be persuaded to exercise his wit on generals. 'For two generations', he said, Italian families had

pushed into the Officer Corps those 'boys whom they did not know
what to do with, the idle and the mentally deficient'.[49] Although
Giolitti allowed the defence budget to rise rapidly in the years before
1914 (£15.6 million in 1900 and £28.2 million in 1914) as part of the
Italian participation in the arms race, Italian expenditure in relation
to the other Powers was comparatively low.[50] Much of the money
was necessarily exhausted in the Libyan war. In any case, the defence
vote was used for the most diverse matters, with relatively little of it
going on munitions or defence works. Despite extra funds granted
from 1908 onwards to fortress works along the north-east border with
Austria, Italy's defences were incomplete there in 1914. The Libyan
war had had a debilitating effect on the Army. Later publicists could
boast that Italian inventiveness there inspired the first military use of
the dirigible and of aerial bombing, but not many learned serious
lessons from these pioneering triumphs. In 1914 the Italian Army
possessed only a few old French planes, and in May 1915 had 72
trained pilots.[51] Generally, the Italian Army, like those of the other
European states, went on believing that the best agent of transport
was the horse. The cost of new mounts and forage took one-twelfth of
the total military vote in 1913,[52] and the Italian Officer Corps
contained 187 'expert' veterinary officers against none in the
German.[53] Equally the technology of the machine-gun, although
utilised in Libya, did not lead the Army chiefs to detect that weapon's
potential any better than did their counterparts in other European
states.[54] Of course, the Libyan war was resolved by diplomacy and
not by arms, and military involvement there, with its accompanying
running down of material, continued with little change from 1912 to
1915.

The Risorgimento had also ensured that the Army would not be
popular with the Left. For radicals and republicans, the archetypal
hero was Garibaldi, a soldier, but not an institutionalised soldier; the
Hero wounded so sacrilegiously by the Army at Aspromonte.
Cavallotti, Imbriani and Garibaldi's own sons preserved a tradition
of individual action, contemptuous of Army conservatism, which
would eventually have some connection with Mussolini's squads and
their *ras*.

The Army was a monarchist body; officers belonged to a caste and
were the servants of the King. One recalled in his memoirs that he
became a soldier with splendid simplicity. His father came into his
bedroom and said: 'Listen, son, in our house, one member of the

family has always been a soldier. Do you want to be?' I replied . . .
'Yes, papa'.[55] After the Risorgimento, Bourbon and Austro-Italian
officers had been added to the old Piedmontese structure, and their
traditions blended easily into a generic monarchism, a conservative
disdain for the parliamentary institutions of liberalism, a dislike of
lawyers, intellectuals and journalists, and most of all a profound sense
of pessimism and depression. An officer's lot was not a happy one.
The Monarchy was not inspiring under Umberto I or Victor
Emmanuel III. Money was scarce; promotion was slow. Jews in the
Officer Corps (one, Ottolenghi, was even from 1902 to 1903 Minister
of War) and the record of military defeat made it hard for Italian
officers to hold up their heads at international gatherings. Even the
natural conservative ally, the Church, was denied to the Officer
Corps, given that the Italian state had been founded on
anticlericalism. So Italian officers joined the Free Masons, were
bored, drank and dreamed without hope that their Army could one
day be like that of Germany.[56]

Duty was largely domestic. The Army was needed to preserve the
fragile political and social unity of the state. Shots in anger were not
fired gloriously against the nation's foe, but ingloriously in mountain
raids against bandits, in ploughed fields against striking peasants, in
city squares against dissident socialists, Catholics or republicans. The
Army's function was not clearly separated from that of the police.
The *carabinieri* took up some 10 per cent of the budget of the Ministry
of War, and in June 1914 Army and *carabinieri* were needed to repress
a threatening social revolution during the so-called 'Red Week'. An
officer had little contact with his men. It was decreed that a regiment
must always consist of men from two regions of Italy and be stationed
in a third.[57] The men too could be bored, sullen and hostile. An
Italian major found no distinction between them and *ascari*, the black
mercenaries enrolled in Eritrea.[58] Taught only enough Italian to
comprehend their officers' commands, the ordinary soldiers spoke
dialect to each other and often could not understand the language of
the 'Italians' among whom they were stationed. A report of the crack
Sassari Brigade, for example, notes that the men served out their
term of duty passively, waiting to go back to their island, and, on the
mainland, rarely bothered to take any of the leave allotted to them.[59]

In a way, then, the Italian Army was a sort of reserve army of
occupation, the hidden strength and justification of the Liberal state.
But this power had necessarily to be concealed since it was contrary to

the myths of the free 'nation risen' of the Risorgimento. In these circumstances, and given the traditions carried over from the Bourbon and Habsburg armies, it is not surprising that the Italian Army's most evident characteristics before 1914 were its bureaucratisation and its isolation. The Army ran its own tomato canneries and biscuit factories;[60] the Army knew about technical matters; politicians would deal with the political.

Civilians seemed to endorse this state of affairs. They too did not want to expose the myths of the Risorgimento, but they needed an army. Military men, who liked to dabble in politics, were allowed to control the Ministries of War and the Navy. Only one civilian, Severino Casana, was ever Minister of War (1907–9) and his modernising reforms ran into much caste-based resentment and opposition from officers. His successors, Spingardi, Porro, Grandi, Zupelli, were again all generals.

There was thus a certain ambiguity in the role of the officer corps in Italian politics and society. Formally, the Army was a model one for a constitutional state, separated from politics, loyally on the alert to check the King's enemies. In practice there was always a hint of something more. In addition, just before the First World War, the Army Officer Corps displayed the tensions becoming evident in the rest of the Giolittian system. A campaign against Free-Masonry[61] in the Army, a newly public association with the Roman Catholic Church, a returning usage of domestic repression (Red Week produced the most naked example of military power in action at home since 1898–9) – all these events tended to show that the Army preferred more conservative and straightforward politics to those offered by Giolitti.

If the domestic story of the Italian Army is one of formal exclusion and a certain practical necessity, a similar story can be told of foreign policy. Formally, the Army had nothing whatever to do with foreign policy. It is notorious, and true, that the Italian Chiefs of General Staff did not know the terms of the Triple Alliance. This fact is striking testimony to the primitiveness of civil-military contacts in Liberal Italy. As late as December 1912, when Spingardi, the Minister of War, asked the Foreign Minister, San Giuliano, for the details of the recent renewal of the Triple Alliance, he was told merely that no military provisions were contained in the agreement.[62]

So much is formally correct. But the Army and the Navy also pursued foreign policies of their own, in the sense of being permitted and encouraged to talk to their counterparts in Germany and Austria, and thus 'to plan' for the eventualities of war. The tale of Italian military planning within the Triple Alliance is a bizarre one. Italian generals blithely plotted, for example, the violation of Swiss neutrality, or the transport of 46,000 men (and 14,000 horses) across the Gulf of Lyons to the mouth of the Rhone. When the Italians arrived, planners noted optimistically, the city of Marseilles would show that its citizens knew its real name was Marsiglia and that it was a natural part of Italy.[63] Moreover in 1913–14, Italian generals and admirals reached military and naval agreements within the Triple Alliance which entailed such extraordinary provisions as the certain conjunction of Italian armies with German ones before Paris, the possible transport of Italian troops to an Eastern Front, and even the union of the Italian and Habsburg fleets off Messina under an Austro-Hungarian commander.[64] This last arrangement was made despite the facts that Italy and Austria–Hungary were then engaged in a mini-arms race of dreadnought-building against each other in the Adriatic, and that the officers of the two navies had been trained on their mutual rivalry. (In the Italian Navy, especially rankling was the fact that the Austrians had erected at Pola a monument to their victory at Lissa.)[65] Military collaboration within the Triple Alliance had grown so close that General Pollio, in April 1914, could astound his Germanic colleagues by remarking that, since Franco-Russian forces would be in a more threatening condition in 1917, the Triple Alliance should imitate the example of King Frederick II: 'Why', Pollio demanded superbly, 'don't we begin now this inevitable conflict?'[66]

Diplomatic historians have puzzled over the detail of the military agreements or of Pollio's out-kaisering the Kaiser even to the extent of invoking in his justification the ancestral memory of Frederick the Great. But certainly neither the legal terms nor the officers' rhetoric should be regarded as too significant or binding. For Giolitti and San Giuliano these military arrangements were merely new cards which could be added to the pack being used in the diplomatic game. What, then, if there was war? But the military agreements show just how little Italian statesmen believed in or considered the prospect of general war. It was an age of peace. If there was war, soldiers would do their duty, and very likely do it with their usual incompetence. So, Giolitti did not tell Pollio about the decision to intervene in Libya until a few days before the event. So, in the Scutari crisis, the Army was instructed to commence a secret mobilisation without any explanation why it was necessary or how it could be done. So, in the July crisis, Cadorna, the new Chief of General Staff, continued war preparations against France until 2 August, with no word from the politicians. So, in August 1914, the Army was badly deficient both in equipment (for example, winter clothing) and in munitions, but scarcely bothered to inform the civilians about such problems except where soldiers could join politicians such as Sonnino in mutually cathartic complaints that Italy's continued military weakness was somehow all Giolitti's fault.[67]

The key assumption underlying Italian foreign policy was not therefore that military concerns did not matter, but rather that nothing could be done to redeem the stupidity of soldiers and the likelihood that they would soon surrender gains cunningly won on the diplomatic table. In military questions, in questions of real power, Italian foreign policy was at its most unrealistic. But then, given the character of the Italian Army, its place in Italian politics and society, and, more importantly, the conjuring which lay behind any appearance of Italy as a Great Power, it is hard to see that either civilians or soldiers had much of an alternative if Italy was to continue to have the foreign policy desired by the ruling classes after the Risorgimento.

It is also not astonishing that informed opinion and the press exercised only a distant and equivocal influence on the making of foreign policy. Liberal Italy had a numerous, flourishing and inventive press. It was typical of the vivacity and enthusiasm, of what Italians call the *fantasia* of their political life, that no sooner had Giolitti made his famous remark that he had 'relegated Marx to the attic' than a faction of the socialists began producing a paper, cheerfully or brazenly called *La Soffitta (The Attic)*.[68] Contemporaries already spoke of the press as the fourth power of the state.[69]

There were three main aspects of this press. The first was the regional press, the papers and journals of smaller cities. With limited circulation, antiquated technology, and overwhelmingly parochial interests, these papers were the local power base of many a politician and, taken together, were one of the more important parts of the Giolittian system. But theirs was not the world of high diplomacy. These small local sheets were being challenged by more modern alternatives. There was the party press – for the socialists, *Avanti!* which, symbolically, transferred its editorial office from Rome to

Milan in October 1911, and from 1912 to 1914 was edited by the demagogic radical, Benito Mussolini. For Roman Catholics an editorial trust developed, giving greater unity to political Catholicism, especially in *Corriere d'Italia* founded in Rome in 1906. By 1911 an Association of the Italian Catholic Press had been set up in Milan.[70]

Socialists and Catholics may have carried with them portents of a more democratic future, but Italy's major press remained 'liberal', tied to financial interests and, especially, to great editors. In Milan, there was Albertini's *Corriere della Sera*; in Turin, *La Stampa*, edited by Alfredo Frassati and loyal to Giolitti; in Rome, there was the Sonninian *Giornale d'Italia*, edited by Alberto Bergamini, and *La Tribuna*, edited by Olindo Malagodi and preserved for the Giolittian cause in 1909 after considerable effort on Giolitti's part.

These papers were the Italian equivalent of *The Times* or the *Frankfurter Zeitung. Corriere della Sera*, for example, reached a printing run of 100,000 in 1899, and had risked new-fangled technology in 1895 when its offices acquired its first telephone. It also engaged in the soundly *belle époque* activity of financing cycle contests and car races.[71] Barzini sent his despatches from the Gobi desert during the Peking-to-Paris 'raid' on to *Corriere della Sera*'s offices.[72] Most exciting of all, in 1911, the paper backed a Paris-to-Rome air race which a French lieutenant won by dauntlessly flying across the Tyrrhenian Sea and thus out-distancing fellow contestants who were timidly hugging the coast. *Corriere della Sera* would have preferred an Italian victory but put on as good a face as possible confronted with such heroism and such good sales.

As in other countries, these papers paid major attention to foreign affairs, headlining on their front pages the latest skirmish in the Balkans or rhetorical flourish by Kaiser William II. In 1911 all the major papers, despite their differing political opinions, favoured the Libyan campaign and indeed hired nationalist special correspondents to report on the delights and prospects of Libya in the spring and summer months before Italy's declaration of war.

More formal contact between the press and foreign policy is difficult to establish. The Italian Foreign Ministry possessed only the most primitive press office, and any 'management' of foreign reporting was not really attempted until the creation of an Under-Secretaryship of Press and Propaganda in 1917 after the battle of Caporetto.[73] In 1914, De Martino had drafted a detailed report bewailing the absence of a (nationalist) 'public opinion' which could be 'used' by diplomatists to back up Italian claims and ambitions. He regretted, too, that the Italian press had so often to turn to big business for financial subsidies since, he averred, this created too many embarrassing and damaging conflicts of interest. De Martino's ideas were endorsed by San Giuliano,[74] but no suitable method of better channelling public opinion had been thought up before the outbreak of war. Government funds were given to Italian and foreign journalists by the Consulta, and foreigners, notably the French, in turn subsidised the Italian press, but this 'corruption' was more part of the social system of Liberal Italy than a cause of particular decisions about foreign policy. The press was not part of a conspiracy but merely reflected and expressed the unspoken assumptions which conjoined the ruling class of Liberal Italy to its agents conducting Italian diplomacy.

An examination of more specialised pressure groups provides further obvious evidence of the close but informal relationship between the making of foreign policy and domestic structures. The Italian equivalents of the Pan German League or *parti colonial* were the Italian Navy League (set up in 1897 and allowed to finance itself by a parliamentarily approved lottery), the Dante Alighieri Society, the Geographical Society, the Istituto Coloniale Italiano (founded after a conference at Asmara in 1905) and other still more narrow bodies. None of these institutions aimed at anything like mass membership. Membership lists often overlapped. San Giuliano was, before he became Foreign Minister, President of the Geographical Society and Vice-President both of the Navy League and the Istituto Coloniale. Members came from the court, and from politics, diplomacy, commerce, the intelligentsia and the press, with no one section clearly predominating. All the patriotic institutions expected, needed and received government subsidies in order to survive.

Beyond these elite bodies there were other, mass organisations paying some attention to foreign policy. Socialists (and sometimes Catholics) favoured internationalism. Republicans and radicals patronised irredentist and sometimes also pacifist societies. But these ideas, even irredentism which had been so strong in the 1870s and 1880s, merged into the general political context and rarely directly affected specific diplomatic action.

If a sociological category has to be found to typify the group in Italy with interest in and influence over foreign policy, then the best term is 'the intellectuals'. Gramsci endorses its usage. And Mussolini provides the splendid example of an Italian politician pining after intellectual recognition. He expected his wife to address him as *professore* until after the birth of their fourth child![75] The 'best and the brightest' have had enormous prestige in Italy since the Risorgimento, paralleling, to a considerable degree, the situation which Zeldin has discerned to be true in the Third Republic in France.[76] But then there is the comment of a poor man, questioned by a journalist after the Messina earthquake: 'A Messina chiamano professori tutti i borghesi'. ('At Messina we address all the bourgeoisie as "professore".')[77] In Liberal Italy the terms intellectuals, the political world and the ruling class were near enough to being synonymous.

In the final analysis the major characteristics of the relationship between domestic and foreign policy, and of all the unspoken assumptions of Italian diplomacy, is the unanimity of those interested in foreign policy about Italy's needs. Even the most notorious conflict in the Liberal period, that between Giolitti and his supporters, on the one hand, and Salandra and Sonnino and their supporters on the other, over war entry in 1915, sprang from a difference in method and not in aim. Giolitti and many other neutralists did not reject the concept of Italy cold-bloodedly entering the First World War; they merely did not believe that the time was ripe in May 1915.

Italy's record, then, is very different from that of Imperial Germany, which was a country with many different interest groups, each of which, at times, had its own foreign policy. In Italy there were also many interest groups which contested against each other, but, with the possible exception of the socialists, the political leaders and the ruling class agreed that Italy must have a foreign policy, and that it must be that of a Great Power. The policy operated best in peacetime, and could be passive, but if opportunity offered Italy should employ as much cynicism and opportunism as was needed in order to get closer to being a genuine Great Power. Any abandonment of passivity, any colonial let alone any general war, was perilous in the extreme. But then if failure came, as it very likely would, the system could hope to escape by putting blame on an individual –Crispi in 1896, Tittoni in 1908, perhaps Mussolini after 1940. The individual could be dropped, but the sense of ambition, however chastened for a time, would continue.

In December 1903 Tittoni piously began his maiden speech on

diplomacy to the Chamber of Deputies with the statement: 'the principal quality of any foreign policy must be its continuity'.[78] For once, piety was not out of place. Despite changing social, political and international circumstances, despite the appearance and disappearance of certain individuals, Italian foreign policy from 1860 to 1915 (and perhaps to 1945) did have remarkable continuity. In imitation of her betters, or, rather, of those with more power, Italy sought to forget social crises at home and ignore the emigrants who were making abroad their own foreign policy of the poor, by finding 'a place in the sun', by being a Great Power. Trieste and Trento must eventually be redeemed. In general war, they would be the priority. But there were plenty of other areas for hope and cupidity. In the Mediterranean and Adriatic there were Tunis, Malta, Corsica, Libya, Egypt, Turkish Asia Minor, the Aegean Islands, Albania and Montenegro. Beyond beckoned the Somaliland, Eritrea, Yemen and Ethiopia. Few Foreign Ministers making their diplomacy in the traditional world, few segments of political and public opinion commenting on foreign policy, disagreed with this triple policy of peace, fear and ambition.

3 Italy Among the Powers, 1900–11

Italy was the diplomatic 'quantité negligéable'; the nation of 'sturdy beggars'. By 1900 few European statesmen saw any reason to doubt the accuracy of these words of Lord Salisbury in dismissing all Italy's pretensions to be a Great Power. Italy was a 'poor country [which] . . . will always have their hand out for a "piccola elemosina" '.[1]

The 1890s had been a very bad decade for Italy, both at home and abroad. At home there had been the spectre of social and regional revolution in the activities of the Sicilian *fasci* in 1893–4,[2] and then the national rioting and unsuccessful repression under the governments of Rudinì and General Pelloux from 1898 to 1900. In Milan, some hundred civilians died as soldiers tore down barricades in the events of 6 to 9 May 1898.[3] Parliamentarism seemed a sham or a disgrace. In a notorious incident in the Chamber on 30 June 1899, Leonida Bissolati, the intellectual young socialist, punched the conservative Sidney Sonnino on the nose and knocked him down, while another socialist, De Felice Giuffrida, with a band of supporters, smashed up the ballot boxes which recorded parliamentary votes.[4] Italians cemented their international reputation as anarchists, brigands and *mafiosi* by their involvement in celebrated assassinations. It was an Italian who assassinated the Austrian Empress Elizabeth in 1898. It was another Italian, a returned emigrant from the United States, who brought the decade to a close by assassinating King Umberto at Monza on 29 July 1900. One Italian conservative thought that these years meant that 'revolution is not yet here, but it will end by being a fact in reality since all believe that it must be'.[5] Another conservative, more succinctly, noted that the trouble was parliamentarism, which had brought 'great woe' to Italy.[6]

On the international scene, Italy played a lowly part in the 1890s. When the decade began Italy was still the third naval power in the world, and in 1893 Lord Salisbury thought that, as far as Britain was concerned, 'the key of the present situation in Europe is our position towards Italy'.[7] But the next years brought calamity in Ethiopia, where Italy committed the sin not so much of losing a battle as failing massively to avenge a defeat and thus restoring the 'honour' of the white man.[8] Moreover, by 1896 when the humiliation at Adowa occurred, Italy was isolated diplomatically. The strong men of Europe, Bismarck and Salisbury, had been appalled by Crispi's blatant attempts to get Germany and Britain to act as Italy's noble seconds. Italy failed to keep up her arms spending just as the other Powers began to accelerate theirs. By 1900 most expert opinion agreed that even the Italian Navy was now of only derisory significance.[9] Financially, too, Italy was in a bad way. From 1887 to 1896 Crispi had destructively engaged in a trade war with France just at a time when the vine disease, phylloxera, was devastating a major area of Italian agricultural produce. There were harvest failures in 1897 and 1899, and in 1898 the average Italian calorie intake was, among the major European states, only greater than that in Spain and Russia.[10] A Tory English journal commented tartly:

Italy has been bled to death by a corrupt bureaucracy, and the heavy expenses of an utterly unnecessary army and navy are wrung from the half-starved masses . . . . She was better off in the old days of Papal rule or even of King Bomba. At least men then had bread.[11]

However, the new decade, symbolised by the new King, Victor Emmanuel III, and by the new governments of Zanardelli and Giolitti, would be much better. Shortly after Crispi's fall, Italy's diplomatic position had begun to improve. In Africa, Rudinì offered a policy of retrenchment, a public abandonment of Crispi's adventures against Ethiopia. Because soldiers had lost the war at Adowa, a civilian, Ferdinando Martini, an elegant belle-lettrist who, one day, would attempt, unsuccessfully, to write lyrics for Giacomo Puccini, was sent as governor to Italy's surviving colony, Eritrea, which lay along the Red Sea.[12] By 1901, a visitor reported unfavourably on the Italian imperialist effort: 'They seemed to be making no progress whatever with their . . . possession, there were really no colonists and only a few shopkeepers. The colony was not popular and officers only came to it attracted by the higher pay they received.'[13] In 1913 the grand total of permanent Italian settlers in Eritrea was still only 61.[14]

Yet the turning away from Africanism was more apparent than

real. After Adowa, for the next two decades, 'Africa' was always the word which could most easily arouse popular resentment against colonialism and the Army, and politicians were therefore very reluctant to be caught out meddling in the Horn of Africa. But the desire lingered to meddle, to overturn Adowa, one day, when opportunity offered, to take Ethiopia. Martini, even though a civilian and a man of the world, occcupied himself building a new capital at Asmara. The site on the inland plateau, and the pseudo-Renaissance arcades planned for in the architecture, all indicated that Italy intended to stay in Eritrea. Martini had never wavered in his dislike of the prospect that Eritrea would become instead the colony of Britain or France.[15]

By 1903–4, as the glory of Emperor Menelik II, victor at Adowa, grew tarnished by old age and tribal rivalries,[16] Italian diplomatic action towards Ethiopia revived, albeit hesitantly. In 1903 Bertie, the British ambassador in Rome, was approached, first by Tittoni and later by King Victor Emmanuel himself, with the suggestion that the interested parties, Britain, Italy and probably France, come to an agreement whereby Italy could be granted a concession in the Juba land on the borders of Somaliland, and perhaps also a division of spheres of influence in Ethiopia.[17]

Since 1892 a section of Somaliland, the 'Benadir coasts', had been administered in Italian interests by private companies with dreams of the exploitation of cotton and government subsidies.[18] Progress in the former area was slow, and in 1903 it was reported that there were only 20 Italians living in the Benadir territory, that they could not travel even the shortest distance without armed escorts and that they were otherwise occupied merely in contesting each other's financial claims.[19] Italian governments reacted with extreme suspicion and studied procrastination to the numerous British suggestions that Italian troops apprehend the 'Mad Mullah', who was using the Italian sphere as a recuperating base against British-controlled lands.[20] Despite this, the compulsion, characteristic of Italian foreign policy, never to surrender anything once gained, led, in 1905, to the Somaliland formally being raised to the status of a national colony. In 1910 the colony was given as governor an active colonialist, Giacomo De Martino, uncle of his namesake, the later Secretary-General of the Foreign Ministry. De Martino began to construct the first roads which the colony had seen, a new residence for himself, and even dreamed of a complex railway network.[21] None the less the colony only limped towards civilisation. In 1913 plague broke out at Mogadiscio,[22] the Somaliland's capital and main port.

Real Italian interest remained focused on Eritrea and, on its borders, Ethiopia. From the first soundings in 1903, after three years of unhurried negotiations, on 13 December 1906 an Anglo-Franco-Italian agreement was initialled in London. Its first clauses affirmed the three Powers' upright loyalty to the *status quo* and honest neutrality, should order in Ethiopia break down. Later clauses sketched a division of interests in Ethiopia for hypothetical reference. Britain would safeguard the headwaters of the Nile; France would protect the hinterland of the railway which she was building from Jibuti to Addis Ababa; Italy would control a swathe of territory which would unite Eritrea to the Somaliland.[23] Further events must await the death of Menelik.

Adowa had not thus destroyed Italian aspirations in the Horn of Africa, but the publicity surrounding the defeat had ensured that, during the next decades, Italian ambition would look more to Europe, and what was often already called the *mare nostrum*, that is, the Mediterranean.

Within Europe, Italy's key diplomatic arrangement was the Triple Alliance. The initial treaty of the Triple Alliance was signed on 20 May 1882 by delegates from Germany, Austria–Hungary and Italy. Article II pledged aid if either Italy or Germany was attacked by France, and other clauses provided assistance for a signatory if attacked by two or more Great Powers, and benevolent neutrality if a signatory, having been threatened, was driven to make war itself. There were also provisions for military and economic interchange. The terms were to be secret, and the treaty would last five years.[24]

Apart from the domestic attractions to King Umberto of alliance with the monarchies of the north, the agreement had arisen very much out of the international manipulations of Otto von Bismarck. In 1881 he had encouraged the French to occupy Tunis, which lay just across the Mediterranean from Sicily, and had been an object of potential colonial and imperial interest to Italian states even before the Risorgimento.[25] In Bizerta, Tunis possessed the best port on the North African coast.[26] Moreover 11,000 Italians lived in Tunis itself (in 1915 the number, for the whole territory, had grown to 130,000,[27] being another example of the difference between the foreign policy of the poor and that of the government). The Italian ruling class was always inclined to be suspicious of France, which, patriotic publicists liked to recall, had stolen Corsica in 1768 (thus falsely making Bonaparte French instead of 'Italian'), and which had so graspingly insisted on the cession of Savoy and Nice as the price for their incomplete help in the wars of the Risorgimento. Tunis made the cup of Italian fear and hostility towards France overflow, and, in 1882, Italy was easily persuaded to join the Triple Alliance.

Not that Bismarck's stratagems were directed at seducing Italy because of her own attraction. Rather, in allying with Italy, he aimed at a tacit agreement with Britain[28] which was Italy's patron or 'traditional friend'. Thus in 1887, the renewal of the Triple Alliance until 1892 was accompanied in addition by a Mediterranean Agreement between Italy and Britain for 'mutual support' in every problem that might arise in the area.[29]

Italy had little reason to quarrel with Britain, her patron and coal supplier, or with Germany, the other new, great nation, which was an object of Italian emulation and envy and also of increasing importance in Italy's commerce, finance and industry. The problem of the Triple Alliance lay rather in Italy's relationship with the third signatory, Austria–Hungary.

The major external enemy of Italian unification had been the Habsburg Empire. For many of the Italian ruling classes, the acquisition of Venetia in 1866 left the contest against Austria unfinished. Eventually official propaganda would define the First World War as the war to complete the Risorgimento.[30] Beyond the borders of the new Italy lay the major city of Trieste, in 1914 the eighth greatest port in the world.[31] The ethnicity of its population was hard to define, but its governing language had long been Italian. Moreover its architecture, and, even more so, that of the smaller cities of the Istrian peninsula and the Dalmatian coast –towns such as Pola, Fiume, Zara and Spalato, which had once been part of the Venetian Empire – could easily stimulate Italian nationalist sentiment in the hearts and pens of publicists. In 1882 they gained a fresh martyr for their cause when the Austrian authorities executed a certain Guglielmo Oberdan (or Wilhelm Oberdank), a Triestine deserter from the Habsburg armies, who had become an Italian nationalist and planned to assassinate the Emperor Francis Joseph.[32]

Apart from Trieste and its hinterland, the city of Trento, famous once for the Council of the Counter Reformation and today for a university whose sociology courses inspired the leadership of the Red Brigades, was another object of Italian nationalist ambition, or, as it was called, 'irredentism' – the desire to regain the *terra irredenta* or the unredeemed lands. In Trento, as in Trieste, the realities of the situation were complicated. Trento was, ethnically, an Italian city, but it would be strategically vulnerable unless Italian ambition extended to cities further north, notably Bolzano (Bözen) and Merano (Meran), and to the Alpine watershed, that is to the top of the Brenner Pass. But Bolzano and Merano were German-speaking cities, and the peasants of the area were also German.[33]

In Trieste any reality behind Italian pretensions weakened with the passing of the years. The population of the city increased from 45,000 in 1815 to over 200,000 in 1914. Financially Trieste grew because it was the southern outlet for much of the commerce of Central Europe, and the terminus of the Südbahn railway from Vienna. Indeed Trieste's prosperity allowed her to become a major employer of Italians from over the border, so-called *regnicoli*, who found more and better paid jobs in the Habsburg Empire than in their own kingdom. Annexation to Italy would be likely instead to convert the city to a backwater. The political emergence of the Slav peoples, Slovenes and Croats, which accompanied the peasant drift to the city, and was favoured by the Austrian authorities, meant a major challenge to Italian predominance. In 1914, the nationality of the city of Trieste was still confused,[34] but the peasantry of the land behind the city and some of the urban working classes were Slav.

In the wake of these events, and of the wider diplomatic situation, irredentism became a more and more equivocal force in Italian politics. In the 1850s and 1860s, hating the Austrians was a popular activity. Then, in the Marches, it was reported that even the Lord's Prayer had been converted to carry an anti-Austrian message: 'Our Father who art ... the first Soldier of Italian independence ... make our nationality respected as we respect that of others; lead us to enjoy peace but deliver us from the infamous Austrian'.[35] A number of irredentist societies were established, the most famous being the Pro Italia Irredenta association founded in Naples in 1877.

However, in the next decades, irredentism lost ground as a serious force. The existence of the Triple Alliance made irredentism seem unrealistic as a basis of foreign policy. By 1896 Rudinì had coined the dictum: 'if the Triple Alliance did not exist it would be necessary to invent it'.[36] By then, irredentism remained the creed of republicans and radicals, of sentimental Mazzinians such as M. R. Imbriani who neither accepted the Savoyard system nor were attracted by the new theses of socialism. In contrast, respectable monarchists grew accustomed to the idea of alliance with Austria, and to proper collaboration by the House of Savoy with the great dynasties, Habsburg and Hohenzollern. Socialists, too, disliked irredentism. Italian socialists admired and imitated their more organised comrades in Berlin and Vienna. The Party newspaper, *Avanti!*, took its title from the German SPD's *Vorwaerts*, and, after 1900, a complicated series of contacts developed between Italian socialists and those of Germany and Austria. In Trieste, socialism stood for the working class rather than Italian or Slav nationality. These contacts, both legal and practical, meant the existence of a sort of socialist Triple Alliance.[37] In 1910, Bissolati curtly dismissed irredentist traditions: 'Don't talk to me about irredentism. No serious person among us even suggests the plan of a war with Austria in order to regain Italian lands'.[38] In 1912, a local Triestine socialist pointed out that, if irredentism wanted to have an appropriate task, then Italians were worse off in Nice, Corsica, Malta or the Ticino than they were in Trieste.[39] Even an irredentist admitted that the most likely way by then that a Triestine became an irredentist was to be born into an irredentist family.[40]

To conclude from this evidence that Italy and Austria had become natural allies would be absolutely wrong. With the onset of the war, Ferdinando Martini was to say that Austria had been Italy's ultimate enemy for the past 50 years.[41] And, as far as almost all Italian political leaders were concerned, he was right. In the short term, over-enthusiastic irredentism seemed obsolescent, because its associated policy of republicanism was losing a domestic base both in Trieste and in Italy. But the long-term ambition to complete the Risorgimento, to give Italy strategically sound and what were alleged to be ethnically just borders, remained the basic credo of the Italian ruling classes. In a peacetime which might last for ever, it was useful and even necessary for Italy to ally with Austria. After all, Italy had ambitions beyond those in Trieste. In the unlikely event of general war, a war which brought Italy opportunity, then Italy's first goal, whether by diplomacy within the Alliance or by military action against it, must be Trento and Trieste. As a left-liberal politician noted cynically in 1909: 'All [our statesmen's] efforts must unite to preserve the Austrian alliance until the day when we are ready for war. That day is still far off'.[42]

This cynicism was reciprocated within Austria. The alliance with the contemptible Italians had its uses especially when Austria attempted, as under Aehrenthal from 1906 to 1912, to make foreign policy as independent of Germany as was possible.[43] The alliance had a domestic significance also. The Hungarian section of the Empire had little to fear from Italian irredentism, and sometimes liked to invoke the historic contacts between Kossuth and Garibaldi.[44] Economic bonds were increased between the two countries with the agricultural agreements of 1891 and 1906. Although there was sometimes commercial competition, as in insurance, Adriatic shipping or investment in the Balkans, Austria enjoyed a favourable balance of trade with Italy. By 1913, the value of imports and exports to and from Austria was similar to Italy's trade with France.[45] But Austrian foreign policy was no more dictated by her trade interests than was Italian. Austrian soldiers still talked of the prospect of launching preventive war against Italy (in January 1909, for example, after the Messina earthquake, or during the Libyan war). The Austrian Navy also constructed its Dreadnoughts in direct competition with Italy.[46] An Italian naval plan, in 1913, which demanded the building of Italian ships in a 4:3 ratio against Austria, a 2:3 ratio against France, with no other countries mentioned,[47] expressed well enough the military reality (or unreality) of the Triple Alliance.

Thus, the edifice of Italian foreign policy in the Triple Alliance rested uneasily on matters stated and unstated, on myth and on reality, and on the constant interchange occurring between the two. The nature of Italo-Austrian relations was yet another reason why pre-1914 Italian foreign policy was equivocal and even tortuous, and why, in retrospect, it seems so dishonest and absurd.

None the less the legal side of treatying and the daily round of peacetime diplomacy carried a certain weight of contact and habit. Successive renewals had amplified the terms of the Triple Alliance. In 1891, Articles VI and VII pledged Italo-German and Italo-Austrian recognition of a mutual interest in the *status quo* 'on the Ottoman coasts and islands in the Adriatic and Aegean Seas'. Also confirmed in Article VII was an agreement of 1887 between Italy and Austria, which had asserted that any change in the *status quo* in the Balkans would 'take place only after a previous agreement between the two Powers . . . based upon the principle of reciprocal compensation for every advantage, territorial or other, which each

[Power] ... might obtain beyond the present *status quo*'.[48] It was this clause which would eventually give Italy the legal justification for her declaration of neutrality in 1914.

In 1892 Romania, a state with similar irredentist ambitions towards Austria–Hungary, became an associate to the Triple Alliance.[49] In December 1900 Italy and Austria signed a special agreement on the Ottoman territory of Albania, where both were developing strategic, commercial and cultural interests. Again the clauses piously pledged a defence of the *status quo* or a search to reconcile reciprocal interests.[50] although, in practice, an Italo-Austrian cold war for the souls and balance sheets of the Albanian leadership steadily intensified. On 28 June 1902, the Triple Alliance was again renewed,[51] and two days later Prinetti, the Italian Foreign Minister, could rejoice that Austria–Hungary, 'having no special interest to safeguard in Tripolitania and Cyrenaica', had also agreed 'to undertake nothing which might interfere with the action of Italy, in case, as a result of fortuitous circumstances, the state of things now prevailing in those regions should undergo any change whatsoever'.[52]

Prinetti had been a busy man during that summer in Rome. After Adowa, Visconti Venosta had turned back from Crispi's disastrous policy of political and economic confrontation with France. In 1897–8, with major assistance from Luigi Luzzatti, the garrulous Jewish financier and politician, Visconti Venosta was able to end the trade war with France.[53] An Italo-French *rapprochement* was also favoured by Camille Barrère, the new and very able French ambassador, and by Théophile Delcassé, who took office as French Foreign Minister in 1898 and had as one of his basic aims the wooing of Italy away from the Triple Alliance.[54]

Characteristically, political differences were less easy to resolve than financial ones. But, in December 1900, in an exchange of notes, Visconti Venosta and Barrère pledged a mutual recognition of Italy's special interests in Libya, and of those of France in Morocco. Visconti Venosta, despite his reputation as a model of restraint,[55] did nothing to prevent Italian intervention, along with the other European powers, in events in China, that Empire which, expansionists boasted lustfully, was 'the great carcass of Asia'.[56] In 1901, Italy participated ingloriously in the European expedition to suppress the Boxer rebellion.

Prinetti took over as Foreign Minister in February 1901. Though a businessman, he pushed Italy's political rather than her commercial interests and did so with a crude opportunism which was in practice not a break in diplomatic traditions, but was so in appearance, and was therefore notably unsuccessful.[57] Despite Italy's reliance on Britain, in June 1901 Prinetti chattily suggested to Barrère that, if the circumstances of the Boer War continued, Italy might well have to join a hypothetical continental league against Britain.[58] In 1902, Prinetti's policy grew still more active. First, Italy reached an agreement with Britain. Under unremitting pressure from Rome, Lansdowne, the British Foreign Secretary, on 12 March, added Britain to the list of Powers who recognised that, should there be a change in the *status quo*, then Italy's special interests in Libya would be recognised.[59] Yet, on any realistic assessment, the agreement was practically worthless, being founded on the most unlikely principle that so major an event as the break-up of the Ottoman Empire would occur with such surgical neatness that hopes elsewhere would not interfere with Italy's special hopes in Libya. The treatying was accompanied by notably 'incorrect' diplomatic behaviour: Prinetti showed the British the text of the 'secret' Italo-French exchange of 1900, and the British promptly conveyed to the Germans the 'secret' text of the eventual agreement of March 1902.[60] Only a few weeks after the agreement was signed, Viscount Cranborne, Under-Secretary of State for Foreign Affairs, told the House of Commons that Britain's position on Tripoli was quite without obligation to Italy, and he probably believed what he said.[61] In 1911, San Giuliano and the Italian ambassador, Imperiali, tried to remind the British of the 1902 agreement, but the Foreign Office had difficulty locating its copy, and British inaction before Italy's invasion of Libya owed very little to the words uttered in 1902. Rather the agreement indicated a continuation of Salisbury's earlier advice about what to do with Italy:

To my mind the Italian alliance is an unprofitable and even slightly onerous corollary on the German alliance . . . . We have to make words do as much work as can be got out of them; for it is out of the question that we should show our gratitude to the unreasonable extent they desire.[62]

The more notorious of Prinetti's diplomatic 'triumphs' of 1902 was not the agreement with Britain, but that with France. On 30 June 1902, that is two days after the renewal of the Triple Alliance, Prinetti and Barrère signed a secret agreement pledging that Italy would remain neutral in any conflict to which French entry had been 'provoked'. Privately Prinetti defined provocation as having occurred in the Ems telegram, the Schnaebele incident and in some aspects of the Fashoda affair.[63] Neither the formal post-dating of the agreement to 2 November, nor its secrecy, hid the fact that Italy had admitted more openly than ever before that the Triple Alliance, for all its legal terms and military exchanges, was an agreement which could operate in peace but not if there was war between the Great Powers.

Prinetti scarcely understood these subtleties. He went on urging that the Triple Alliance had not been infringed, claiming for example, that the declaration that there were no differences 'in the respective interests' of Italy and France 'in the Mediterranean' was irrelevant to the Triple Alliance, which dealt with 'Europe'. Other Italian Foreign Ministers would later try to exploit this geographical vagueness in Italy's legal arrangements with the other Powers.

What Prinetti was probably aiming at in the welter of his policies was the imminent seizure of Libya. (Interestingly, for a businessman-statesman, his ambition ran in an area of most unlikely financial advantage where Italy had, as yet, developed very few commercial interests. In 1901, only 704 Italians lived in Tripoli.[64]) But, in this ambition, Prinetti was blocked from within the Zanardelli Cabinet, especially by Giolitti, the powerful Minister of the Interior, who threatened to resign if there was any move across the Mediterranean.[65] So Prinetti, to his chagrin, achieved no 'grand design' and in March 1903 was driven to resign. Soon after his resignation he went mad and died in 1908.

What Prinetti had in fact achieved was very slight, despite the claims enunciated by some historians of a 'diplomatic revolution'. The Prinetti–Barrère agreement left Italy, perhaps a little more publicly than before, in a position of independence between the other Powers. It also made it obvious that Italy was the least strong of the Powers, the state which deserved Bülow's gibe in January 1902 about its vulnerability to genteel seduction.

What Prinetti's policy indicated was that, in moments of opportunity or enthusiasm, the centre of Italian expansionism would be the Mediterranean, that sea which washed the 'Fourth Shore' of Libya. At the same time, if Italy did look for advantage in the Mediterranean, then the country with whose interests she must compete was France (and, perhaps, just conceivably, Britain). Should events drive France to concentrate more on the Mediterranean, then the Power which would cause her immediate problems was Italy.

Prinetti had thus left unresolved the basic dispute at the heart of Italo-French relations. Italian publicists continued to regard Paris with affection and envy, and be readily slighted by France's effortless superiority towards her little 'Latin sister'. Financiers continued to be grateful and jealous that so much French (and Belgian) money was invested in Italian governmental, municipal and private bonds. For most Italian statesmen, France continued to be Public Enemy Number Two. In an ideal world, as San Giuliano put it in September 1914, Austria would be beaten in the Adriatic and surrender Trieste; France would be beaten on land and abandon Savoy or Nice or Corsica or Tunis to her deserving poor relation, Italy.[66]

There were few signs in the decade before 1914 that God would be so generous to Italy. Instead, greater events in the diplomatic constellation worked to Italy's disadvantage. In 1904, Prinetti's promises about Fashoda were rendered irrelevant when Britain and France reached their Entente Cordiale. From then on, Italian statesmen were confronted by the insoluble dilemma that Britain and Germany, Italy's two traditional patrons, fell more and more into a conflict which Luigi Luzzatti saw as 'the final catastrophe for civilisation'[67] and which, for many Italians, signalled the end of Italian hopes and ambitions. The desire for Anglo-German friendship had been the motive which persuaded Bismarck to form the Triple Alliance, but now German leaders increasingly believed that Britain could not be won over to reason. British leaders, on the other hand, were glad that Italy remained in the Triple Alliance. Her greed and levity could be relied on to embarrass her partners, as could the latent conflict between Italy and Austria. When the Anglo-Russian agreement of 1907 created a Triple Entente, the Foreign Office in London became still more convinced that Italy was best left in the Triple Alliance. Why try to tempt the faithless Italians out of their current ménage when an exchange of partners might encourage Russia to look again at the attractions of Germany? As Hardinge, the Permanent Under-Secretary of the Foreign Office in London, explained: 'We have no desire to seduce Italy from the Triple Alliance, since she would rather be a thorn in the side than any assistance to France and ourselves'.[68]

The foreign policy of the years which followed Prinetti's occupation of the Consulta thus led to embarrassment after embarrassment. The Moroccan crisis played an unwelcome spotlight on Italy's numerous commitments and half-commitments. When a conference was called to Algeciras in order to resolve the Franco-German dispute about Morocco,[69] Tittoni and Giolitti at first opted for the sensible and necessary policy of the lowest possible profile. The Italian delegate was named as Giulio Silvestrelli, Italian ambassador to Spain, and a diplomat whose reliability could be vouchsafed by the fact that he was Tittoni's cousin. Italy, it seemed, was to attend the Algeciras meeting, but hope that no-one noticed her amid the greater powers.

The Giolitti government had resigned in March 1905, and been replaced by one led by an old irredentist, Alessandro Fortis. He kept Tittoni at the Consulta until December, when San Giuliano, fresh from the nationalist excitement of the Asmara Conference, was made Foreign Minister. In February 1906, after the conference had begun meeting at Algeciras, Fortis's new administration fell and, until Giolitti's and Tittoni's return in May, Sonnino became Prime Minister and Guicciardini, a Tuscan landowner, Foreign Minister.

For Barrère, the intrusive and hard-working French ambassador who was renowned for the close, rewarding and rewarded relationship which he had built up with the Italian press, the appointment of Silvestrelli was disappointing. Although it is very doubtful that he was sincere, Barrère began to spread rumours that Silvestrelli had been a Crispian and was a zealot for the Triple Alliance, who would be 'too inclined to take a line of his own'.[70] However, for Barrère, the real problem about Silvestrelli was not his independence, but his insignificance. If he was the delegate accredited to the Algeciras conference, then maybe Italy would try to creep away from a display of the 'new stance' taken in the Prinetti–Barrère agreement.

In order to ensure that Italy publicly exhibited her friendship with France, Barrère favoured the appointment of the elder statesman, Emilio di Visconti Venosta, who was famous both within Italy and abroad. Barrère won over the British ambassador, Egerton, to a solid loyalty to the Entente Cordiale, and Egerton dutifully began to promote the name of Visconti Venosta in government circles.[71] (Privately Barrère and his deputy, Laroche, had a very low opinion of Egerton, who was described as a diplomat with a mania for dinner parties, but who was so dull and unpopular that he had to invite all and sundry whether he 'knew' them or not.[72])

The intrigues of the ambassadors had little effect on Tittoni, who understood much about intrigue himself. But the replacement of Tittoni by San Giuliano changed circumstances. Silvestrelli's family relationship to Tittoni reduced his attractiveness to San Giuliano, a Sicilian aristocrat who wanted to be his own *padrone*. By the end of December 1905, it was announced that Visconti Venosta would be the Italian delegate. Visconti Venosta then showed that northern aristocrats also knew something about patronage and families by appointing two of his sons, successively, as his private secretaries for the duration of the conference.

Barrère's triumph was a little hollow. He had won in terms of personalities, but Visconti Venosta's appointment did not really represent a change in Italian policy. Indeed, Italy really did not have a policy, except to expect apprehensively that all would be well. As Visconti Venosta immediately explained to Egerton, it would be best if the Algeciras conference concentrated on the technicalities of the Morocco problem and not on high politics: 'He trusted the discussions of the Congress would not take a wide range and would not be complicated by subsidiary details'.[73] In these circumstances, he hoped Italy would with wisdom shoulder a Great Power's burden, as she had done in Macedonia or Crete, those other areas of international dispute.

At the conference, Visconti Venosta behaved with caution and good sense, and did some useful work in preserving a middle ground, especially in association with the delegates from Austria and the United States. But he really could not resolve the dilemma of Italy's conflicting ties in a dispute which divided the Great Powers more definitely than had the Macedonian or Cretan affairs. It was all very well for Sonnino to tell the Chamber that Visconti Venosta was pursuing 'a disinterested and active line of conciliation which is a testament of our loyalty towards our allies and our friends';[74] but, in the emotional atmosphere engendered by the crisis, both allies and friends grew testy about Italy's untrustworthiness. Visconti Venosta was soon explaining in embarrassment to Rome that the best that could be hoped for was for Italy 'to emerge from the conference in the same international position which she had before she went into it'.[75] Nicolson, the British delegate, irritatedly complained that Visconti Venosta was old, tired and unhelpful.[76] Monts, the German ambassador to Rome, already in 1905 had said: 'So tricky a customer as the pseudo-Great Power, Italy, is nothing but a deadweight [on the

Triple Alliance] which our policy has to drag along behind it', and he continued to advise Berlin that alliance with Italy was not worth the trouble.[77] On 13 April 1906, the Kaiser, William II, ostentatiously thanked his 'noble second', Austria, for her backing during the conference, and, just as ostentatiously, failed to acknowledge Italy's role.[78] The British ambassador in Berlin reported home, with a certain satisfaction: 'There can be no doubt that Germany is very indignant at what she considers the undutiful behaviour of Italy at Algeciras'.[79]

In practical terms, rebuke from Germany and self-interested praise from France only showed Italian foreign policy to be what it was. Nothing had changed. With the alarums of the conference over, and with Tittoni back at the Consulta in May 1906 as a member of Giolitti's third government, Italian foreign policy soon settled back into its accustomed ambiguous course. Many Italian publicists were appalled by the openness of the dissidence between Britain and Germany,[80] but Italian diplomatists, averting their eyes from the perils of the future, again steered Italian policy along the line between 'friends' and 'allies'.

In October 1908, another international crisis exposed Italian weakness and unreliability. The Austrian Foreign Minister, Aehrenthal, on 6 October, announced that Austria–Hungary was annexing the ex-Turkish provinces of Bosnia and Herzegovina which she had administered since the Congress of Berlin in 1878.[81] Tittoni had been, somewhat half-heartedly, trying to preserve an Austro-Russo-Italian accord in the Balkans,[82] and perhaps even to make some gains in finance and prestige in Albania, or in the proposed Adriatic-to-Aegean railway. Tittoni had met both Aehrenthal and Izvolsky, the Russian Foreign Minister, in the weeks before the annexation of Bosnia–Herzegovina; he seems to have known that Adriatic to Aegean railway. Tittoni had met both Aehrenthal and to it, perhaps thinking that, in time, there might be some crumbs of compensation negotiable for Italy.

However, the reaction both at home and abroad rendered such expectations illusory. Faced with international division, Tittoni applied the usual Italian policy of seeking a haven under the protection of Britain,[83] but his manoeuvres and the recent character of Italian foreign policy had not made him a popular figure in London. When he complained that Aehrenthal's coup had been 'rather that of a baccarat player than of a serious statesman', a clerk in the Foreign Office minuted disdainfully, and without challenge: 'Signor Tittoni is a past master in the art of lying'.[84] The other patron, Germany, was even more unhelpful. In April 1908, Bülow had assured Tittoni that 'Italy will never find herself with the need of having to choose between the German alliance and English friendship';[85] but this pledge, comforting at the present, was, in the long term, an alarming indication that Germany did not regard Italy as a serious ally. Certainly there were few grounds for Italo-German collaboration in the weeks which followed the Bosnia–Herzegovina annexation. In January 1909, the German Chief of General Staff, von Moltke, cheerfully told his Austrian colleague, Conrad (who was then contemplating a preventative strike against Italy) that the Italian Army was in a pitiable condition.[86] Aehrenthal, too, not very politely, requested Tittoni for a statement whether Italy remained Austria's ally given 'the attitute of [Italian] public opinion'.[87] Two years later, the Minister of War, Spingardi, remained bleakly pessimistic about the long-term prospects of Italo-Austrian relations:

I could be wrong, but I see our situation towards Austria as insecure: perhaps our diplomatic ties may be of the best; perhaps the will to peace is sincere, but tension exists in the country and what is more serious in the Army: one spark, the death of the old emperor, the succession of the new who is openly hostile to us, can provoke a conflict, however contrary to the interests of the two countries.[88]

Italo-Austrian relations rarely showed any likelihood of settling into genuine harmony.

But Tittoni's efforts to move closer to Russia, the major victim of Austria's Balkan coup, also had brought little result. It was true that there were dreams within Italy that Russia might become an inexhaustible market for Italian citrus and wines.[89] On the level of ceremonial, the Tsar and Izvolsky, in October 1909, paid a state visit to Victor Emmanuel and Tittoni at the royal hunting lodge of Racconigi, near Turin. There Tittoni managed to extract a promise that Russia, too, recognised Italian interests in Libya should the *status quo* ever be changed. Tittoni was also alleged to have admitted that 'we shall come out [of the Triple Alliance] some day, but it will be to go to war [against Austria]'.[90] Later commentators have seen Racconigi as betraying 'the same morality on Italy's part as 1902 did',[91] but more significant is the nadir it represented in Italy's fortunes. By 1909, it seemed, Italy was keeping up her ancient policies of importuning everyone, but was finding most Powers more and more reluctant to talk to her seriously, and less and less willing to offer her any rewards. 'A Friend of Italy' such as the new British ambassador, Sir James Rennell Rodd, could find little inspiration in Italy's prospects or in his own metaphor:

Italy is in the position of having in a moment of pressure and difficulty made an unsympathetic marriage of interest. The law of divorce does not exist for her and though her best friends counsel reconciliation, she finds each successive plea for the restitution of conjugal rights more repugnant to her. Such situations rarely end happily.[92]

At home, Tittoni had a most unpleasant year in the wake of the Bosnia–Herzegovina affair. Italian political opinion had been appalled as usual by an open display of national weakness. Sonnino recalled the devastating complaint made against Cairoli in 1878; and Tittoni's hands were not merely empty but soiled as well. Italy, Sonnino complained, had lost her self-respect.[93] When, on 28 December 1908, the country was struck by the terrible Messina earthquake, which, in human and financial cost, was likened by the press to a military defeat,[94] then calamity, international and domestic, was complete. Italy seemed to have forfeited the status of being a Great Power.

While Tittoni's foreign policies of public quietism and occasional secret manipulation were leading to this low point in Italian fortunes, new currents of nationalism and expansionism were beginning to eddy around the Italian political world. The first indication came in the Asmara Conference of October 1905.[95] Initially the conference was the idea of Ferdinando Martini, the Governor of Eritrea, in order to celebrate his new capital and the achievements of his long governorship. The majority of delegates invited were Sonninian, conservatives who doubted the wisdom of Giolitti's policies and who had remained believers in the concept that Italy must have a colonial future.

By the time the conference met, it had obtained government patronage, had attracted representatives from all segments of the political world interested in foreign affairs and imperialism, and had extended the definition of Italian colonialism well beyond 'Africa'. The future of Eritrea and Ethiopia was exalted but so too were Italy's 'special interests' in Libya, and the need was proclaimed 'to affirm' a policy of more effective 'pacific commercial penetration by Italy . . . in the Mediterranean basin'. The relationship of the always increasing flood of emigration to the necessity for a colonialist future was underlined.[96] It was agreed that the Istituto Coloniale Italiano be set up in Rome, and that it would publish a journal, *Rivista Coloniale*, which would disseminate patriotic 'colonial culture' and comprehend the emigration question: 'Faith and energy are not enough; nor are passing enthusiasms and big words'. What the Italian foreign and colonial policy demanded was 'clear ideas [and] precise aims' which would not, as in the past, see the wasting of 'fine initiatives'. Soon 'experts' were suggesting that Italy ought to enunciate a Monroe doctrine towards other Powers' interference in Libya; that archaeological or agricultural expertise could be Italy's special gift to the areas washed by the Mediterranean; that emigration and commercial expansion should go together; and that the Tigrè or Yemen or Constantinople or the Jubaland was especially attractive to Italy.[97] De Martino, the future Governor of the Somaliland, in a presidential address in April 1907 warned of the general struggle occurring between the British and Germanic 'races', and prophesied that, if Italy wanted to preserve any economic foundations of her own, she too must sooner or later join the struggle for colonies.[98]

The problems experienced by the Italian economy in 1907 added some impetus to this colonialism. Yet Italian capitalists did not direct foreign policy and remained a little naive in their comments on foreign affairs. Bonnefon Craponne, the French citizen who was director of the Lega Industriale of Turin, specifically disclaimed any interest in social imperialism and with his friend, Luzzatti, continued to pronounce that international peace was absolutely essential for Italy.[99]

In October 1908, the month of Bosnia–Herzegovina, Tittoni was again embarrassed when the ICI held in Rome its first great patriotic ceremonial, the First Congress of Italians Abroad. Although the rhetoric was more cautiously official than on some other occasions, the ICI again suggested that Italian emigration should, at least partially, be directed to Italy's own colonies, and that the ICI should be recognised as the spokesman of all Italian emigrants.[100] In the first days after the Bosnia–Herzegovina crisis, San Giuliano, then ambassador in London, and one of the most politically important figures in the revival of colonialism, dropped a thinly disguised hint that Tittoni should be replaced as Foreign Minister, presumably by someone such as San Giuliano himself, more in tune with colonialist opinion.[101]

The more renowned critics of the passivity of Giolittian foreign policy were Enrico Corradini, Giovanni Papini and Filippo Marinetti, those Nationalists and Futurists who were stirring among the young generation of Italian intellectuals. Their role will be discussed in more detail later, but it is important not to view it out of context. In 1909, a feeling of futility and frustration with the current line of foreign policy was experienced by many Italians interested in foreign policy, and was not unreasonable while the chimera of Great Powerdom was still to be sought.

In high policy, Tittoni, at the end of 1909, left a legacy which was little changed by the humiliation of Bosnia and Herzegovina. Racconigi did not mean any serious new *entente* with Russia. Predictably, in November and December 1909, an exchange of notes between Vienna and Rome bringing new definition to future Austro-Italian relations towards European Turkey had acted as compensation within the Triple Alliance for the Italo-Russian *rapprochement*. The Austrians admitted that a move by them against the Sandjak of Novi-Bazar would justify an indemnity to Italy under Article VII of the Triple Alliance.[102] Apart from Izvolsky, who had his own reasons to search out any ally or friend whatever, few Russian statesmen showed major interest in Italy. In 1912 Sazonov, the new Foreign Minister, accepted the long-existing British view of Italy's place in the Triple Alliance: 'we do not regard it as in our interest to work for the formal withdrawal of Italy from the Triple Alliance'.[103]

After the First World War, F. S. Nitti and other commentators propounded the thesis that many Italian statesmen in the last years before 1914 were worried by the growth of Russian power, and by Russia's potential arrival in the Mediterranean or Adriatic.[104] It is true that Pollio was willing to mouth words about preventive war against Russia, and that San Giuliano, especially in discussions with the German ambassador, could talk sagely about the 'Slav peril'. Yet, too often these remarks have been taken out of context. Italian diplomats often said, for their own purposes, what they thought that their listeners would like to hear. In contrast to what he told the German ambassador, San Giuliano, for example, joked to his own colleagues that Russia was the Great Non-Power ('grande impotenza'), and his policy was rarely troubled by a belief that Russia directly threatened Italy's interests. In 1914 Giolitti already predicted that Russia would be the Power whose domestic system was most likely to collapse in war.[105] Russian policy, too, was less exercised by Italian ambition than was that of the other Great Powers. The belief that Russia was already beginning to play a major part in Italian strategic and diplomatic planning before 1914 seems to have sprung from the contestation by Russia of Italy's territorial aims in 1914-15, and even more from contemporaries' fears of Russia after 1917. What Nitti perceived in 1918–19 was not what San Giuliano or Giolitti had seen in 1914.[106]

If Tittoni did little to sort out Italian priorities on the general international scene, he did not abandon Italian aspirations. In the traditional areas of national interest, in Montenegro, Albania, Asia Minor and especially Libya, Tittoni was eager to give government assistance to Italian entrepreneurs who might be able to construct a future base for an Italian commercial or territorial empire. In Albania, for example, Tittoni preserved the continuity of Italy's cultural contest with Austria. But his most significant involvement in cultural or commercial expansionism was in Libya. There, the agent of new Italian interest was the Banco di Roma, that Vatican-financed institution in which Tittoni's brother, Romolo, held high office. From 1905, the Banco di Roma, with government blessing, began a major investment programme in Tripoli, and in other parts of the Eastern Mediterranean.[107] Once again, Italian dreams about the possibility of a change in the *status quo* in Libya were reviving.

In December 1909, when Giolitti's government fell and Tittoni left the Consulta, Sonnino and Guicciardini took over the management of foreign affairs. But Sonnino, as usual, was unable to apply his policies successfully at home, and in March 1910 Luigi Luzzatti became Prime Minister with Giolitti's blessing. He recalled San Giuliano from the Embassy in Paris to be Foreign Minister for the second time. San Giuliano's involvement in Africanism in the 1890s, in revived colonialism under the patronage of the Istituto Coloniale, and in the emigration question, made him appear a Foreign Minister of unusual expertise and one who might favour a more forward policy. In practice, however, in 1910, San Giuliano timidly preserved continuity, acknowledging the peril of open adventure and the reality of Italy's subordination to the other Great Powers.

The first sign of change came at the end of the year. Ibrahim

Pasha, a new Turkish *vali*, hostile to the Banco di Roma's pretensions to monopoly in Tripoli, had begun to treat Italian interests there unsympathetically. In a debate in the Chamber on 30 November, deputies friendly to Tittoni were unusually critical of San Giuliano's foreign policy and especially of his failure to protect Italian financial interests. San Giuliano gave a poor oratorical performance in rebutting his critics[108] and, despite his public statements that Italy was a loyal advocate of the preservation of the *status quo* in the whole Ottoman Empire,[109] he was shortly after forced to confess to his ambassador in Constantinople that Italo-Turkish relations had been driven to a crisis point by 'public opinion'.[110]

In the next months, the crisis showed no signs of going away. Instead, there was every indication that, among all political groups except the socialists, there was a widespread sense that a 'new period' was beginning,[111] and that Italy must grasp any opportunity which came her way. The Nationalist Association held its first Congress in Florence on 3 December 1910, and on 1 March 1911, the anniversary of Adowa, began publishing a weekly, *L'Idea Nazionale*, which echoed Corradini's cry that now was 'the hour of Tripoli'. But it was not only the nationalist press which urged action in Libya. A series of correspondents from the other major papers, including even *La Tribuna* and *La Stampa*, agreed that the Cyrenaican plateau was a potential Garden of the Hesperides.[112] By 20 September, a meeting of the respectable Dante Alighieri society in Rome was broken up by cries of 'To Tripoli, to Tripoli!'.[113]

Throughout 1911, there had been a series of patriotic manifestations celebrating the Cinquantennio, the fiftieth anniversary of the Risorgimento. In June, the Istituto Coloniale organised at Rome a Second and larger Congress of Italians Abroad held in the immediate aftermath of the ceremonies formally inaugurating the huge Victor Emmanuel monument.[114] On all such occasions, patriotic rhetoric was hard to avoid, and time and time again San Giuliano was impelled to repeat to Constantinople and the other capitals that 'the real mood' of 'public opinion' might force him to take 'energetic action' in Libya.[115]

Most threatening was renewed criticism in the Chamber of Deputies. There, on 7 June, while the Second Congress of Italians Abroad was meeting elsewhere in the city, the ex-Foreign Minister, Francesco Guicciardini, launched a major attack on the government. The trouble, he said, was that foreigners grew sentimental about

Italy, but did not respect her. Alliances and friendships meant merely that Italy was always talked out of any advantage. Italy must be ready to act by herself, and, in Libya, must be 'more energetic and more decisive'.[116]

Guicciardini was not only implying that he would be a more successful Foreign Minister than San Giuliano; he was also foreshadowing a move against Giolitti himself, who had taken over as Prime Minister from his 'lieutenant', Luzzatti, in March 1911. Guicciardini, after all, had twice been Sonnino's Foreign Minister. What the courtly words of the debate of 7 June indicated was that the Sonninian conservatives might use a prolonged passivity in Italian foreign policy to attack and destroy the whole Giolittian system, and thereby to out-distance the pretensions of the young men of the Nationalist Association to become the new 'constitutional opposition'.

In the Consulta, too, the bureaucrats of foreign policy were beginning to draft memoranda explaining how Italy could justify the taking of Libya. On 17 July, the ambassador in Constantinople was recalled, and it was announced that, once the heat of summer was over, his replacement would be Camillo Garroni. In the meantime, the Embassy would be managed by the Chargé, Giacomo De Martino, a diplomat who had the closest political and personal contacts with San Giuliano.[117] (They were even rumoured to share the favours of De Martino's wife.) There was also a change in personnel at the consulate in Tripoli, where, on 29 July, the youthful, intelligent and very patriotic Carlo Galli arrived to be Italy's 'last consul' there.[118] And San Giuliano, fearfully and in tortured prose, began to explain to Giolitti that the present, or at least the discernible future, was probably the moment of opportunity for Italy in Libya.[119]

Even pacifists and some socialists accepted the need to act. E. T. Moneta, the pacifist theorist who had won the Nobel Prize in 1907, declared that Italy had to go to Libya to avoid being caught in an 'iron-ring' in the Mediterranean.[120] Even that great moralist, Filippo Turati, was not insensible to the appeal of patriotism and opportunity.[121] By September, Giolitti, usually such an able judge of the political atmosphere, was convinced (wrongly as it turned out) that the Italian government would not be met by large-scale socialist hostility if he launched a colonial war.[122]

However, the supposed unanimity of Italian 'public opinion', which in any event comprised only the opinion of the political leadership, does not mean that Giolitti, who himself rarely showed signs of excessive patriotic excitation, was driven to make war because of it. International pressures were also propelling Italy towards decisive action. The international constellation had shifted in a way which suggested that 1911 might be the year of opportunity, and the only year of opportunity. Certainly that was the advice of the Italian military attaché in Constantinople.[123] With every year, the Anglo-French Entente Cordiale and its corollary, Anglo-German dissonance, seemed a more natural and inevitable accompaniment of the concert. In the Mediterranean, there were hints that naval strategies and deployments were beginning to be discussed in a way which did not bode well for Italy. In 1912, without any formal agreement, but with what would seem to Italy the maximum of implicit understanding, Britain and France decided to alter the disposition of their navies. Britain would concentrate on the North Sea; France on the Mediterranean. At sea, Italy was even more vulnerable than on land, and now it seemed feasible that the capricious and prepotent French would become the dominant naval power, and that the fleets of her kindly patron, Britain, would be far away.

In 1911, Italy had particular as well as general reasons to be doubtful of her future relationship with France. On 1 July, the German gunboat *Panther* anchored off the Moroccan port of Agadir, and the resulting crisis threatened, yet again, an open conflict between Britain and Germany. This danger passed, but only with the probability that France and Germany would formally resolve their differences in Morocco, and that any uncertainty about the French position there would be removed. In the treaty of 4 November, Germany acknowledged French mastery over Morocco.[124]

Legally, the clear probability of a French acquisition of Morocco meant that Italy could appeal to the terms of the Visconti Venosta–Barrère and Prinetti–Barrère exchanges, and perhaps even to the pledges of each of the other Powers that Italy had special interests in Libya should there be a change in the North African *status quo*. Italy's legal case was far less watertight than many Italian historians have maintained, but for Italy to have even an arguable case was unusual and very tempting.

Italy had other powers to think about apart from France. Germany would be unlikely to try to stop Italy (even under Austrian prodding), given her paramount involvement in the Moroccan crisis. Britain was sounded on 28 July, and Grey replied vaguely and courteously enough for San Giuliano to believe or maintain that he had received a green light.[125] But, as so often for Italy, the final pressure to act developed within Italy's relationship with Austria.

Throughout 1911, suggestions had been raised, in Rome and in Vienna, that soon the Triple Alliance should be renewed (even though legally this need not occur until 1914), and these hints grew more insistent in September. If Italy did not use the Moroccan affair to legitimise action in Libya, and thus preserve Prinetti's distinction between the 'Mediterranean' and 'Europe', then, in the renewal of the Triple Alliance, Austria might well ask for an extension of the terms which would allow her to claim compensation for Italian advantage in Libya.[126] Moreover, if Italian public opinion learned, or could be persuaded to believe, that it was Austria which prevented Italy from taking Libya, then irredentism and republicanism would be given extraordinary stimulation which might threaten general war, and/or a danger to the Savoy dynasty and the whole political system. Italo-Austrian relations were as good an explanation as were Italo-French relations why Italy finally acted in September 1911. Italy could rely on neither the friendship of her friends nor the alliances of her allies, but, if she did not act now, the various friendships and alliances would be worth even less than in the past. By 20 September, Giolitti and San Giuliano had made an irreversible decision to invade Libya as soon as possible. On 26 September, an ultimatum to Turkey was despatched to De Martino. It was presented to the Turkish government on 28 September, with a totally cynical assumption that no Turkish reply could now be satisfactory. By the time the ultimatum elapsed at 2.30 p.m. on 29 September, Italian troop ships were already sailing across the Mediterranean towards Tripoli.

In the final analysis, Giolitti's decision for war was based on the primacy of external over internal politics. Italy had acted because the time was ripe for her in the system of international relations. Domestic pressures for war there certainly were, the clamour of 'public opinion' and the more subtle possibility that Giolitti did not object to a colonial campaign as a way of letting some of the poison of nationalism and domestic tension be drained from the Italian body politic. Maybe a colonial victory would help the adolescent 'Third Italy' to manhood; but, without the Agadir crisis and the threat of the renewal of the Triple Alliance, it is difficult to imagine that Giolitti would have felt the need, or that San Giuliano would have had the confidence, to go to war. In a less advantageous or pressing international situation, Italy would have merely sought further diplomatic advantage, more 'kind words' about her 'future' in Europe.

Perhaps the most striking evidence of all is provided by the variety of war which Giolittian Italy proposed to wage. The Italian leadership displayed a marked and premature version of what would be called the 'short-war illusion'. It was Giolitti, and perhaps San Giuliano, rather than the service Ministers or the Chiefs of the General or Naval Staffs, who made the decision for war. The military were told almost nothing about political events. On 3 September, the conscripted class of 1889 had been allowed to disband.[127] Even in mid-September, while San Giuliano and Giolitti talked vaguely about action in 'winter' or 'October', Pollio was not kept closely informed of developments. When he suggested that 20,000 troops might bring victory, Giolitti scored easy points off the dull soldier by declaring that 40,000 would be needed.[128] Neither did much to work out how these might be organised, and, even after the ultimatum was despatched, Pollio had only the sketchiest ideas about probable military dispositions in Libya.[129]

Giolitti and San Giuliano seem to have believed that they were launching a coup, that it would all be over in three or four weeks, as long as the military did its job with a modicum of alacrity and efficiency. That the war would last more than a year and that military victory would not be won until the 1920s, that peace, in the sense of an acknowledgment of the Italian annexation of Libya, would be gained at the tables of international diplomacy and because of the actions of the small Balkan states, were unlooked-for complications. Such stresses in turn gave time for the domestic fissures in the structures of Giolittian Italy to widen, and for some Italian politicians to gain in ambition and optimism and to learn that, at last, even if by the most blatant diplomatic manipulations, Italy had reached a position from which it might join the 'great contest of the nations'.

One of the most interesting contemporary analyses of the Libyan war was written by the great political scientist, Roberto Michels, discerner of 'the iron law of oligarchy'. Michels naively regarded the war as a great turning point and abdication by Italy of the morality of the Risorgimento, which had made her a rock against which imperialist currents beat in vain. On the other hand, Michels had some very sensible things to say about the domestic base of this new Italian imperialism. He emphasised the constant pressure provided by the emigration problem; he was sceptical about the prime significance of economic factors, especially for such an apparently worthless territory as Libya. Rather, Michels explained, Italy had acted for psychological reasons; it had taken on what was likely to be a 'mediocre affair' in order not to cut a still more 'mediocre figure' on the international stage.[130] Michels's judgement is persuasive. Italy went to Libya because her ruling class wanted her to be a Great Power, and because Giolitti believed that it would be a quick victory like the French conquest of Tunis or the Austrian coup in Bosnia–Herzegovina. But Giolitti, to his cost, to Italy's, and perhaps to Libya's, was wrong.

4 The Italian People and Foreign Policy

One of the major themes of debate about the coming of the First World War underscores the latent role of public opinion in the causation of that war. Unleashed in the 'strange death of Liberal England', or manifest in the discovery of the irrational by so many contemporary intellectuals, a popular 'will to violence', it is alleged, surged beneath the surface of many a European mind. The Vienna from which Sigmund Freud was able to plumb the meaning of the unconscious and to comprehend the animal drives of the *id* was precisely the place where the genteel hierarchy of Kakania was giving terrible birth to the hate and destructiveness of Nazism.

Another facet of the Fischer debate, and a possible alternative resting place for those whose sentiment has yearned, or whose intellect has decided, to reject Fischer's condemnation of the German ruling classes, has lain in the theory that the glitter and growth of *fin de siècle* Europe was too good to be true. The approach of democracy must also mean the approach of totalitarianism, when the 'beast' of war and of social conflict would emerge from 'the abyss'. An early and predictable partisan of this view was Pope Benedict XV. In his first encyclical, *Ad Beatissimi Apostolorum Principis*, delivered to a troubled world on 1 November 1914, Benedict detected the real reason for men's travail. The present war was only part of another, greater, madder war which was caused by materialism, the unchecked spirit of independence and individualism, lack of respect and 'the insubordination of the masses'. The sin of modern society was that it no longer appreciated religious or social authority.[1]

Such naive conservatism, whether from Benedict or from later historians, is hard to take seriously, but there is an important and more plausible variation on the thesis of a popular will to violence. There can be no question about the alarming zest with which *belle époque* intellectuals hurled themselves into the knowledge of the irrational. Even socialist parties whose ideology asserted their untrammelled devotion to internationalism and the class struggle were themselves deeply penetrated by nationalism and by xenophobia. Confronted by the challenge of the July crisis, the socialist parties collapsed into an acceptance of patriotism, and pledged their allegiance, each to the war effort of his own fatherland. As one German socialist would muse in a metaphor characteristic of the moment:

Suddenly – I shall never forget the day and the hour - the terrible tension was resolved – [one had been in suspense] until one dared to be what one was; until – despite all principles and wooden theories -one could, for the first time in almost a quarter-century, join with a full heart, a clean conscience and without a sense of treason in the sweeping, stormy song: 'Deutschland, Deutschland, über alles'.[2]

The irritation set up between the manliness of socialism and the hegemonic direction being provided by nationalism had ejaculated into war.

What evidence is there for a similar story of tension and release in Italy? The most obvious candidates for analysis are the nationalists, those young intellectuals loosely grouped around the Associazione Nazionalista Italiana, and its paper, *L'Idea Nazionale*.[3] Already in 1909, Luigi Federzoni, an intellectual who was the most important political figure in the movement, had proclaimed:

In order to make civilisation fecund, hatred is no less necessary than love. And to whoever reproves me for not feeling a single throb of brotherhood for a Croat I ask whether he would regard himself as the brother of a Patagonian or a Kaffir .... The new generation of Italians, if it has any consciousness of its historic mission, can only be nationalist and imperialist.[4]

The nationalists addressed themselves to domestic affairs, and sought to reinvigorate conservatism. One spokesman for the party Alfredo Rocco, another who would move on to a distinguished career under Fascism, defined Parliament as 'a third-rate club, frequented by a varied collection of broken down wind-bags, of letter writers who like official stationery, of old misanthropes who like to read a free newspaper, of rabid gamblers who could not live without their daily game'.[5] Still more emphasised than anti-parliamentarism was anti-socialism. In July 1914, *L'Idea Nazionale* preached an 'implacable hatred' for socialism and internationalism. This hatred should be 'a racial hatred, a hatred of men who belong to the race which

constructs for those who belong to the race which destroys'.[6] Or as
Giovanni Papini, the silliest of the nationalist intellectuals, had put it
ten years before: the 'democratic mentality' is

that sorry mixture of the lowest sentiments, of empty ideas, feeble
phrases and bestial ambitions which embraces all from the
homebodies of soft radicalism to tearful Tolstoyan anti-militarists,
from ingenuously progressive and superficially anti-clerical pseudo-
positivism as far as its apotheosis in the thunderous *blagues* of
Revolution, Justice, Fraternity, Equality and Liberty.[7]

There can be little doubt that as wordsmiths the nationalists had
real prowess and versatility. It is thus not surprising that serious
capitalists were willing to pump hard-earned money into their
movement. Despite frequent criticism of lawyers, intellectuals and
politicians' time-consuming love of rhetoric, many businessmen were
not averse to the belief that happiness was a hired pen.

Yet it is hard not to conclude that existing historiography has
wildly overestimated the significance before 1914 of the ANI (and,
even more strangely, underestimated their importance after 1922).
The main ambition of many nationalists was a directly political one to
supplant the tired and inadequate 'constitutional opposition', typified
by the austere and woolly-minded Sonnino. As Papini put it with his
accustomed facility and envy: 'For a new, fresher, younger
generation to gain power is always a good thing'.[8]

But the nationalists' direct political ambitions were always
thwarted. Papini's career led to that summit of rhetorical banality,
the authorship of a life of Christ. Federzoni, Rocco and some of the
others were prominent and influential figures under Fascism but only
after they had accepted the suppression of their political party and
made obeisance to Fascist hierarchies and language. The simple fact
is that the nationalists always lacked a social base.[9] Their significance
could only be intellectual. Even so their ideas did have some
importance; but not because of their difference from those of their
society, rather because of their similarity. Before 1915, the
nationalists said, more loudly or more prettily, what major sections of
the political classes already believed. Their words have continued to
be regarded as more decisive and original than they were because of
the almost unchallenged prestige accorded to intellectuals under
Liberal, Fascist and Republican Italy. The achievement of Paolo
Farneti in uncovering the sociology of the Liberal parliamentary

classes has already been noted. What is also urgently needed is a satisfactory sociological analysis of the Italian intelligentsia,[10] with the aim of discovering not so much what intellectuals said, as why they said it.

Nationalist ideas were not merely trite, but also feebly co-ordinated. The nationalist group was riven by dispute and schism. It was appropriate that, in July 1914, the ANI had no single policy to pursue. Its cadres bickered instead about whether the fruitful war should be waged on Austria's side or against her.

Still more loosely linked to political action were other famous intellectuals. The futurists, led by the often delightfully imaginative and witty F. T. Marinetti, mocked sobriety and tradition in art, drama and even grammar. Marinetti, as an observer in the Libyan war, decided that the best way to depict battle to the folks back home was to assemble an array of letters which might be mouthed into suitable clashing sounds. His poem 'Zang Tumb Tumb' ends:

> zang-tumb-tumb-zang-zang-tuuumb
> tatatatatatatata picpac
> pampacpacpic pampampac *uuuuuuuuuuuuuuu*[11]

Despite their freshness, and despite their employment in Tripoli or Bulgaria, the futurists scarcely influenced government. Their cleverness was brittle. What would the brilliant young men who preached the worthlessness of all over 30 do as the years passed? For Marinetti, the sad years after 30 brought the robes of Mussolini's Academy and nurtured a fondness for being photographed below with a chin jutting in imitation of *professore* Mussolini. For Carrà, the man who, futuristically and grandly, renamed himself Carrrrrrrrrrrrrà, middle age offered the loss of artistic dynamism as expressed in a painting such as *The Funeral of the Anarchist Galli*, and its replacement by a sordid repetition of pretty country scenes.

A still more renowned intellectual in Liberal Italy was Gabriele D'Annunzio, one of the few Italian writers with fame and credit sufficient to live abroad, but he was disliked by the new generation of nationalists and futurists as an exemplar of what was most decadent about Giolittian Italy. D'Annunzio occasionally dabbled in politics. Luigi Albertini employed him to write odes suitable for the waging of the Libyan war. But D'Annunzio's real political career lay ahead after he had added the status of War Hero to his self-proclaimed potency as the World's Greatest Lover. It does, however, deserve pondering why, in October 1922, D'Annunzio, the Poet, Hero, Lover and dilettante, was widely seen as an imaginable alternative to Mussolini as leader or inspiration of a government of National Unity.

Certainly before the First World War, for all their influence on each other and on those young men such as Mussolini or Gramsci who aspired to join their ranks, the dissident intellectuals scarcely reflected the will or life-style of the Italian people. What then were the attitudes to and influence on foreign policy of those broader segments of the population whose emergence was giving some credence to the thesis that Italy was a 'democracy in the making'? One such force was political Catholicism. The *rapprochement* at the highest levels between Church and state in Liberal Italy, based on a mutual recognition that at home the enemy lay on the Left, and on a mutual understanding that patriotic co-operation was an appropriate policy for both the Third and the Second Romes, has already been noted. In China by 1911, all Catholic missions staffed from Italy flew the Italian flag.[12] In Malta, Mizzi, the Catholic leader of the opposition to British colonial rule, proclaimed his 'Italian nationality'.[13] In Libya, Egypt and Turkey, Argentina and the United States, the same harmony sounded. Pius IX's anathemas, which in 1871 had denied any possibility of reconciliation between Church and State, 'Christ and Belial, . . . light and darkness, truth and falsehood',[14] were wearing thin by 1915.

The most interesting aspect of the Vatican's return to an Italian policy is the financial one. It is also an area closed to detailed analysis by an archive policy pursued by the Church with a variety of touchiness and obscurantism equalled only by the Soviet Union. The revival of Catholic finances in the decades after 1870 is plain. The 'obolo' for St Peter encouraged generosity abroad. Within Italy, the Church became a major inspiration of co-operatives and local banks, notably in traditionally 'white' regions such as the Veneto. These co-operatives were in turn associated with an emerging Catholic press. By 1914 *Corriere d'Italia* was a loyal advocate of Italian expansion abroad, and could be heard to deplore the absence of an economic side to Italian diplomacy.[15]

By then, the major Catholic bank, the Banco di Roma, was labouring to repair that deficiency under the guidance of Ernesto Pacelli, uncle to Eugenio, the intellectual and pro-German young *monsignore* who in 1939 would become Pope Pius XII. The Banco di

Roma punted on an Italian future in Alexandria, Tripoli and in Asia Minor. Believing that the sword was sometimes mightier than the account book, Pacelli long tried to sponsor an Italian occupation of Libya. In July 1911, he was the sort of person deemed worthy to receive an obsequious letter from the nationalist, Enrico Corradini, which humbly remarked that the Banco di Roma alone had been 'daring and serious' in the 'peaceful penetration' of Libya. In case deferentially patriotic uplift was not enough, Corradini added the stimulating advice that Pacelli's pressure on the craven government of Giolitti and San Giuliano could *one day* [sic] pay off at one hundred to one'.[16]

Yet, as archival evidence stands at the moment, there is no indication that Pacelli was able to decide government foreign policy. The kinship between his bank and Tittoni perhaps assisted financial expansion before 1910, but San Giuliano disliked and distrusted both Tommaso Tittoni and his friends and relations. Pacelli's wagers in Alexandria, Libya and Turkey failed to produce not merely one hundred to one, but any profit at all. By 1914, the Banco di Roma was in severe financial straits due to its losses abroad, and both Giolitti and San Giuliano savoured the pleasures of delaying and rejecting government assistance. The First World War did not improve matters, and by 1916, with prosecution hanging over him, Pacelli was forced to resign his offices. He was saved from the ignominy of conviction through a loyal and public defence of his character by a number of politicians, including Luzzatti who wrote at length, and Giolitti who was succinct indeed.[17]

Pacelli is thus not a very convincing entrepreneur of the grand manner. Rather, as with the more flexible and clever Volpi, Pacelli's skills were those of the middle-man, the lawyer who knew which doors to open and who was able and bland enough to ingratiate himself not just with one Pope but with three. His great-uncle had been a Cardinal, his wife was a Liberal Minister's daughter. However, even Pacelli's achievements had limits. Leo XIII, Pius X and Benedict XV all smiled on the Banco di Roma and blessed Pacelli as a family friend. But, despite his advice and despite the religious probity of a Catholic bank, the Church's current account stayed with Rothschilds in Paris.[18]

As for the Catholic masses, who were beginning to assemble themselves in 'white' unions and from whose ranks were emerging political figures such as Romolo Murri, Luigi Sturzo and Filippo

Meda, evidence about their views on foreign affairs is slight. Catholic politicians were often vulnerable to patriotism. Murri, a priest whose zeal for democracy earned him unfrocking, excommunication and a Swedish wife, and Sturzo, both defended the Libyan expedition. Meda, from 1916, was willing to serve in War Cabinets, appropriately for a Catholic as Minister of Finance. But, generally, the problem with political Catholicism before 1915, after 1919 and indeed today is the uncertainty and eclecticism of its ideology. The inter-class nature of Christian Democracy can often seem little more than a trick whereby the more conservative elements of the movement confuse and conserve their foot-soldiers. In Liberal Italy, Catholicism, as it reappeared openly on the political scene, was the natural ally of reaction and nationalism, the friend of the ANI and the associate of Salandra. The Roman Catholic Church, rather like the Prussian Junkers or like the other, once cosmopolitan monarchies of Europe, was becoming nationalised, and its nationalism, albeit only partially formed, was Italian.

In traditional historiography, much the purer opponent of nationalism, colonialism and war has been the Italian socialist movement. On the surface, the record seems limpid. Italy was the country where colonial expeditions, such as those to Ethiopia in the 1890s or that to Libya in 1911–12, produced condemnation from socialist intellectuals, and strikes and demonstrations from the rank and file. The vivacity of Mussolini's and Nenni's opposition to the latter war led to their arrest at Forlì in September 1911. Elsewhere in the Romagna, women stopped troop trains by prostrating themselves across the railway tracks. For a reformist such as Leonida Bissolati, Italy's great virtue was that, alone among the Powers, she possessed no territorial ambitions.[19] Turati, in 1910, defined an Italian's patriotism: 'The real fatherland is the commune'.[20]

In the First World War the conduct of Italian socialism seems equally praiseworthy. Whereas other socialist parties capitulated into voting war credits for their governments, the deputies of the Italian socialist party did not approve the Salandra government's action in May 1915, and subsequently pursued their famous policy of 'neither support nor sabotage'.[21] Only a few syndicalists or a few rhetoricians, of whom Mussolini was the most notorious, vulnerable to the appeal either that war might mean revolution or that the trendiest intellectuals favoured fighting on France's side, then deviated from this proper neutralism.

Organised socialism had begun in Italy in the 1880s in humbleness and innocence.[22] Andrea Costa was elected deputy for Imola in the Romagna in 1882. He was that variety of patriarchal figure who, ten years later, fought (and won) a duel against another internationalist who doubted the honour of Costa's local financial administration.[23] A socialist party had been founded in 1892. After surviving the repression of Crispi, who, with the sensibility of a Garibaldinian and a Sicilian lawyer, opined 'our plebs are barbarians',[24] and of Rudinì and Pelloux, the movement grew steadily through the Giolittian decade. After the 1913 elections, the socialists held 52 seats. Around Ferrara they won more than half the votes, and the Socialist Party had already commenced in Bologna the tradition of Red administration, notable for its municipal wisdom, caution and achievement in a superior Italian version of gas and water socialism. The movement, split into the intellectually and socially diverse factions of reformists, maximalists and syndicalists, had a lively intellectual life. Major journals, such as Turati's *Critica Sociale*, were published, as was *Avanti!*, a daily which inaugurated its issue, with manifest anti-clericalism, in Rome on Christmas Day 1896.[25]

The socialist movement similarly had achieved much in the spread of trade unions. From 1906, these were banded together in the Confederazione Generale del Lavoro. Cities, such as Turin where the young Gramsci and Togliatti attended university, were already earning a reputation as redoubts of the organised working class. Nor was socialist unionism restricted to the proletariat. Since 1901, the great peasant union, Federterra, had organised the *braccianti* and some sharecroppers and small landowners, especially in the Po Valley where agricultural capitalism was well developed. Later historians would claim that it was precisely this rural aspect of Italian socialism which distinguished it most plainly from that of other European states (and which made it the most appropriate forefather for the inter-class ambitions of today's PCI).[26]

Social conditions often underlined the necessity of socialism. In Ancona, a *signore* was defined as someone who ate twice a day.[27] The lack of effective labour legislation meant that exploitation was rife, notably among the women and children who made up such a major element of the workforce. In the Bergamo silk industry of the 1880s, men worked a 16 hour day.[28] In the south and the countryside, life was even harsher. In Naples, a third of the adult population was unemployed.[29] Such was the pre-industrial innocence of that city that those arrested in a riot during 'Red Week' consisted of one steel worker, one railwayman, two coachmen, a baker, a tinker, a shop-assistant, a hair-dresser, two waiters, a contractor and two street traders.[30] In the Sicilian sulphur mines after 1860, mining techniques were allegedly those originally employed by the Etruscans.[31] In the very environs of Rome, in the Agro Romano, undrained marshes illustrated

the squalor of centuries of utter desolation. A few large estates, of which even their names – Casal della Morte, Campomorto, Pantano, Malafede [Death Village, Dead man's field, Swamp, Bad Faith] – recalled often the annals of malaria and feudal violence; men dressed in untreated sheep-skins, mounted on unbridled horses, who chased wild buffalo through ditches and who drove in front of them across the desolate plain their flocks and herds. Not a house nor any refuge for many miles around. Only, every so often, a Roman tomb or a feudal fortress, turned into a resting-place by inhabitants, reduced to savagery; on the threshold naked children with stomachs monstrously distended, of men and women . . . all marked in their wan and pallid faces by the unmistakeable signs of fever, of [malaria] the ancient goddess and implacable queen of the Agro.[32]

This was the real Italy, far removed from the Glory of Rome about which nationalists orated within the walls of the city, with shutters barred against the mosquito.

The story of one young socialist, Alfonso Leonetti, deserves comparison with that of the liberal politician, Marcello Soleri, whose rise was described in chapter 1. Leonetti was born in 1895 in the Puglian city of Andria to a modest artisan family. Andria was expanding rapidly as peasants, forced off the land, came to the city to live in 'dark hovels below street level' or in caves.[33] Alfonso was bright and stayed at school until the 5th *elementare*, after which he had to leave because of the pressures of belonging to a family with six children. He obtained employment, without pay, as an assistant to a local chemist, and a happy future beckoned. But, from 1910, a series of deaths including, catastrophically, that of his father, reduced the family to penury. His mother spent her last savings on a publicly acceptable funeral. The family then moved into one room, and the mother yielded her *letto matrimoniale* to her two eldest sons. Leonetti recalls in his memoirs: 'When I endeavour to reconstruct the history of the year after the death of my father, I try in vain to judge how it was possible to live on nothing or almost nothing.'[34]

Leonetti was sufficiently proud, stubborn, able and lucky to survive. He could earn a pittance helping peasants do their accounts at harvest time, and he also found a friendly priest who obtained entry for him into a local high-school. Although as a young intellectual in the making he flirted with the dramatic appeal of futurism, by 1914–15 he was a follower of the radical Neapolitan communist, Amedeo Bordiga, and his paper, *Il Socialista*.

The engendering of one southerner's socialism can be paralleled to the growth of northern socialism in Ernesto Ragionieri's beautiful history of Sesto Fiorentino. In Sesto, the Ginori ceramic works had been established in the eighteenth century by an enlightened nobleman. During the Risorgimento, the scion of the family was a liberal who achieved a massive vote for unity by explaining the referendum as 'an act of homage to the superior political wisdom of a landowner and an industrial entrepreneur'.[35] By 1883 the factory had expanded to employ 900 workers, but the Ginoris preserved the old order through strict paternalism. The next decade was troubled: Sesto had been connected to Florence, and thus to the outside world, by a tram line; a radical school-teacher was sacked for his political views; May Day began to be celebrated; the Ginori factory in 1896 became a public company, and local Catholics established a rural bank; a member of the Ginori family was a prominent Crispian deputy. The crisis deepened in 1898–9 while the Ginoris challenged the election in Sesto of a socialist deputy and communal administration. After the failure of reaction, Sesto became a socialist citadel where reformists controlled the Council (which introduced electricity), the Chamber of Labour (which greatly favoured educational programmes) and some of the co-operatives, but where the maximalists had a majority of branch members. The Ginori family and their middle-class associates remained suspicious of Giolitti and preferred the conservatism of their fellow Tuscan, Sonnino. In 1907, a Ginori lock-out culminated in victory for the workers, but a share-croppers' strike in 1906, after the harvest had been wiped out in a flood, was repressed by the police. Thereafter, the Chamber of Labour had meagre appeal to the peasantry.

In this little world, socialism by 1913 had done much to solidify its base and to improve the lot of the poor. But working conditions could still be harsh. In one factory, workers were pledged not to 'talk, eat, smoke and do anything else which distracts from work. It is absolutely forbidden to curse and to use bad language or to play jokes of any kind.'[36] Moreover the party was intellectually divided, and socially threatened by its failure with the share-croppers. After 1913, the local bourgeoisie regained confidence and sought better class organisation behind a national programme.[37]

The story so far narrated is one dear to Italian socialist historians. The Italian people emerging towards democracy combined ancient charitable localism with modern ideological internationalism. They rejected war and nationalism because the state, created in the Risorgimento and controlled by the bourgeoisie, did little or nothing for them except to tax and conscript the peasantry, or to repress the social and economic structures of the proletariat. The Italian people, unlike their ruling class and unlike many foreigners, did not believe in any way in the myths of the Third Italy and the Third Rome. As the final verse of a bitter peasant song from Umbria about the Libyan war ran:

> Comanda Cristo oppure il padrone
> maledetta sia sempre la guerra
> chi di sangue ha sporcato la terra
> che non possa il sole veder.[38]

But this picture, however gratifying, needs some revision. Were the Italian people as consciously innocent, as admirably untainted by patriotism and xenophobia, as leftist historiography suggests?

There are some reasons for doubt. First, there is evidence from outside Italy. There, it has long been clear that parties formally committed to pacificism or international brotherhood were deeply infected by the nationalist currents which swirled throughout their societies. The classic example is the German SPD. This party, conservative rhetoric made believe, was staffed by 'enemies of the Reich', whose maws ached to drip with genteel and patriotic blood. But the SPD was really the party of Gustav Noske, the young deputy who, in his maiden speech to the Reichstag in 1907, demanded a Germany 'as well armed as possible', and stated that all German socialists had accepted the 'principle of nationality'.[39] In 1914 the SPD voted war credits to the Imperial government; in 1918–19, it sought an alliance with the Officer Corps in order to give Germany a 'legal revolution' with minimum social change. Nor was nationalism restricted to German socialists. In Britain, the working classes included many loyal imperialists, perhaps a third of whom were

jingoist partisans of the national cause in the Boer War. In Austria–
Hungary, the different ethnic groups created their own national
socialist parties, anxious to break away from the German leadership
of the Austrian SPD. That leadership, in turn, was sceptical about the
genuineness of socialism among the suppressed nationalities, and
pondered whether Austrian socialists should bless the troops of
Francis Joseph if ever they were sent to Budapest on a mission to
destroy the tyranny of the Magyars.[40] In colonial Australia, world
pioneer in 'Labor' governments, the Labor party preached not
merely socialism but also racism which would block the importation
of Asiatics and of Italians, 'the Chinese of Europe' as they were
locally denominated, into White Australia.[41] Even in Russia, among
the Bolshevik party which would oppose Russian entry into the First
World War, the seeds were germinating which would be harvested in
the nationalism of Stalin's 'Socialism in One Country' and in 'the
Great Patriotic War'.

Given that nationalism, despite its manifest absurdity and
destructiveness, has been everywhere the triumphant ideology of the
last century, it seems *prima facie* unlikely that a vast majority of
Italians could remain immune to it. Much more research needs to be
done, but it is probable that a markedly patriotic strain did exist in
segments of the Italian Left before 1914.

One excellent example of the vulnerability to patriotism of men
whose major ideology proclaimed an aversion to it, is provided by the
Italian pacifist movement. Other pacifist movements dissolved into
nationalism in 1914, but the small Italian pacifist group had already
demonstrated its patriotism by justifying the Libyan war. For middle-
class 'liberals', who looked back to Mazzini and Garibaldi and to a
state born in warfare, it was extremely difficult not to believe that
some wars were just. The tortured ideologising of a theorist such as
E. T. Moneta provides many fine examples of the limits of pacifism.

But the pacifists were not numerous and they were bourgeois.
What of socialists; did not they reject any deviation from
internationalism? One immediate issue is sociological – which
socialists are being analysed? The admirable work of Paolo Farneti,
so sadly cut short by his death, has demonstrated how little socialist
deputies differed in class or urban background from their liberal and
conservative fellow parliamentarians. Thus, even after the 1913
elections, men whose first profession was law made up more than 50
per cent of socialist deputies; only 15 per cent were not university

educated and 65 per cent had graduated in law. Farneti finds that only 4 per cent came from outside the 'political class'. In the 1913 Chamber, despite the application of Giolitti's electoral reform, no peasants sat, although rural life then employed a majority of Italians. There were 'four workers or artisans' in a Chamber of 511. (Similarly there were only six deputies whose major social definition was 'businessman'). Socialist parliamentarians did not break the basic rule that Liberal Italy was governed by an 'urban, professional and intellectual political class which assembled its vote largely in rural areas'.[42]

A class analysis of deputies has its implications; so, too, does an analysis of the words and of the social background of the various ideological factions which made up Italian socialism. One notable problem for the party was the regional diversity of Italy, particularly that between north and south. The Socialist Party did exist in the South, but southern socialists, given the social conditions from which they sprang, were more given to extremism, to revolutionism and, potentially, to patriotism than northern ones. Lacking the hard and salutory experience of the Turin proletariat, or of the modernising and unionised *braccianti* of the Po Valley, southerners were impelled towards socialism by the appalling social conditions around them. At the same time, such socialists could both look to drastic solutions, and be themselves conditioned by some of the ancient hierarchies of their region. Even Antonio Gramsci, son of a southern bureaucratic family which, through political misjudgement, had fallen on hard times in Sardinia, was suckled by a wet-nurse, and was being looked after by another nurse when he suffered the accident which was blamed for his hunch-back.[43] However saint-like in his humility, Gramsci never entertained doubts about the supremacy of the intellectual life over other callings and expected recognition and support for his intellectual labour. The austere Salvemini, the radical who so censoriously prosecuted Giolitti's limitations as 'Minister of Crime' ('Ministro della Malavita'), was not averse to writing letters of recommendation requesting government assistance for his own needy friends.[44]

Other southern socialists deviated more seriously from ideal internationalist practice. Giuseppe De Felice Giuffrida, hero of the *fasci* and the most prominent Sicilian socialist, favoured the Libyan war. Indeed, the Libyan war was often popular at first in the south. In the Salento, the populace showed signs of a recollection of the ancient crusading spirit of the Christians against Turks. In remote villages, 'the entire population accompanied soldiers going off to the Libyan front, farewelling them with displays of emotion and patriotic fanaticism'.[45] The small and embattled local socialist groups split over the war, but radical attempts to arouse anti-war protest from the poorest classes failed.

Still more generic is the outraged patriotism which can be found among the extremist faction of syndicalists, the leadership of which was often southern even if such leaders often looked to the north for the quickest solutions to Italy's many pressing problems. The classic example is the Neapolitan, Arturo Labriola, who, in 1912, called the Libyan war 'an act of national defence' which had not, in reality, been opposed by the working classes.[46] Labriola rallied to Fascism when his patriotic sentiment was aroused by the unfairness of the international campaign against Italy during the Ethiopian war. Other syndicalist writing contains many manifestations of a bitter resentment against foreign power and superiority. A. O. Olivetti, in attacking the Giolittian bourgeoisie, blamed them for being the carriers of

the virus of ... foreign dominations ... our outlook is still degraded by all the humiliations we have suffered; the cunning we learned in the age of servitude takes the place of real competence in us. We are still dragging behind us the rags of our baroque and Arcadian seventeenth century ... we still have in our veins the Papacy, the Saracens, the Spaniards, Aretino, Loyola, and our shoulders still ache from the Croat's club.[47]

Such anger could evolve easily into that variety of despairing nationalism which would persuade Labriola to describe the Libyan war as a way 'to break out of our customary stinking laziness'[48] and which would lead most syndicalists into interventionism and Fascism.

If the barrenness of syndicalism could be converted to exasperated nationalism, the calmness and achievement of the reformists could also contain a not unexpected love of country. Bissolati and Bonomi left the Socialist Party in opposition to the noisy campaign by radicals such as Mussolini against the Libyan war. Filippo Turati, however saddened by maximalist excess, held his reformist faction within the main socialist structure. He opposed imperialism in Libya, as he would also refuse to vote war credits for the Salandra government in May 1915. But, for Turati in 1911, as in 1915, it was not war or patriotism *per se* which he repudiated but rather the unscrupulous methods of Giolitti and of Salandra. In 1911, Turati, with considerable diffidence, opposed the premeditated attack on Turkey, all for a valueless desert where few Italians lived. In 1915 he objected to a war capriciously entered by a minority and reactionary government in the cause of *sacro egoismo* abroad and authoritarianism at home. On neither occasion did Turati or the other reformists reject defensive war, or the validity of the fatherland. As Turati himself wrote in *Critica Sociale* in 1909, he was not opposed at all to having a foreign policy; rather all that he desired was that Italy should cut her diplomatic cloth according to her means.[49] Where the cause was just, most definitely, for example, in her claims to the Trentino and Trieste where Austria was an 'irreconcilable enemy', then reformists should approve Italian expansion, if the preferred method to achieve border rectification was by international negotiation and not by war.[50] Most socialists objected to the Italian Army, but more because of its reactionary Officer Corps and its frequent usage as a police-force against strikes in city and countryside, than as a result of a thorough-going intellectual hostility to militarism. Giorgio Rochat, one of the very few left-wing historians to investigate matters related to the Army and to foreign policy, has deplored the innocence and levity of Italian socialists' knowledge of military questions compared, for example, with the profundity of the work done by Engels and his successors in the SPD.[51]

Even about that majority group of socialists, anti-colonialist in 1896 and 1911 and neutralist in 1914–15, some questions may be asked. Socialism was for most of her followers a doctrine which offered solutions to internal woes. Indeed there was a marked suspicion both of centralisation and of Rome. In phrases echoing those of their capitalist enemy, socialists warned against Rome and its myth, against 'the bureaucratic and parasitic city, consisting of nothing but government and *sottogoverno*'.[52] Within the Italian union movement, a constant battle was fought between centralisers, who wanted a national and unified policy, and partisans of the local Chambers of Labour, who were much more convinced that all virtue and all solutions lay in the *paese*. In this socialism, which arranged itself beneath the *campanile*, foreign affairs in the Balkans or 'Africa' only entered as a bogey, fear of which could better focus attention on domestic ills. The visit of the Tsar, that 'Hangman of Europe', colonial adventures, the conspiracies of Throne and Altar which ensured the execution of the 'freethinker', Francisco Ferrer, in

Spain, were of much the same significance. All could be objected to in much the same way – a demonstration, some fiery speeches in generic and even blood-thirsty praise of peace. But apart from the reformists, whose leadership laboured to improve contacts with the German and Austrian SPDs, few Italian socialists thought hard or read widely about foreign affairs.

Moreover, despite all the internationalism and the *campanilismo*, nationalism could yet come in by the back door to the most loyal socialist hearth. Education, as elsewhere in Europe, was a potential nationalising force. Socialist school-teachers praised Garibaldi, free-booting and nationalist Hero of Two Worlds, who had overthrown repressive evil enemies who could be deemed 'Germans' or 'Croats'. At the same time an inchoate but resilient idea survived that foreign policy was not an affair for ordinary people but something superior, almost automatic or inevitable. This acceptance that foreign policy was a cause apart, justly, at least for the moment, left to the King, and always to be left to 'the Nation', can be found in the mind of a radical democrat such as Giovanni Amendola.[53] But even socialists did not always disagree. In 1910, the reformist Luciano Magrini noted: 'In a nation, political parties arrange internal life, abroad the party spirit must be silent and allow the spirit of nationality to speak.'[54]

It is not surprising then, that, in the July crisis and its immediate aftermath, Italian socialism was much embarrassed. A major section of the party felt the tug of the idea that war between the Great Powers implied an overthrow of the eternal verities of liberalism. Mixed uncomfortably together were the tantalising prospect that war meant revolution, that international war, as Bordiga put it, in ironical agreement with Benedict XV, was only a continuation of the already existing social conflict, that capitalist war could be replaced by civil war.[55] The idea of revolutionary war itself carried the alluring and confusing memories both of Garibaldi and of Robespierre. On 5 August, these confusions were well expressed in a double motion by PSI and CGL members that 'Italy must maintain her neutral line until the end of the war' and, as well, that 'Italy must not abandon her neutrality in support of the Austro-German bloc'.[56] No wonder, ten days later, that Bordiga felt it necessary to write to *Avanti!* warning against a love of the French Republic.[57] But the most frank comment of all was that of the maximalist, Costantino Lazzari, who admitted in *Avanti!* on 18 September as the Battle of the Marne held up the victory of the Central Powers: 'A correction of frontiers [i.e. at least in the Trentino] is an extraordinarily attractive idea, however bourgeois it might be, for all Italians from the King down to the lowest of the low'.[58]

From the evidence available, it would be wrong to conclude that Italian socialists were unscrupulous machiavels or crypto-nationalists. Most socialists, especially those in the rank and file, did not believe in, or did not know, the myths of the Risorgimento or of the 'Third Italy'. On the other hand, nationalism is an extraordinarily potent and pervasive force. There are indications that Italian socialists were, by nature, little more immune to nationalism than were their brothers in Germany or in Britain. The special history of the Italian socialist movement, with its rejection of the Libyan war and its neutralism during the First World War, was caused more by the mistakes and greed of the Italian ruling classes and by the social underdevelopment of the Liberal state than by some special virtue of the Italian people whch might make them for ever averse to war or imperialism.

The same comments can be made about the still poorer, more exploited and less nationalised social groups of the peasantry and of emigrants. There, again, many commentators have been decidely sentimental in the image which they have constructed of an arcadian peasantry whose love of their fellow man was only matched by hatred of the 'plague' of war. There can be no doubt whatever that, contrary to the myth of the *rivoluzione nazionale*, the Italian peasantry was not integrated into the Italian state during the Risorgimento. The wars of the 1860s against brigandage in the south were of social origin and resulted in a bloody victory for 'Liberalism', that is of the agrarian bourgeoisie and landowners over the landless or poor peasantry through simple military repression.[59] If this was the situation in 1870, there are few reasons to assume that it had changed much by 1915. The prefectural reports, commissioned by Salandra in April 1915, were clear that the agrarian masses felt no enthusiasm for entry into the First World War.

It is also obvious that peasant hostility to war was not intellectually developed or sustained. Piedmontese women, forced, after 1915, to take over the heavier labouring jobs, given their husbands' absence at the front, knew that their men were fighting 'Austria', but comprehended no more than that Austria was somewhere 'over the mountains'.[60] Much rural hostility to the Army was explicable given the Army's major role as rural police; Giolitti had required neutrality towards urban strikes but repression in the countryside.[61] Conscription, too, is never welcomed by a peasantry dependent on the strong arms of its sons for physical survival. None the less, this picture is not a unilinear one. In rural areas, there could be admiration for the display side of the army, its uniforms, its parades, its brass bands. The peasantry was nothing if not sexist and acknowledged that a soldier's life made a man of a lad.[62] However low the pay and severe the discipline, military service was often better remunerated than life in the *paese*. In the 1930s peasant communists, imprisoned in Fascist gaols, were able to save some money even from their prison stipends in order to send it home to their wives and children.[63] A conscript could do the same. Peasants would fight bravely, stubbornly and loyally in the Italian armies in the First World War.[64]

Equally, violence was scarcely alien to a peasant's life. Indeed successful violence, be it that of the banditry or the *Mafia*, organisations in which some peasants in some regions found the channel of upward social mobility, could well be admirable. Within the family itself, violence was endemic in the role of *padre, padrone, padreterno*.[65] Emilio Lussu recalls in his memoirs that the most prized quality for a boy in the hills of Sardinia was that he could shoot straight; if a peasant crossed the communal border, he must be armed.[66] The tiny but crucial divisions of wealth and status, which far more than any unity are characteristic of peasant society, encourage suspicion, competition and, where possible, violence. It was peasant xenophobia, in process towards nationalism, which became the well-spring of rural resistance in Yugoslavia and Italy in the last stage of the Second World War.

In 1914 peasant loyalties were local, familial or institutional. The 'nation of Italy' was irrelevant to their lives except as the fitful tyrant of taxation or conscription. At the same time, this innocence of nationalism had a curiously fragile quality. It was, potentially, not so difficult to commence the course of nationalising the peasant masses, of turning peasants into Italians, even though the insensitivities and prejudices of the Italian ruling classes prevented them from favouring this process until 1943.

Emigrants are yet another group for which, apart from the inanities of celebratory historians, the commonplace speaks of an absence of nationalism. Italian migrants went abroad in huge numbers. F. S. Nitti pedantically noted that, by 1910, 5,547,746 Italians legally lived outside the national borders[67] and that there were many more who had abandoned their nationality. Pre-1915 nationalists were particularly alarmed by this loss of numbers. San Giuliano, in December 1911, warned his ambassadors to remember that 'emigration is . . . not any more the inevitable result of poverty, [but rather] is the voluntary export of power to the benefit of foreign [interests]'.[68] Another Liberal politician complained that migrants were absorbed abroad like 'drops of rain on the sand'.[69] Corradini, for the ANI, bewailed this loss of power, denying any population excess by comparing Italy's social and military history with that of Japan.[70]

By 1910, only 2800 Italians were resident in Eritrea and 240 in the other colony, the Somaliland, but 35,000 Italians lived in Egypt, 135,000 in Switzerland and even 20,332 in England and Wales.[71] The figures for trans-oceanic migration were even greater, especially from the south where emigration in 1901–9 was ten times more than it had been during the decade from 1876 to 1886.[72]

Many emigrants eventually came back to the *paese* from which they had come. Even among the migrants who had gone to 'America' – the United States, Argentina or Brazil – perhaps half returned to Italy. It has been estimated that between 1900 and 1917, 1.5 million Italians left the United States.[73] Rhetoricians declaimed about the tie between the Italians and 'their common mother', the *madrepatria* as it was frequently and somewhat confusingly denominated. But most 'Italians' were *paesani*. The emigrant carried still the simplicity and innocence of early modern life. Perhaps 50 per cent of pre-war emigrants to the United States were illiterate.[74] In far-off Western Australia, well beyond the end of the world, it has been tabulated that an Italian emigrant group in 1901 comprised 7 farm owners, 1 hotel keeper, 2 wineshop owners, 1 antique dealer, 2 fruit shop owners, 1 foodstuff importer, 4 government employees, 3 painters, 4 cooks and waiters, 1 sculptor, 2 fishmongers, 1 baker, 2 tailors, 3 cobblers, 3 carpenters, 1 plumber, 1 accountant, 20 organ grinders, 45 agricultural labourers and 20 brick or quarry workers.[75] In their clubs and churches, in the very process of 'chain migration', Italians abroad assembled themselves not as 'Italians' but as men from a particular *paese* or region. Italians left Italy without being Italians, and came back to their *paese* still without having been nationalised into being self-conscious patriots. Emigration for them, be it to

Switzerland or to Brazil, was little more than a pattern of movement by employable males in search of sustenance followed by many of the world's poor, according to the season, for many centuries.

This is probably true as a generalisation, although it could repay further research if even more historians of migration could be dissuaded from singing paeans of community pride or dirges of community lament. There is some contrary evidence. Giorgio Amendola, as a *fuoruscito* from Fascism in inter-war France, found Italians who had lost both their language and even their dialect but who none the less possessed a strong sense both of class and of nation.[76] 'Italians' abroad were certainly apt to be treated as Italians by their hosts, although there was some distinction made between northerners and southerners. Frequently the reception was hostile, the result sometimes of an economic resentment of scabs and hard-workers, sometimes of a racial dislike of Mediterranean 'blacks'. Social workers in the United States were saddened to have to report of Italians 'still eating spaghetti . . . they have not yet become Americanised'.[77] Sometimes racial prejudice led to racial violence. In New Orleans in 1891, 11 Italians were lynched after rumours that the 'Black Hand' had been behind the murder of a local police chief.[78] In France in 1893, a riot at Aigues Mortes against the low wages accepted by immigrants produced the death of 9 Italians, the disappearance of 2 more, the wounding of 96 and assault on 521.[79]

In these circumstances, it is not surprising to find that some returning migrants had a more defined sense of being Italian than they possessed before they left Italy. The 'intellectual leadership' of emigrant communities was seldom of a high level.[80] The isolation, which is a product of emigration, encouraged a devotion to petty gossip, and partisan politics tended to freeze at the moment of departure. Genuine, old-style Mazzinians could thus be found in pre-1914 Argentina; and in Egypt, a government report of 1908 deplored the survival of Risorgimento-style anti-clericalism.[81] But in a moment of crisis, during the Libyan war, the *intervento* and the First World War, as later in the Ethiopian war, many Italians abroad felt more Italian than ever before, and their patriotism was strengthened by the scorn with which their neighbours attacked Italy's failure or the crudity of her aggression. The young Achille Starace came back to Italy in 1911 to attend a patriotic conference. Edmondo Rossoni, later a Fascist syndicalist, discovered abroad the inadequacies of orthodox socialist ideology: 'We have seen our workers exploited and held in low regard not only by capitalists but also by the revolutionary *comrades* of other countries. We know from experience how internationalism is nothing but fiction and hypocrisy'.[82] An abandonment of Italy could thus sometimes, ironically, lead to a new devotion to the *madrepatria*. As an Italo-Argentinian told Romolo Murri in 1913: '[Here] we find in ourselves for the first time, our country and its mark .... . Gone to discover America [a man] has learned, in America, how to know Italy'.[83] Emigrants, too, were not invulnerable to the allure of nationalism. They could sometimes imagine that the world would be a better place if Italy were a genuine Great Power, and if Italy possessed her own colonial empire.

It is thus arguable that the Italian people were a reserve army which, potentially, could have been mobilised behind some aspects of Italian foreign policy. However, neither Giolitti nor San Giuliano, and certainly not Salandra or Sonnino, was interested in such a mobilisation. For them, in so far as foreign policy was concerned, the 'popular will' was irrelevant. Foreign policy was a matter for the King and his closest advisers. Nationalist 'public opinion' as expressed by Federzoni or Corradini was tiresome, although, if organised and directed, it might have positive virtues. But it must never make decisions.

Nor was there much challenge to that longstanding view. The ANI might wax strident about Italy's pretensions to Tunis or Rhodes, but another more traditional and perhaps more representative Italy existed in the provinces. An excellent example can be found in that Sassari where, in 1910, the young Palmiro Togliatti was being educated. There, local politics followed a well-worn path. The political class of Sassari was determined to oppose the despotism of Cagliari and its Giolittian boss, Francesco Cocco Ortu. Anti-clericalism could also move a man. In October 1909, the execution in Spain of Ferrer inspired a massive protest demonstration. One local notable, from the important Berlinguer family, denounced the Spanish clericals for having sponsored 'the greatest infamy of the twentieth century'. Garibaldinian sentiments, anti-Austrian and potentially republican, still flourished, and in 1911 converted readily into colonialism. During the Libyan war, the local paper, *La Nuova Sardegna*, which after Adowa had been responsibly anti-Africanist, now made space for a journalist who thought Italy should 'regain' Malta, Trieste and Nice and who opined that Italy's future national choice lay in being 'either an oppressed and continually wounded slave, or queen and mistress of the world'.[84] Official myth-makers would proclaim the First World War 'the last war of Italian independence', the culmination of the *rivoluzione nazionale*. For the ruling elite of Sassari at least, that myth was not completely false.

5 Italy and the Last Years of Peace, 1911-14

The Libyan war has rarely been seen as such, but as, arguably, the only war of aggression waged by a recognised Great Power against another traditional member of the Concert since 1870, it was in many aspects a microcosm of the greater war to come. The Italian government had entered the conflict with a complete 'short-war illusion', with the most rudimentary war aims and without any definition of civil-military relations. On the afternoon of 29 September 1911, Italy was at war with Turkey. What that meant was still to be worked out.

The first and most urgent parameters had to be drawn in the military field. What did war 'against Turkey' involve? Was Turkey to be regarded as vulnerable in its whole huge extent? Could Italian might unfurl the banners of the new Rome in Arabia, in Asia Minor and in Albania; could Italy contemplate the storming of Constantinople; or was she merely waging a local war which must be restricted to an assault on the ports of Tripoli and Cyrenaica or the oases of Fezzan?

Most of the Great Powers had received the news of a war between Italy and Turkey with a certain embarrassment. That the two most dubious members of the Concert were in conflict was one problem. Another was admitting Italy's special privileges in Tripolitania amid that multiplicity of 'agreements' and half-agreements which Italian statesmen had so pertinaciously extracted from condescending European statesmen for so many years. With the Moroccan affair Italy appeared to have a legal case. As Izvolsky, the Russian ambassador in Paris and a diplomat who thoroughly disliked the thought of any Power gaining a march over Russia, advised, nothing could be done to oppose Italy.[1] The unspoken assumptions about Italy's military and moral inferiority had not been forgotten. The liberal press of Europe was crosser at the sight of Italian imperialism than they would have been at any other brand. In Munich, it was reported solemnly, the locals persistently sang anti-Italian songs in their beer-halls in order to provide some moral revenge to counter Italy's escapade in Libya.[2] Metaphors about brigandage came easily to non-Italian lips, although some refuge was found in the fact that Italian arms were only advancing into uninhabited and unusable deserts. As a young clerk at the British Foreign Office recorded loftily: 'We deprecated these goings on but deemed them less ungentlemanly than [they would have been had they been directed against] more civilised parts'.[3] By far the more influential reason for restraint by the other Powers was that mixture of fear and ambition which had long kept the Eastern Question unresolved. The collapse of Turkey, men had assumed for decades, would trigger a European war.[4] Some classically trained politicians welcomed the return of the Mediterranean to the centre of world history,[5] but most statesmen anxiously sat out the Libyan war. Under the leadership of Germany and Britain, the Powers tolerated Italian aggression and Italian victory on the grounds that they were, after all, only Italian, and expressed the hope that the conflict was a *coup* and not a war to the death. 'Expert' commentators were soon explaining to their own satisfaction that it was only Italy's notorious incompetence and feebleness of will which prevented her from concluding such a modest campaign in three weeks.[6]

There was one immediate and predictable exception to this bemused tolerance. In the first flush of military enthusiasm, an Italian naval squadron in the Adriatic exchanged fire with some Turkish torpedo boats off Prevesa, and attempted to blockade some Austrian vessels running to Turkish Albania. The result was a drastic diplomatic incident in which Aehrenthal, an Austrian statesman unusually sympathetic to Italy, abruptly forbade further incursions into the Adriatic. In deference to the terms of the Triple Alliance which spoke about compensation for one if the other gained advantage in Europe, but made no mention of Africa, Italy, after the Prevesa incident, accepted that she must engage in a limited conflict.[7] Neither Libyan sands nor even a regained Byzantium were worth the sacrifice of Trento and Trieste. In 1911–12, Italy waged war robustly in the Mediterranean, but her major interests were defended or veiled by continuing peace in the Adriatic.

There were a number of other international incidents in the course of the Libyan war. In the last months of 1911, rumours about the 'Charykov kite' produced flutterings in European chancelleries lest Russia take action to achieve her own designs to be the third Rome and to restore the cross to Constantinople. It remains obscure whether the 'kite' was fabricated merely by one diplomat or had been blessed in St Petersburg. What is plain is the relief of all the Powers, and especially Italy, that the kite did not get off the ground.[8] Once the war was confined to Libya, Italy did not desire a prepotent fighting ally.

A more public conflict arose in January 1912 between Italy and France over what would, after 1914, become the familiar issue of the rights of neutral shipping directed to belligerent regions. The Italian arrest of three French vessels, the *Carthage, Manouba* and *Tavignano,* on the not unjustified suspicion that they were carrying contraband men or material to the Turkish forces in Libya, provoked howls of protest in Paris. These were returned with interest in the Italian press. Since Poincaré was not the sort of politician who believed in mincing words with Rome, a major public deterioration in Franco-Italian relations ensued. It took all the coolness and sanity of Giolitti to relieve the antagonism by seeking adjudication from the International Court of The Hague. There, Italy, eventually and responsibly, accepted the need to compensate the allegedly injured ship-owners.

The *Carthage* incident has sometimes been regarded as a major indicator of an Italian drift away from her friendship with the Triple Entente to her alliance with the Central Powers. Yet it is important not to exaggerate the matter. Franco-Italian relations were never completely cordial and, all other matters aside, a war between them was never out of the question. But all other matters were never 'aside' while Austria–Hungary existed, and while France was on such excellent terms with Britain. The very publicity associated with the *Carthage* incident was a signal of its superficiality. Giolitti's despatch and commonsense ensured its rapid defusing, and Italy thereafter behaved sensibly in allowing no repetition of such open interference with neutral shipping.[9]

The Italian Navy, which was much more active and confident than an Army enfeebled by sand, heat, cholera and its generals' conservatism and timidity in Libya, provoked the third major incident of the war when, in April 1912, it launched an attack on the forts of the Dardanelles. Subsequently the fleet occupied the Dodecanese islands and Rhodes, which lay just off the area of Asia Minor where Italy had developing political and economic interests. The raid was officially described as accidental, although it had been planned beforehand and had political approval.[10] The occupation of the ethnically Greek islands was self-righteously explained away as temporary. However, the extension of combat into the Aegean indicated the pressure building on the Italian government to finish off the war. Once again Italy's vulnerability to expressions of international displeasure meant that her leadership, thereafter, accepted with only minor demur the demand of the Powers that there be no further raids against the Turkish mainland. The obscure and frustrated suggestion by the Chief of General Staff, Pollio, in July 1912 that Italy shut her eyes, attack Smyrna and plunge a knife into the heart of Turkey was ignored by Giolitti and San Giuliano and dismissed as an expected example of a general's simplicity and crudeness.[11] Instead peace had to be sought internationally, on and under the tables of diplomacy.

In the memoranda which had circulated in the Consulta in July and August 1911 San Giuliano had made some effort to appraise Italian war aims and to work out what constitutional and religious policy Italy should pursue in Libya. However, nothing had been decided by the end of September. Moreover, with the war not producing immediate victory, a certain fearfulness resurfaced in the Foreign Minister's mind. Generals, with recollections of Adowa, and politicians alike knew that a command position in Italy during a period of colonial war was an ill-omened one. Caution and procrastination were therefore the best policies.

San Giuliano, in October 1911, thus surmised that Italy might not need outright legal control of Libya and could tolerate some residue of authority for the Sultan. But international events and Giolitti's sense of logic eliminated the chance for complex compromise. On 4 November the Franco-German agreement on Morocco came into force. Giolitti, recalling no doubt that neither France nor Austria must be permitted to claim compensation for Italian advantage, at once published a royal decree, on 5 November, annexing Libya. Italy's new territories would not be another Egypt. Giolitti had comprehended that, for a Power as weak as Italy to be able to make territorial gains, the simplest possible legal position was obligatory. During the next year, San Giuliano's subtlety occasionally suggested timid criticism of this sternness, but Giolitti remained unmoved.

Contemporary critics from the Right retailed the legend that Giolitti, numbers man and wheeler-dealer, did not know how to wage war. It was suggested that the war effort of Italy was feeble because of the levity and corruption of her politicians. In fact the evidence is to the contrary. It is true that Giolitti scarcely relied on his military to win the war. But there were excellent strategic, psychological and international reasons why the Italian Army might be unlikely to cut to pieces all opposition within Libya. Certainly, once he had moved, Giolitti displayed not the slightest intention of surrendering the fruits of victory. It was characteristic that Giolitti used the occasion of the Libyan war to justify the foundation of a Ministry of Colonies, and thus implicitly to announce to the world Italy's arrival as a colonial force. In October 1912, Giolitti offered the Ministry to Pietro Bertolini, the politician closest to the Prime Minister and a man who had often been used on delicate and difficult missions where absolute reliance had been placed on his probity and calm.[12]

Making war and providing a structure of administration for the conquered territories were the less pressing of the issues confronting Giolitti's government. Of more immediate concern was peacemaking. How, when necessity decreed that only a desultory and limited war be waged in Libya, was Turkey to be brought to admit defeat? Although San Giuliano often hinted that Italy would be interested in Great Power mediation (so long as it was mediation favourable to Italy), it was soon evident that the Great Powers could do no more than hold the ring. Italy would have to find her own peace.

In this question, too, it was Giolitti whose mind was most lucid and wide-ranging. At the very start of the war, Alberto Theodoli, the clerical Italian delegate of the Ottoman Public Debt, had gone on a mission to Constantinople, probably at the behest of Vatican financial circles and the Banco di Roma. The mission ended in fiasco; neither Giolitti nor San Giuliano was ready to be cast in the role of the puppet of clerical banking, and Theodoli's obscure messages about the wages of compromise were ignored. Theodoli was expelled from Turkey,[13] and the Banco di Roma began to learn that financial imperialism in the East could put balance sheets in the red as easily as in the black. Whatever else the imperialism of Liberal Italy might have been, it was not to prove merely a collecting agency for Peter's pence.

But, despite the failure of Theodoli, and despite the sardonic pleasure that San Giuliano drew from the difficulties of the pious initiatives of the Banco di Roma, Giolitti had not forgotten the message that the path of reconciliation with Turkey could be paved with gold. Giolitti's paladin for deals in the East was Giuseppe Volpi, a Venetian entrepreneur and middle-man *extraordinaire*, who loved to see himself as the father of a reborn Venetian Empire.[14] Volpi's durability and skills would lead him through many vicissitudes in which he would be both a cultured patron of the Biennale and the greedy sponsor of the polluting growth of Porto Marghera on the Venetian lagoon. He also served as the Governor of Tripolitania, appointed by Giovanni Amendola and retained by Mussolini, who launched the genocidal 'pacification' of the Libyan interior. In 1938, at the end of a life of much distinction and reward, Volpi, as President of Confindustria, happily suggested to Ciano that it would, naturally, be a good idea for Italy to take over Albania, but then asked why stop there when the benefits of Anatolia beckoned an Italy on the march?[15] This First Servant of the Doge-Duce is a splendid symbol of the continuity of ambition and method in Italian foreign policy.

In June 1912, Volpi, in close contact with Giolitti, visited Constantinople where one of his agents, Bernardino Nogara (a financier who was *persona gratissima* in the Vatican), had continued to reside and inform throughout the war. Although Volpi personally liked to discuss loudly the imminent disintegration of the Ottoman Empire, he found himself able to talk to Turkish financiers and politicians. In July 1912, Volpi moved to Switzerland where he was joined by Fusinato, a legal expert, and by Bertolini. There, the Italian team began serious, if lengthy, negotiations with Turkish officials searching to coin a formula with which to end the Libyan war. As summer lengthened into autumn, the negotiators, at Lausanne, Caux and then Ouchy, beneath the magic mountains, kept at their austere work. Giolitti, it was plain, believed that words and money could be better relied on than arms to sue for peace with the Ottoman Empire.[16]

In retrospect, it is not at all certain that Giolitti was right to believe that bribery was the way ahead. On 29 August, Volpi could only report with frustration that the talks were deadlocked,[17] and the impatience of the negotiating team and of Giolitti's domestic opposition tightened. But Giolitti and Italy were saved by external events. By the end of September, Turkey and the other Great Powers were confronting not merely a war for Libya, but imminent action by the small Balkan states who intended to destroy Turkey in Europe. With Germany leading the way, the Great Powers hurriedly 'suggested' that Turkey had better cut her losses in Libya; too late, because on 8 October Montenegro launched the Balkan wars by attacking Turkish Albania. By the time the delegates in Switzerland had initialled a peace agreement at Ouchy on 15 October and signed the Treaty of Lausanne on 18 October, Libya had already returned to its accustomed insignificance, a desert outpost of no concern to international diplomacy. Foreigners were politely amused by the concept of an Italian Empire and chuckled quietly as an Italian Senator proclaimed that General Caneva was a *Duce* who, in the earlier Rome, would have been granted a triumph.[18] Some historians have seen the Libyan war as a 'Prelude to World War I', to paraphrase Salvemini's famous description of Mussolini's Ethiopian war. Certainly, both the Libyan war in 1911 and the Ethiopian in 1935 were followed by a sequence of events which would produce world conflict within four years. In neither case was Libya or Ethiopia in herself of direct moment to the Powers. History is upside down if Italy, the least of the Great Powers, is made the cause of general disaster. However, for a student of the structures of international relations (and of their continuity) what is interesting is the parallel between events 1911–14 (–15) and 1935–9 (–40). It is almost as though a rule could be essayed that expansion by the least of the Powers is an excellent indicator of a malfunctioning Concert and of the peril of approaching war.

Historians of war and society have instructed us to examine war as a test of the war-maker's society and institutions. How did Liberal Italy fare with respect to the conflict of 1911–12?

In many ways, the administration of the war reflected the strengths of *giolittismo*; perhaps it was a 'triumph of all that was best and fairest' in Liberal Italy. Civilians showed no signs of handing over real authority to the military. None of the presumed puppet-masters behind the parliamentary stage emerged to take power away from Giolitti. The King, although paying scrupulous attention to military formalities, remained in the background. The Church saw its financial ambitions thwarted. Big Business stayed in its place. Even those certain critics of a Giolitti government, Sonnino, Albertini and the nationalists, did little more than celebrate the war and criticise the war-making. Contrary to the thesis of a military-industrial-ANI complex behind Italian 'new imperialism', the nationalists were notably hostile towards Giolitti's reliance on what they regarded as the unsavoury 'plutocratic' skills of Volpi.[19] They were similarly vociferous in objecting to Giolitti's appointment of Camillo Garroni, ex-prefect of Genoa, his long-time crony and agent, and intermediary with Genoese ship-building and other heavy industrial interests, to the Embassy at Constantinople. The nationalists, those alleged sponsors of the imperialism of finance capital, preferred that the post be manned by one of the accustomed litterateurs of the Consulta who might beguile the Porte with his knowledge of Canto XXVIII.

Instead, in the short term, the war was very much Giolitti's war; begun and confined by him, administered by him and, to an extent, ended by him. Under the test of war, Liberal Italy displayed Giolitti's best abilities as a bureaucrat and a politician. However much he worked with San Giuliano, Bertolini, Frassati, Malagodi, or other colleagues in Cabinet, Parliament and the press, it was Giovanni Giolitti who held power in Italy in 1911–12.

Short-term triumph carried with it the symptoms of long-term failure. In October 1912, to the scarcely concealed relief and amazement of the Army, the King and San Giuliano, Italy had won its first colonial war. But with victory came its military and social costs, and they were high.

Waging war was expensive even in Libya. Giolittian stratagems prevented public knowledge of the fact,[20] but the Italian budget fell into deep deficit while defence spending spiralled upwards. The war had required expenditure more than 50 per cent above the normal annual level, and the money could only be found in loans. Moreover, Giolitti had to put up with inane but continual complaints from Sonnino and his friends that not enough was being spent on the Army and that part of the military budget was diverted to nourish a pro-Italian international press.

Moreover, the stress of war-making had profound effects on Italian society. The comfortable norms of the political process were jostled out of place. The socialists split; the Catholics became more determined not to lose their money next time and the nationalists were convinced, quite inaccurately, that the war had been theirs and that therefore the future belonged to them. The Giolittian system wavered and went into crisis. Elections in September 1913 brought gains to nationalists, Catholics, socialists and the anti-Giolittian 'constitutional opposition'. In March 1914, in at least temporary admission of defeat, Giolitti resigned to be replaced by the southern professor of law, Antonio Salandra, a 'uomo di classe' who soon revealed ambitions to undermine all Giolitti's authority and to divert any processes which might have led Liberal Italy to be a 'democracy in the making'.

Salandra's rise was a demonstration of a new confidence (and a new desperation) appearing among Italian conservatives as a result of the Libyan war. Colonial success, a foreign adventure brought to fruition, meant that conservatives could look abroad for further solutions to the strains of modernisation at home. Adowa and the failures of Crispi and Pelloux had at last been overcome. Now, again, conservatives could dream of 'returning to the Statuto' and thus relegating Giolitti and his socialist fellow-travellers to the attic.

It is always important in Liberal (and Fascist) Italy not to over-emphasise the significance of differences among ruling class groups, especially about foreign affairs. So, in 1912–14, first under Giolitti, and then at Giolitti's direct behest under Salandra, the guide along an Italian path to imperialism was the Foreign Minister, Antonino Di San Giuliano. The war in Libya had taught this intensely patriotic and coruscatingly cynical Sicilian aristocrat that there was still a chance for his Italy. Emerging from Giolitti's shadow, although always with Giolitti's approval and now confident in legerdemain and manipulation to the point of fool-hardiness, San Giuliano intruded into the affairs of the Greater Powers with an aplomb rarely displayed by an Italian since the time of Cavour. In 1912–14, Italy became an active Great Power in a way which belied the decade of restraint before 1908. In 1914, the 'Giolittian system', arguably, was on the point of domestic collapse. From 1912–14, the norms of Giolittian Italy's international practice were already broken, although the change was managed surreptitiously, by a reliance on peace and not on war, and with Giolitti's support. Italy, in her own way, had taken her first steps on her own path to imperialism.

Italy's diplomatic machinations were favoured by the pall of gloom which hung over the Great Powers as a result of the Balkan wars. While armies marched to and fro across Macedonia, and while it was likely for a time that Constantinople would welcome Foxy Ferdinand, 'Tsar' of Bulgaria, as its Christian liberator, there was an imminent and obvious threat of war between the Powers. Could Austria or Russia tolerate gains or losses for their clients and enemies among the Balkan states? Big Bulgaria, Transylvania, the Sandjak of Novi-Bazar, Macedonia, Antivari – phantasms of an outlandish and barbarous world tested the patience (and the spelling) of every European Chancellery.

However, while the threat of war was so immediate, the Great

Powers reacted to the squabbling in the Balkans with remarkable decorum and sanity. A Conference of Ambassadors of the Great Powers was established in London in December 1912. Italy was naturally offered a place with the garrulous Neapolitan, Guglielmo Imperiali, ambassador in London, acting as her delegate. It was not long before all participants agreed that Balkan affairs were 'intolerably wearisome',[21] but with Grey and the German ambassador, Lichnowsky, giving the lead, the Great Powers stuck to their last. A year later, the Conference was able to dissolve, with its members secure in the knowledge that public fighting in the Balkans had ceased, and that the small Balkan states had arranged new borders and all but eliminated Turkey from Europe without apparent damage to the interests of any of the Great Powers. It was almost as though the Concert had been reconstituted, and the courteous if nervous Grey had taken up the baton once wielded with such authority by Otto von Bismarck.

Countervailing factors existed. A war by the weakest Great Power in Africa succeeded by a series of wars in the Balkans made risky a prophesy of permanent peace. Moreover, Austria–Hungary, Russia and Italy, the Powers with the most direct interest in what was happening, were stimulated, depressed and irritated by the changing panorama in the Balkans. Once the local skirmishes were over, and politicians in Vienna, St Petersburg (and Rome) had time to think hard about the meaning of new Balkan borders, there was every likelihood that the international picture might not seem as rosy as it did in Christmas 1913.

Within Italy, the conflict in the Balkans had heightened nationalist excitation. Politicians of all persuasions had reinforced their belief in 'the coming struggle of the nations' and in the survival of the fittest and best prepared. On the pages of the newspapers, international relations preserved their primacy and events in London sustained anew the myth that Italy was a Great Power. Nitti, Sonnino and Guicciardini all joyfully greeted the 'Risorgimento' in the Balkans,[22] and opinion in the press[23] and in the Consulta hardened that the total collapse of Turkey was inevitable and imminent.

Italy did have some commercial interests in the Balkans. Although her technological concern in the subject was as yet slight, she bought oil from Romania. Tsar Ferdinand, 'the last of the Bourbons', sometimes seemed prepared to regard Rome as the near-equal of Paris. Volpi, who was reputed to be able to speak Serb, had many deals bubbling nicely in Serbia and in Montenegro, where in each case he had been adept at ingratiating himself with the princelings of the local court. Even Greece, perennial rival legatee of Italy to the testatment of Rome and Byzantium, and a country whose $M\epsilon\gamma\alpha\lambda\eta$ $I\delta\epsilon\alpha$ aspired to the 'Greek territories' inland from Brindisi, was showing an interest in Marconi's communication systems.

But, as in most other areas of Italian foreign policy, trade was not the key. Compared to her commerce with the Great Powers or with Argentina and Switzerland, Italian interests in the Balkans or even with Turkey were meagre. Moreover a country such as Montenegro, whose financial and royal contacts with Italy might have suggested a client relationship, was, in fact, ruggedly independent or ruggedly anxious to seek loans from Vienna, Paris and St Petersburg rather than from the relatively poor Rome. Giolitti made a virtue of necessity by warning, with the wisdom of a good house-keeper, that too much economic involvement in Montenegro meant merely 'money thrown away in complete loss'.[24]

The real mainspring for Italian policy in the Balkans, the Eastern Mediterranean and elsewhere in 1912–14 remained, as usual, psychological and set in the tactical requirements and opportunities created by Italy's relationship with the Powers. The triumph in Libya and continuing war in the Balkans offered many openings for a ruthless and adroit Italian Foreign Minister.

One minor but characteristic region of Italian endeavour in 1912–14 was Ethiopia. It has already been noted that, contrary to the common assumption that Adowa spelled the end of Italian ambitions inland from Eritrea, many Italian politicians merely regarded the defeat as a disastrously public set-back which necessitated caution but scarcely renunciation. In 1910 apprentice officers still looked wistfully on coins marked Umberto 1st, King of Italy and Emperor of Ethiopia.[25] The nationalists chose the fifteenth anniversary of Adowa, 1 March 1911, to launch their paper, *L'Idea Nazionale*, and thus to remind their readers of an anti-anniversary to the general celebrations of 50 years of Italian unification occurring in that year.

Within many other ruling-class minds, similar ideas stirred. The Amharic Empire, constructed by the great Emperor Menelik, might not last for ever. In 1906 Ferdinando Martini, the gentlemanly Governor of Eritrea and recent sponsor of the Istituto Coloniale Italiano, and a man who also propounded an 'iron severity' against miscegnation and in favour of the death penalty and even genocide in dealing with black subjects of Italy,[26] had already suggested that the Ethiopian state might itself perish as Menelik aged and died. Then there might be need for revision of the formal policy, as suggested to Martini's successor: 'not to pursue a policy of adventure [but rather] to create the cheapest administration possible'.[27] By 1912, when Menelik, stricken by general paralysis, was a sad, dumb prisoner in his own palace, another sometime advocate of stern realism, the patriotic journalist, Giuseppe Piazza, warned that the Great Emperor had no heirs and that his kingdom would soon be of nothingness.[28]

By then, within the Consulta and the new Ministry of Colonies, if often in irritable bureaucratic competition, San Giuliano, Bertolini and their juniors dreamed of reinforcing Italy's position in Ethiopia, lest, as one put it, Italy have to accept that 'Eritrea be for ever what it is now'.[29] San Giuliano, characteristically, was dismayed by the low level of Italy's commercial penetration of the area. Credito Italiano was making some initiatives, and the Banco di Roma was theorising about involving itself. But, in June 1914, San Giuliano and his officials were still puzzling how best 'to nourish Italian economic interests' in the Horn of Africa.[30] Historians should perhaps not deal in 'might-have-beens', but without the crisis in Europe there is every indication that, in 1914–15, Italy would have sought better political definition of her longstanding interests in Ethiopia.

Another, more famous area of Italian penetration in 1912–14 was Turkish Asia Minor. Some commentators have been ready to argue that the Eastern Mediterranean had become the fulcrum of Italian policy under the southerner, San Giuliano, and his 'southern Ministry'. There is very little evidence for this thesis, but Italy did busy herself in readiness for what San Giuliano, more publicly than most European statesmen, was willing to call the 'not far off' collapse of the Ottoman Empire.

There were many paradoxes in Italy's Turkish policy. The formal basis had long been what Tittoni had declared it to be in June 1908:

I will say that Italy's policy towards Turkey is clear and straightforward. The unshakeable foundation of this policy is and will be the maintenance of the Ottoman Empire, and when I speak of integrity I do not mean to make restrictions or reservations. This excludes in the most absolute manner any intention of occupation of any part of that Empire.[31]

Given similar circumstances, both before and after 1911–12, San Giuliano was equally capable of such categorical purity of intent. But ambition lurked in Asia Minor as it had in Libya.

Because of the Balkan wars, because of Italy's 'temporary' and uncertain occupation of the Dodecanese islands and because Libya had been scarcely the most cherished child of Ottoman power, in 1912–14 Italo-Turkish relations for a time became remarkably cordial. Italian politicians and entrepreneurs suddenly discovered Constantinople a reasonable place in which to do business. Volpi, Nogara and their friends found the Turks ready to tolerate a dummy local company to assist the development schemes of their Società Commerciale d'Oriente. Armenian middle-men humbly accepted Italian patrons; the Egyptian royal family and the De Martino clan (with contacts to the Secretary-General of the Consulta) organised profitable deals. Generally, San Giuliano began to favour the drawing up of blue-prints of harbour-works, railways, agricultural holdings and mines in the region of Adalia or around Smyrna, although he always regretted that such 'economic interests' remained so sketchy. When Giolitti objected that the sale of an Italian ship to the Turkish Navy would set off an Eastern Mediterranean naval race, San Giuliano demurred, declaring such an event 'less serious than . . . the loss of all our political and economic hopes' in Turkey.[32] He was not assisted, he complained, by a sufficiently mobilised public opinion. Nationalist philosopher, Enrico Corradini, for example, obscurely expressed his disgust over the fact that 'plutocratic pacifism' wanted to uphold the status quo in Turkey since it was, regrettably, such 'an excellent field for business'. At the same time, Corradini's logic persuaded him that it would not matter very much if minerals were not discovered in Libya since too much wealth would retard a colonising nation's spiritual development.[33]

Despite such fondness for the intellectually tangential, in 1912–14, Italy did endeavour to justify her future presence in Asia Minor by arrangements with the other Great Powers. Within the Triple Alliance, San Giuliano worked on the competition and association with Austria in order to persuade Germany to permit Italian desires to be admitted to junior partnership in the steadily growing German economic, military and political penetration of Turkey. The Germans were, at times and especially by 1914, likely to become hostile to what they understood to be the completely 'political' rather than commercial stimulus of Italian pretensions; but, by the summer of 1913, they had wearily conceded that Adalia must be accepted as an Italian 'sphere of work'.[34]

San Giuliano at once sought to delimit and expand this sphere by appealing to bankers and businessmen for action and by continuing his moralistic discussions with the Germans. Quite remarkably, he was able to persuade the British in March 1914 to accept that a concession given to the Smyrna–Aidin railway company must be reconciled to Italian interests. When challenged by Rodd, San Giuliano proclaimed that the Powers must perforce admit that 'a new Great Power has arisen in the Mediterranean ... [which] must get its share [in matters of] economic concessions and political influence'.[35] The British, with some muttering, backed down before what they saw as Italy's 'strictly political' ambitions.[36]

By the summer of 1914, a number of Italian zones were caressed by the Consulta's ardour, although, by then, Italian intrusiveness had irritated both Britain and Germany, had alarmed Austria and was presently regarded with less sympathy by the Turks who had begun to suspect that Italy was not a platonic lover. Italy's commercial schemes were erected only in the mind, and, with the onset of the European crisis, they collapsed. By 17 August 1914, Nogara reported bleakly to Volpi that war had meant 'the legal end of the world' for all Italian ambitions.[37]

The only hard territorial gains which Italy had made in the area between 1912 and 1914 were in the Dodecanese islands and Rhodes. A decade later, the islands were all that remained of Liberal Italy's dreams of commercial, territorial or political advantage from the collapse of Ottoman Turkey. It was only Mussolini, in 1924, who made it plain that Italy did not intend, one day, to evacuate the islands, to surrender them on strategic or geographical grounds to Turkey, or on ethnic grounds to Greece. From 1912 to 1914 Italy's publicly enunciated policy was that her occupation was temporary, pending the resolution of the Balkan wars and the departure of the last Turkish troops from Libya. Privately, both San Giuliano and Giolitti also stated that Italy could not keep European territory which did not belong to her and, moreover, territory which had the potential to provide a powerful naval base from which both the Suez Canal and the Straits could be supervised or threatened. France and especially Britain understood that peril and, from time to time, reminded Italy of their anxiety that the islands be handed over to their real or deserving master.

In fact, the story of Italy's retention of the Dodecanese is a good illustration of the limitations of verbal evidence in the study of diplomacy. For all Italy's protestations in public and planning in

private, it was soon apparent that the islands would not be evacuated
unless severe pressure by the Greater Powers was exerted on Italy to
leave. Such pressure, with the risk that Italy might be alienated, was
unlikely while the international situation remained menacing or
fluid. Thus, before 1945, the moment at which Italy came nearest to
abandoning her occupation was in 1919–20 when the other Great
Powers were united and when Italy's international bargaining
position was particularly feeble. Even then, despite treaties to the
contrary, Italy hung on. In the Dodecanese, for Italy, the general
state of the Concert was everything; the phrases of treaties or
diplomatic parleying and even Italian domestic affairs were nothing.

Thus, in 1912–14, although hardly conscious of it and scarcely
daring to admit it, the Liberal leadership solidified Italian claims.
The possibility of constructing a naval base was raised, and began to
be taken seriously. San Giuliano became habituated to using the
islands as pawns, pledging a future abandonment of them against
present advantage in Ethiopia, Asia Minor and especially in Albania.

For, despite all the dalliance and daydreaming in the Eastern
Mediterranean, Italy continued to place the real focus of her
diplomacy in the Adriatic. One area of particular concern was
Albania, whose coast reached out almost to touch Apulia. Albania,
for the present, was a squalid battlefield of rival religions and
cultures, held fast in a tribal past by the ubiquitous mud and an
almost total lack of communications or economic development.[38] But
publicists could easily recall the great Roman roads to the east which
ran out of Durazzo (Dyrrachium); or they could proclaim the island
of Saseno, which lay off the port of Valona, 'the Gibraltar of the
Adriatic',[39] concealing the fact, which would cause discomfort to
occupying Italian forces from October 1914, that the island had no
supplies of running water. Valona itself was esteemed a port of
strategic potential equal to Bizerta or Malta;[40] and the Corfu Channel
was proclaimed a perilous haven from which could operate a hostile
fleet. Rhetoricians discoursed redolently on the existence of Albanian
communities within Italy. Crispi had been proud of his Albanian
blood. Italian universities were the haven and sponsor of Albanian
languages and history.[41] Italian businessmen or heroes financed or
declared their willingness to fight for Albanian independence. The
sons of the great Giuseppe Garibaldi were often thought to be about
to lift the Turkish yoke from Albania. For some Italians, too, Albania
could only revive under the nourishment which would come from

massive Italian immigration. A figure of 200,000 was mentioned as a starting point.[42]

With the Balkan wars, one problem was that Serbia, Montenegro and Greece started to resolve the Albanian question by themselves. Italy's hostility was particularly directed against Greece. The other Great Powers all from time to time distrusted Serbia, Montenegro, Bulgaria and Romania, but Greece, at the far south of the Balkan peninsula, neither Slav nor Latin, could, from a distance, be proclaimed the successor of Demosthenes and Aristotle, the birthplace of literature, of the theatre, of parliament and 'civilisation'. A poor peasant country, with a particularly vicious tradition of political infighting among the tiny ruling class, Greece threatened no Great Power, except Italy, another 'birthplace of civilisation' and the equal to Greece certainly in past grandeur and perhaps in present weakness.

As Italy developed a Mediterranean policy, this comparison rankled. Italy's relationship with Greece became consistently tense except when annointed by the balm of honied words. The great Cretan statesman, Eleutherios Venizelos, was particularly adept at telling the Italians what they wanted to hear (while aiming at policies to their detriment). But neither the Corfu incident of 1923 nor the Italian invasion of Greece on 28 October 1940, neither the fact that the Greek government still celebrates the victory as the National Day, 'Oxi' ('No!') day, nor historical legend about the virulence of Fascist foreign policy, should conceal the fact that Graeco-Italian conflict has a long history.

Thus, from 1912 to 1914, the only Balkan power whose advantages Italy resented was Greece. At the London Conference of Ambassadors Italy was the proponent of the anti-Greek cause. In particular, Italy was anxious to curtail Greek advances into southern Albania, or northern Epirus as the Greeks liked to entitle it. This area, Italian politicians said with probity and not without justice, was not ethnically Greek. At London, Imperiali, and in Rome, San Giuliano, had recourse to three arguments of significance to the Great Powers. If Greece was responsible now in southern Albania, then Italy might later be so in the Dodecanese. If Greece was not held back in southern Albania, then how could the Powers go on making such a fuss about Serb or Montenegrin advantage in the north? And, finally, Italy was a Great Power, Greece a small one. If their interests clashed irreversibly, the other Great Powers must support their colleague, Italy, and sustain the supremacy of the Concert over all small states.

By 1914, Italy had her way in southern Albania. At least legally speaking, Albania had come into existence, although one British diplomat confided sadly to another that Albania was a wholly 'fictitious creation of Austria and Italy'.[43] Albania's border with Greece had been drawn at a point cutting the Corfu Channel. In practice much southern Albanian territory was a prey to Greek irregulars, against whom Italy twice threatened mobilisation. By then, Albania's ruler, the unfortunate Prince William of Wied, was seated on a most uncomfortable throne. Six months later, faced with competing revolts, William abandoned his throne and the country.

For Italy's Albanian policy, there was a more serious problem even than Greece. When, in 1877, Bismarck had held out to Italy the temptation of her occupation of Albania, he had done so as compensation for a supposed Austrian expansion into Bosnia and Herzegovina.[44] Austria first occupied and then annexed those territories, while Albania remained under Turkish rule, but after 1878 Albania became the crucial southern meeting-place of Austro-Italian collaboration and rivalry.

Italy had endeavoured to establish a cultural policy towards Albania from the 1880s with the government sponsoring schools in some of the larger centres. A patriotic journalist was delighted to be able to report in April 1914 that the Italian school at Durazzo had 450 pupils.[45] There had been some difficulties in establishing the culture of Dante and Manzoni in Albania. The religious leaders of Albania's Catholic minority were sometimes well informed about Liberal anti-clericalism. From 1896 to 1898, the Italian school at Scutari had been placed under interdict because the teaching was being done by Free Masons.[46] In 1914, the Consulta believed that Austria, which had pursued her own cultural imperialism in the area, had established a lead in academic matters and was still the favourite son of the local Roman Catholic Church. Instead, it was suggested, Italy should concentrate not on Dante but on commercial matters, and use modernity to deflect the Habsburgs' traditional power.[47] Financial means were particularly appropriate, said San Giuliano, given Albanians' 'innate venality'.[48]

In practice, Italian economic interests in Albania were small and likely to be contested. In May 1914, the Italian government solemnly pondered the news that Austria had set up a rival hotel to the Italian-owned one in Valona, and was aggressively proceeding to undercut Italian prices.[49] However, in so far as any country had an economic presence[50] in Albania, Italy did. In 1913 Italy and Austria signed an economic accord there, pledging co-operation and promising competition. The two Powers also collaborated in establishing a Bank of Albania. Italian consuls were the predictable advocates of total victory over their rival, Austria, even though at Durazzo, a journalist reported disapprovingly, the Italian and Austrian vice-consuls dined together once a week to compare notes on their hostility, to enumerate the number of pianos controlled by each faction[51] and mutually to recall the delights of civilisation.

However much consuls, journalists or bureaucrats dreamed and plotted about the financial control of Albania, the real initiative in trade usually came from the Italian government. As in Asia Minor, its motive was political. There was the question of strategy. San Giuliano and Guicciardini, who had both had their patriotic memories stirred by travels in Albania, and Tittoni, repeatedly stated that a neutral Albania was fundamental to the national interest. Unspoken, but understood by all, was another, more shadowy, possibility. If Austria moved anywhere further in the Balkans, then it would very likely be into Albania, given the uncertain sovereignty of that region. If Austria did move, then Article VII of the Triple Alliance would come into effect and any Austrian advantage might result in the cession of the Trentino and Trieste to Italy, although it could also, disastrously, be another humiliation in the style of the Bosnia and Herzegovina affair. In 1913–14 a comforting metaphor ran around the Consulta. The day was coming when Albania would be the new Schleswig Holstein and, then, Italy's destiny would be that of Prussia. San Giuliano liked the parallel and soon used it himself in talks with the German ambassador.[52]

Given their potential instability, Italo-Austrian relations in Albania were hedged around by much treatying. Apart from the 1913 accord and the Triple Alliance, Italy and Austria had signed exchanges on Albania in 1897, 1900 and 1902. Each agreement, however, signalled a continuation of rivalry rather than a solution to it.

During the Balkan wars, Austria had her attention focused away from Italy and towards the doings of Serbia and Montenegro, the two South Slav states which occasionally thought of themselves (and covertly were so regarded in Italy) as 'Piedmonts', fated to be the spearheads for the liberation of Slavs within the Habsburg Empire. In 1912–13, on at least three occasions, Austrian patience with the South Slavs threatened to run out completely.

In this period, San Giuliano played an able role in restraining his ally, in preserving general peace and in searching out diplomatic advantage for Italy. The most dramatic moment occurred in April–May 1913 during the Scutari incident. Then, Austria was adamantinely determined to prevent a Montenegrin occupation of Scutari, since she believed that such an event could lead to a Serb (and a Russian) exploitation of the coast south of Antivari and its riverine connection to Lake Scutari.

The London Conference of Ambassadors could offer only rebuke to Montenegro through a naval demonstration, an event which afforded San Giuliano savage enjoyment since he at least understood that Scutari lay over 30 kilometres inland. In these circumstances Giolitti advised clearly that Italy must 'avoid that a European war breaks out; if such a war does break out we must have no responsibility for it and in no way be implicated in it. All the rest has no value whatever for us'.[53] But, setting aside such a dramatic warning, San Giuliano maintained an active diplomacy. It had three aspects. Within the Triple Alliance, he sought to associate very closely with Germany. He constantly reminded Austria, Germany and the other Powers of the Greek problem – what could not be permitted in north Albania must also be banned in the south. And, if Austria still could not be dissuaded from attacking Montenegro or Serbia, San Giuliano offered association – at least in the sense that, if Austria moved against Scutari, Italy would seize Valona and drive the Greeks and their irregulars back to the legal border. It was at this time that San Giuliano suggested to a bemused Pollio that Italy secretly mobilise, whatever that meant.[54]

Such confidence, and even rashness, was in striking contrast to San Giuliano's timidity before the victory in Libya. It is likely that he assumed that the threat of Italian co-operation, and the complexity given to the northern Albanian issue by its constant association with the south, would be enough to delay Austria. Certainly this assumption was correct. But the last days of April 1913 and the first days of May were the time when Liberal Italy went closest to armed collaboration alongside Austria, even if this collaboration was directed against her ally.

The tension of the Balkan wars had nourished a new concern for the Triple Alliance which, in 1910, had seemed almost a dead letter. In the direct aftermath of the Libyan war, on 5 December 1912, the Triple Alliance had been renewed, eighteen months early. The renewal has excited considerable controversy, with it sometimes being depicted as an example of San Giuliano's exasperated triplicism. In fact, the Italian motivation in renewing the treaty was a predictable mixture of fear and a desire to substantiate gains just made. After 5 December 1912, Austria could no longer hint, as she had done in September 1911, that Italian victory in North Africa ought to produce Austrian compensation in the Balkans (and no associated Italian advantage in the Trentino and Trieste).

In 1913–14, as a result of this renewal, but much more as an effect of the evident strain on the Concert of the Great Powers caused by the Balkan wars, the Italian Army and Navy joined in the refurbishing of the military accords of the Triple Alliance. In June 1913, an Italo-Austro-German naval agreement pledged association in event of war against the Triple Entente and in the next months technicians exchanged ideas on how to make this co-operation most effective. In March 1914, Pollio revived the uncertain pledges of a decade before that Italy would directly assist Germany in a conflict with France. It was in these circumstances that, on 1 August 1914, the Italian Officer Corps was still preparing itself to fight alongside its Central Power partners. But these expert agreements must not be taken out of context. In Liberal Italy, the military were subordinate to politicians. Military schemes were for the military and, in crisis, must necessarily be adjusted to political requirements. The Italian generals were not told the terms of the Triple Alliance and were not expected to interfere in diplomacy which they were not trained to understand and which, if Pollio is any example, they did not understand. It is notable that Thaon di Revel, the more politically able Naval Chief of General Staff who led the more technologically developed and expert officer corps, did endeavour to clarify, at least with Salandra, how possible it was to pursue naval arrangements which clashed with Italian interests and which were not reconciled with Italian means.[55]

At the very time that Italian Army and Navy chiefs sought the most comradely ties with the Central Powers at manoeuvres, San Giuliano was engaging in manoeuvres of his own. While fear, policy and advantage suggested a present loyalty to the Triple Alliance, it was best to keep open an insurance policy with the Triple Entente where, after all, France from time to time was insufficiently respectful of

Italian grandeur. For this purpose, San Giuliano adroitly encouraged the Italophilia of Barrère and Rodd, the French and English ambassadors in Rome, and showed interest in their idea of a Mediterranean or North African agreement.[56] Such a treaty would clarify what the arrangements which Prinetti had once signed with Barrère and Lansdowne meant now that Libya had become Italian. San Giuliano's policy had many parallels with that of Prinetti in 1902, except that the more experienced and astute San Giuliano cleverly avoided signing on any dotted line. The vague Mediterranean scheme was deliberately left moribund so that it could be resuscitated at any time when San Giuliano's diplomatising might demand it.

May–June 1914 was such a time. By then, Italy's diplomatic position was more exposed than it had been since October 1912. The trouble really was that the Balkan wars were over. The long-term irreconcilability of Italian and Austrian interests had already been evidenced in August 1913. Then, the publication of the Hohenlohe decrees, directed against Italian citizens who had come across the border to Trieste in search of employment, raised a storm of comment in Italy. Austria's determination to retain Trieste except in the event of military defeat meant in turn that all Italians waited for just such a defeat. King Victor Emmanuel III commented that scheming in Asia Minor or the Adriatic must not obscure Italy's major need to prepare for the 'completion of the Risorgimento'.

Graver events were presaged with the end of the Balkan wars. San Giuliano's expansionism had required unusual diplomatic circumstances to flourish and in the first months of 1914 the Italian room for fruitful manoeuvres diminished sharply. The hot war in the Balkans over, Germany felt free to resume her policies and began to detect the extent to which San Giuliano had been manipulating his function as noble second within the Triple Alliance. Austria was appalled by Serb victory in the Balkans, and her diplomacy became less easily seduced by Italian offers of collaboration in Asia Minor and Albania. In April 1914 a meeting between San Giuliano and Berchtold at Abbazia was regarded in Rome as a complete failure. Austria refused to countenance either new Italian expansion in the Eastern Mediterranean, any face-saving on the Hohenlohe decrees, or even the promise that an Italian-language law faculty be established in the Italian-speaking area of the Habsburg Empire.

In May–June 1914, Italian diplomacy was dismayed by the profundity of Austro-Serb antagonism. San Giuliano was fatigued by his reiterated proclamation of Italy's utter refusal to allow Austria to seize Mount Lovcen (and thus block a South Slav outlet to the sea). He even began to stress to the talkative, neurotic and potentially malleable German ambassador, Flotow, that Italy's ambitions in the Trentino and Trieste must be admitted, should Austria make a forward move in the Balkans. The Albanian situation was in the most perilous crisis. San Giuliano had resisted domestic Italian pressure hostile to William of Wied as Austria's puppet, although he probably did allow money and munitions to pass to William's rivals. After William left Albania, the contradictions of Italy's policy were evident. Disaster already beckoned on 27 June 1914 when a recruitment office opened in Vienna for volunteers to go to Albania.[57] Francis Ferdinand's assassination seemed only a minor problem (indeed his death was received with relief given his famous irascibility, instability, friendship with Conrad and alleged hostility to Italy). In the summer of 1914, it appeared that the time might be ripe for a general reassessment of Italian membership of the Triple Alliance.[58]

A final question must be what part had Italy played in producing that deterioration in the Great Powers' relations which would convert the assassination of an archduke into general war? The answer is very little, except in the short term, and as an additional irritant for European statesmen already tired by the ever increasing burden of international diplomacy. Italy from 1912 to 1914 pursued expansionist policies with a zeal which bore some comparison to her policies from 1936 to 1939, and with a sense of opportunity, restraint and secrecy which did not. While the Greater Powers failed to resolve their mutual conflicts or their domestic crises and while peace survived, the weakest of the Powers sought advantage for herself and gained some, at least on paper. But the epicentre of the coming storm in international relations was not located in Rome.

6 Italy and the Great War

The July crisis has been studied by so many historians in such detail that it scarcely seems possible to learn anything new about it. Notwithstanding the availability of the *Documenti diplomatici italiani*, Italy in most studies is accorded the most minor part in the crisis. The exception, naturally, is provided by Italian historians who, following the lead of Luigi Albertini, have both over-emphasised Italian power and over-concentrated on what Albertini stigmatised as San Giuliano's amorality, his 'second-rate Machiavellism'.[1]

Yet Italy's role in the July crisis is not without significance both for a student of Italian diplomacy and for one of the origins of the war. The first and plainest conclusion to draw is that the Greater Powers, when they finally became aware that a real crisis existed, had almost no thought for Italy. July 1914 exhibited starkly the extent of Italy's weakness, and the even greater feebleness of her reputation. Thus San Giuliano could not repeat his dexterity during the Scutari crisis; and his quite sophisticated mediation scheme of 28 July[2] got nowhere. Italian diplomats could not even arrange appointments with major European statesmen. Italy's place on the Great Power list was hypothetical and, in the great crisis, little proof could be adduced to support the hypothesis.

This generalisation holds true for the last days of July 1914. Perhaps, earlier, there had been a lost moment for Italian diplomacy. It was not so much that Italy lost an opportunity, as that Germany (and Austria) refused it. Despite the long existence of the Triple Alliance and despite Italy's recently active membership of it, Germany and Austria excluded Italy from any foreknowledge of the crucial events of the July Crisis. Although his pumping of the nervous Flotow at Fiuggi did produce some leaks, San Giuliano was not officially informed beforehand of the drafting of the ultimatum to Serbia. Both in Berlin and in Vienna, there had been some appraisal of the merits of loyalty and alliance to Italy. But such thoughts were rapidly put out of mind when it was contemplated that Italy would be sure to 'betray' any information to St Petersburg. 'Fear', Riezler advised, fear of imminent, overwhelming German victory, was the most practical means of ensuring the survival of the Triple Alliance.[3]

This cavalier omission of Italy may merely indicate that the politicians were too busy and the issues too grave for the Italians to be involved directly in the July crisis. After all, Italy's relationship within the Triple Alliance had deteriorated in recent months. But there is another possible interpretation. The peremptory dismissal of San Giuliano as a Slavophile, and the determination not to permit him opportunity to display again his ambiguous skills in preserving peace and seeking his own advantage, do illustrate that the July crisis was being conducted to a tempo diverse from that of the Balkan wars. Had Germany and Austria won a diplomatic triumph in the July crisis, then Italy could only have remained in the Triple Alliance as a client and not as an ally, no longer with even the tattiest shreds of respectability as a Great Power.

The patriotic elucubrations of some Italian historiography have obscured the technical legality and moral justice of Italy's declaration of neutrality, which was made public on 3 August. Throughout the July crisis, San Giuliano may not have been sinless in dreaming of Trieste and the Trentino regained to an Italian bosom, but such dreams were irrelevant when neither Germany nor Austria wanted to interpret them. Italy's allies did not treat her as an ally, nor even as a Great Power. In these circumstances, and fitting with all the traditions of Italian diplomacy, neutrality was the only appropriate policy.

The July crisis and, indeed, negotiations for war entry until October 1914, cast penetrating light on another debated area of Liberal Italy, that is on the processes of decision-making in foreign affairs. Contrary to the prescriptions of those who diagnose for Salandra a more penetrating brain and a more dramatic political significance than he really possessed, decisions in July 1914, even more than in June 1940, were made by 'one man alone', by the Foreign Minister, San Giuliano, if always in the context of Italian needs and ambitions. Distanced from the domestic crisis of 'Red Week', those June days which had so occupied Salandra, sure in the support of Giolitti and the King, contemptuous of his Cabinet colleagues, superior to the buzzings of patriotic and ANI press criticism, scoring points at will off the fussy German and the honourable English ambassadors, backed by a loyal Consulta and ignoring the predictable advice of his ambassadors, San Giuliano ran Italian foreign policy. He would continue to do so until his death on 16 October 1914.[4]

Given that his always feeble body was collapsing, San Giuliano preferred to conduct much of his business from the spa at Fiuggi, south of Rome. There, from 4 August, he confronted an entirely new diplomatic and political situation. Decades of Italian diplomatising, and all the fabulous schemes of the last months, lay in ruins. There was war between the five Great Powers. Was it possible for Italy to be or to remain a Great Power unless she entered, at sometime or other, the Great War?

Although much obscured by the detail and controversy of historiography, this was the fundamental question asked by all members of the ruling classes during the so called crisis of the 'intervento', of the period between the declaration of neutrality and Italy's entry into the war on 24 May 1915. Despite the bitterly divided nation which joined the war in May 1915, almost all the Italian leadership had a similar answer to the above question. The Italy which was Liberal, United and a Great Power, the Third Italy, the Heir of Rome, would have to enter the Great War, somehow, sooner or later.

The only additional problem was that expressed by Giacomo De Martino on 18 October 1914. Italy's policy must also be to find itself among the victorious at the end of the war.[5] Therefore, Italy had to be wary in her choice of partners, although, after the French forces resisted on the Marne, it was soon almost unanimously agreed that alliance in war could only be on the side of the Triple Entente. Some nationalists comforted themselves with the belief that Italy could wage her next war against Britain and France.[6] The greater issue, at least for the more astute participants in the decision-making process, then became to select the right moment at which Italian entry against the Central Powers would be of maximum effect and minimum cost. Giolitti was particularly anxious that Italy prepare herself not merely for war, but also for the peace which would follow. Germany might lose the present war but, should Austria be destroyed, regain her strength and harden her will thereafter. In these circumstances, Giolitti repeatedly explained, Italy, with the realism of the poor, must remember that gratitude had no place in politics.[7]

King Victor Emmanuel, too, had begun by viewing the conflict with fearful suspicion.[8] In August 1914 he experienced one of those nervous crises of the onset of middle age which was partially induced by his dislike of war. The same parsimony which persuaded him to argue for the abolition of Greek and Latin in schools and which would soon instruct him to keep a war diary listing his appointments, their date and duration and nothing else,[9] made him always the enemy of the romantic gesture. The Aostas' evident sympathy for France might have suggested that Victor Emmanuel look favourably on France's enemies, but in practice the King was too much a man of his era not to want to complete the Risorgimento against Austria. By the end of 1914 it was apparent that the *re soldato* would not oppose war entry. But Victor Emmanuel continued to behave with his habitual constitutional propriety. Many of the final decisions of May 1915 were posited on the need to defend and preserve the monarch, but Victor Emmanuel had played little direct part in bringing monarchical institutions into question.

The *intervento* similarly confirmed the subordinate role of the Army in the decision-making process of Liberal Italy in peacetime. During the July crisis there had been some sympathy in the Army for the old allies of the Central Powers, although the Naval Chief of Staff was appalled by the prospect of having to make war against England and warned that he could not guarantee either communications with the colonies or even the loyalty of Italy's exposed coastal cities.[10] Pollio had died on 1 July and been replaced as Army Chief of General Staff by Luigi Cadorna, who sprang from a most distinguished Piedmontese military family. The failure of the Central Powers to win the war straightaway soon convinced Cadorna and the other military chiefs that Italy's proper place lay beside the Triple Entente. As early as 13 August, Cadorna counselled a crushing assault on Austria. He remained a partisan for war thereafter, warning, with some commonsense, that Italy's place in the Triple Alliance was lost in any case. If Germany and Austria were victorious, they were not going to be patient with a state which they already believed had betrayed them.[11]

But the military's desire to display its skills and to seek its promotions in combat did not mean that the orthodoxies of civil-military relations had been overturned. Once war began, Cadorna would be particularly rigorous in his desire to exclude the civilians. While there was peace, he sullenly accepted the rules of the game. Moreover, there were many good military reasons to suggest caution and delay. Sonnino and Salandra liked to boost their own morale by attributing the blame for the lack of combat readiness in the Army to the levity and immorality of Giolitti.[12] Some officers, toadies to their masters of the moment, agreed, although the more deeply felt view was probably that 'politicians' in general were to blame. Despite the huge expenditure on 'defence', in August 1914 the Italian Army was deficient not only in munitions, but even in winter clothing. Forts, themselves already out of date, had not been completed on the Austrian border. In May 1914 over 20,000 troops had been dispatched to Eritrea in fear of and readiness for the collapse of Ethiopia, where the new Emperor, Lij Yasu, only called off Ethiopian 'mobilisation' after Italy's declaration of neutrality.[13] 'Red Week' had further wasted the Army. Most of all, the military situation in Libya had deteriorated. There, news of general war between the Christian Powers provoked the revolt of the local Arab population who, in the eight months after August 1914, inflicted 3,500 casualties on the Italian Army. 60,000 troops were required to preserve a minimum of colonial control.[14] It was characteristic that, four days after the signature of the Treaty of London, a Cabinet member's diary should bewail further heavy losses in Libya.[15]

These reasons help to explain why the Army did not do more to repair its deficiencies by May 1915. Then, summer made the clothing question less pressing, but the Army still only had 618 machine and 112 heavy guns.[16] Many foreign experts, in contrast to politicians, and military philosophers doubted its combat-worthiness.[17] The Italian military attaché in Paris agreed that spring 1915 was not the moment for Italy to make a move.[18] But for Cadorna, or Salandra's new Minister of War, Zupelli, who had been born in Istria,[19] such questions were strangely irrelevant. All would be better when there was war and the Army came into its own. For then, as Salandra put it on 23 May, 'a war government cannot be a free government'.[20] In war, the military could at last cut through the compromise and verbiage of the politicians.[21] But, until that happy day, the politicians went on talking and ruling.

There is similarly little evidence that Business or Finance were especially united or determined advocates of an immediate Italian entry into the war on the Entente side.[22] Specialised modern sectors of the economy such as the hydro-electric industry which depended heavily on German (and Swiss) technology were certainly not pro-war.[23] In July 1914 Ettore Conti could not readily discern which was the more appropriate side for Italy to join in combat, and in any case feared the long-term social and economic effect of war.[24] Agnelli and his rapidly growing automobile concern could build for war as well as for peace, but in July 1914 Fiat had contracts exchanged with Britain, Russia and Germany.[25] Gino Olivetti of Confindustria condemned war as 'a monstrous phenomenon' which resulted only in the 'brutal destruction of men and wealth'. In May 1915, this ideologue of Big Business was half-attracted to the idea that it would be best if the working class launched a general strike to block war entry.[26] Italian agriculture, so dependent for its export markets on its favoured relationship with Germany and Austria, also had many practical reasons to oppose the war.

There were currents in the other direction. Both Conti and Agnelli drifted towards interventionism once war began, because they perceived that organising commerce or credit was difficult while Italy was the odd man out among the Powers. Returning emigrants exacerbated both unemployment and its accompanying social tensions.[27] Moreover, those sectors of finance which had been closest to Germany were now painfully anxious to confirm their Italian patriotism. Thus the Banca Commerciale and its officers, Otto Joel or Giuseppe Toeplitz, soon to be the objects of a vicious nationalist campaign which alleged that they were German agents and that their friend and patron, Giolitti, was guilty of high treason,[28] were carefully determined not to swim against the tide.[29] The nationalist attack on Giolitti and his 'German friends', which, allegedly, even included Volpi,[30] was lubricated by funds from Salandra's business associates, who united on 30 December 1914 to form the Banca Italiana di Sconto. This self-styled 'banca italianissima', which in practice relied more on French expertise than the Banca Commerciale had done on German, did back war entry as part of what had then become an ambition to dismantle the Giolittian system.

But one conspiratorial swallow does not make a conspiratorial spring. A far greater mass of evidence about the Italian business classes in 1914–15 shows them following behind political opinion rather than directing it. There was a certain sympathy for Salandra, and a certain expectation, expressed most clear-sightedly by Olivetti, that a more organised and more controlled state would be one of the benefits of war.[31] But business was divided, as each sector sought its own best advantage. It was also patriotic, sprung from a section of the population which accepted the myth that Italy was a Great Power.

Typical was the co-operative movement, so powerful and extensive in the Veneto and other parts of northern Italy. At first its spokesmen defended neutrality but, from September 1914, it became more interventionist, preaching with naive patriotism that in the crisis Italy must be ready and must show her greatness.[32]

The real leaders of the interventionist cause were the intellectuals, those lawyers and journalists who, whatever their political persuasion, were always at the forefront of the ruling classes of Liberal (and Fascist) Italy. Many traversed diverse philosophical routes in coming to the conclusion that they favoured an Italian entry into the war. For some, ethics decided the question. Luigi Albertini and *Corriere della Sera* preached war for British-style liberalism against the Violator of Belgium and the Oppressor of Small Peoples. As Albertini put it in characteristic metaphor, Italy must join the passengers of the stage-coach resisting the attentions of highway-robbers.[33] Salvemini or Bissolati similarly propagandised the cause of France, Home of Revolution and the People, enemy of militarism and authoritarian empires.[34]

Less responsible in their rhetoric were the various bickering nationalists who continued to long for their day when Italy would no more be 'in the hands of old men and greybeards'.[35] Some pondered dreamily for a time how to wage a war against both Austria and France. When it was finally understood that alliance groupings could not be dictated by Italy, the ANI became partisans of the Entente. Soffici, in October 1914, thought neutralism equalled 'the triumph of shit', the sort of leavings which could be expected, he said with unkind but characteristic reference to the dying San Giuliano of the 'invalid' inhabitants of the 'rest-home' at the Consulta.[36] Separate from the main ANI group was Gabriele D'Annunzio, who in 1914 had almost become a French citizen. For D'Annunzio, Paris was the Home of Art and France the country in which kicks were most easily acquired and creditors most easily avoided. D'Annunzio was soon repaying French hospitality by blessing the French cause. Rheims, he declared, had never been as beautiful as it was under bombardment.[37] Many nationalists and patriots showed the courage of their delusions by volunteering. Marinetti, for example, signed up with the Lombard Cyclist Volunteers who hoped to pedal towards adventure, victory and revolution in France.[38]

It was this last word 'revolution' which soon became the one most bandied about among intellectuals to justify their war fervour. Some historians of ideas are so anxious to plumb the profound philosophies of the past that they absurdly over-emphasise the unity and wisdom of certain intellectuals' ideas instead of their levity and self-interest.[39] Certainly in 1914–15 'revolution' became a catch-all word, widespread in its usage and unclear in its meaning except as a justification for war. Thus nationalists, syndicalists, Mussolini, Gramsci for a time, and many others could all submit to the siren song of 'revolution' which really meant little more than better days ahead in which their own peculiar abilities would receive greater recognition and payment. 'Revolution' became a fine-sounding word to justify to others and to oneself the sacrifice of war.

In so behaving, Italian intellectuals were not being particularly silly or particularly inventive. Rather, they were mimicking the behaviour of their peers in other European states, although the delay of the *intervento* gave Italians plenty of time to craft complicated words which would vindicate their behaviour. After all, in August 1914, Freud had said that his whole libido went out to the Habsburg armies;[40] and the ex-pacifist, G. M. Trevelyan, was soon hard at work arguing that his hero, Garibaldi, had been the real sponsor of the battle against Prussian militarism. Trevelyan did add disarmingly that this motive had not been well understood at the time.[41] Although not the cause of the war, the sense of relief, of an end to *ennui*, among bourgeois intellectuals was the basis of that atmosphere favourable to conflict much remarked on by later historians.[42]

In Italy, it was all the more significant given the nearness of the intellectual classes to the exercise of power, and given their absolute acceptance of the myth that Italy was a Great Power. The Risorgimento had allegedly been a time of poetry; the First World War would recreate the moment in which the dull masses were moved by poets and poetasters. War meant an escape from parochialism and failure. Local histories have illustrated that in April–May 1915 the fortresses of interventionism were located in the many large towns of Italy, those famous civic centres, with the grandeur of their past and the uncertainty of their present. In Ferrara or Lecce, a professor or a writer was uneasily Liberal (but disliked the great unwashed), was uneasily Italian (but always averred that his town was best), and wanted Italy to be Great (since there was so much evidence, brought by passing tourists or in the rejection slips of prestigious foreign journals, that she was little). Many Europeans in 1914 spoke of war as a release, an end to a torment of irritation from the inconsistencies and ambiguities of their life. Few had better reasons to feel released than the educated citizens of Liberal Italy.

These currents, united with and often challenged by the innocent pacifism of the masses as outlined in Chapter Four, flowed together to form the 'public opinion' of whose direction Italian politicians had to take some account in 1914–15. These politicians were unlikely to reach decisions at variance with all national opinion. But in decision-making, they kept considerable autonomy. San Giuliano played his cards alone before his death, much enjoying the game, not the least because of the opportunity to be sarcastic about the stolidity of his Prime Minister, the fatuity of his Cabinet colleagues and the levity of 'public opinion'. In November 1914, Salandra promoted his old patron, Sonnino, to be Foreign Minister and the two, thereafter, operated in unwholesomely ethical alliance. 'We two alone', said Salandra to Sonnino in March 1915, must make the decisions, grasp the nettles confronting Italy's path; 'We two alone'.[43]

Perhaps it seems an unlikely boast. What of Italy's position among the Powers; could they allow Italy to make up her own mind about war entry? Again, much legend to the contrary, Italian diplomacy had remarkable independence during the *intervento*.

For all European states, war diplomacy was a difficult and unfamiliar task. Diplomats and their Foreign Ministers were uncertain where they stood in relation to the often amended power structure at home, in which the military had now occupied such a crucial post. For many diplomatists, war diplomacy was something of a waste of time unless its path was smoothed by victory. As Sir Edward Grey repeatedly informed subordinates anxious to seduce this neutral or that: 'it all depends on the progress of the war'.[44] While San Giuliano lived, this caution was apposite since he was one of those politicians who understood most quickly and most clearly that it was going to be a long war. In a world where most believed that the troops would be home by Christmas, it is a testimony of San Giuliano's ability and experience that he saw no need whatever to hurry Italian intervention.[45] From August to October 1914, whatever words were actually spoken, all Italian negotiations were posited on the assumption that what might be true today would be false tomorrow, if one side or other made dramatic military gain. For the present, San Giuliano at no stage was eager to finalise his dealings with the Triple Entente or with the Central Powers.

On any realistic assessment, the Triple Entente and Austria also had little reason to conclude any agreement with Italy. (Germany perhaps did, since any concessions the Central Power would have to make to Italy would patently have to be made by Austria, to no particular German disadvantage). None the less, there was a second fundamental factor in war diplomacy, a sort of diplomatic equivalent to the military tactics being pursued on the Western Front. This was the simple belief that numbers counted. Conrad and Falkenhayn, for example, feared in 1915 that a joint Italo-Romanian entry on the Entente side would precipitate an Austrian collapse. Italian troops would enter Zagreb in three weeks and Vienna in six.[46] In retrospect, these fears seem bizarre. Indeed, as A. J. P. Taylor has taken pleasure in noting, nearly as many Austrian troops were engaged garrisoning the Italian front before entry as were employed fighting on it afterwards.[47] Contrary to the *miles gloriosus* image, pessimism is a frequent accompaniment of a general's metier. Whatever the reason, both generals and diplomats strove to bring Turkey, Italy, Bulgaria, Romania and Greece into the war, and at least justified their ambitions by statements about the decisive effect of such intervention.

Such optimism squared uneasily with the dismissive assumptions of Northern Europeans about Italy in general and Italy's military proclivities in particular. In May 1915 there was some evidence that semi-racist beliefs in Italian inferiority had not weakened. Even the most friendlily disposed foreigners readily recoursed to phrases about Italy's 'nervousness' and 'impressionability'.[48] It is also noticeable how diplomats and politicians started to cover themselves with statements that it was not Italy's military might which should be welcomed, but rather the 'moral effect' of winning over the last Great Power.[49] Despite much distrust of the hard-bargaining of Italians –people whom Asquith said wanted a pound and a half of flesh[50] – it took an unusually depressed or tough mind to believe that, after all, a nation of 35 million would not be of much use.[51]

For both alliance groupings, after August 1914, negotiation with Italy was thus a tricky business. For Germany, it was particularly difficult. Although he had declared Italian neutrality, San Giuliano had not denounced the Triple Alliance, maintaining instead that the nature of the war waged by Germany and Austria meant that Italy could not legally be called on to contribute as an ally. An ally who implied that his allies were aggressors was an unpromising one. In Austria, tradition and racial beliefs combined with these events to confirm the ancient prejudices that the Italians were 'brigands' to whom Austria should never have been allied in the first place. The singing of the Garibaldi hymn in the Volksgarten of Vienna, which had startled one Italian visitor in July, soon gave way to snarled threats that Italy's turn would come.[52]

Some German experts, notably the Centre Party deputy, Erzberger, and ex-Chancellor Bülow who had close personal ties to Italy, realised that this sort of emotion was no basis for a realistic policy. Italy had not made up her mind, and her intervention could be postponed by some carefully defined indemnification of her. If Trieste must remain Austrian for commercial and strategic reasons, could not some concessions be baited in the Trentino, Albania or Asia Minor?[53]

In December 1914, Bülow arrived in Rome as ambassador to try to promote these policies. He worked hard at his contacts with the academic and financial worlds, and tightened his bonds with politicians such as Giolitti. Bülow, a man who seldom resisted the opportunity to shine and who hoped to revive his career in German politics through brilliant success in Rome,[54] was not an ideal player of a weak hand, but whatever chance he had was rendered non-existent by the prolonged German failure to put serious pressure on Austria. Perhaps it was a matter of caste loyalty; perhaps it was a problem of the convoluted decision-making process of Imperial Germany which had not been made simpler by the first months of war administration. But, in 1915, the Germany which, by 1916–17, had turned Austria into little more than its puppet,[55] sacrificed the chance to preserve some credit in Italy to the Austrian alliance.

For the Triple Entente, dealings in Italy were easier, although not straightforward. Russia, at times rendered confident by the appearance of military success, and encouraged by war to augment her ambitions on Constantinople and even to plan a Slav outlet to the Adriatic, was critical of too easy a surrender to Italian whims in Asia Minor or Albania. Even Trieste might prove one day to be a Slav town.[56] When Russia was involved, negotiating with Italy provides many examples of another dictum about war diplomacy – it is conducted as much against one's allies as against one's enemies.

During the *intervento*, France displayed remarkable skill, sensibility and understatement in coping with Italy. It was another moment of success for the Italophile ambassador in Rome, Camille Barrère,[57] who, after a display of interfering nervousness in the July crisis, thereupon behaved with propriety and restraint. The French were solicitous of Italy's independence and welfare; they were excellent propagandists of their own suffering and that of 'poor little Begium'; they were generous and polite in handing over funds to pro-Entente Italian journalists.[58] Little was heard of those family squabbles between Italy and France or of France's traditional sense of superiority about its 'little Latin sister'. Perhaps the impulsion of the military situation was the real explanation, although it should also be stated that, from 1870 to 1918, there were many other moments at which French diplomacy showed itself the most professional and hard-headed in the world.

With the tenor of France's labours set in a low key, the tempo of Italian war entry was defined in London. It was not that Britain much endeavoured to force the pace. Instead Grey ably permitted Italy to take the initiative. His task was to listen, to be considerate, to be encouraging and to be accommodating. It was a policy which fitted readily into his oddly warm friendship with the talkative, emotional and superficially cultured Imperiali, the Neapolitan *marchese* who was Italy's ambassador in London. Perhaps Imperiali was Grey's idea of what an Italian was like.

The centrality of London in Italy's negotiations with the Entente had been established not by Grey, but by San Giuliano. In August–September 1914 San Giuliano converted with remarkable aplomb from peacetime diplomacy to that of war. In a series of exchanges, especially with the honest and gullible British ambassador, Sir James Rennell Rodd, he mapped out well sign-posted paths to intervention.[59] Most action should occur in London since there was less danger of press leaks or politicking in the British capital than there would be in Paris or in Rome. London was also the choice because, although San Giuliano did not state it, it was certain, unless there were drastic developments at the front or a complete Austrian backdown over the Trentino and Trieste, that, when Italy entered the war, it would be on the Entente side.

Choosing the moment of entry was the task at hand. Here San Giuliano at once separated the wood from the trees. Italy's war would be against Austria; the Entente's war was against Germany. The Central Powers' great strength was military, the Entente dominated with their navies. Therefore, San Giuliano mooted the idea gently to Imperiali and Rodd that the way 'to create the *casus belli*'[60] would be for an Anglo-French fleet to enter the Adriatic and to overwhelm the

Austrians. He did not state the obvious corollary. Such a defeat would inevitably mean an Austrian retirement from Pola and Trieste, which could then necessarily be garrisoned by the strongest army in the region, and that was the Italian. San Giuliano thus understood the crucial psychological necessity of having Italy and its allies fighting the same enemy. With his accustomed subtlety, he was preparing the way for an Italian victory, even if the war on the main Western or Eastern fronts ended in a compromise peace – to select audiences he went on stating magnificently that the best war for Italy was one which both Austria and France lost. Then Italy would be in occupation of Trieste, the Trentino, Istria and perhaps Albania. Who could want more?

San Giuliano hastened to resuscitate Italy's dormant friendship with Romania, that Latin outpost on the Black Sea which, like Italy, was an 'ally or enemy' of Austria. On 23 September an agreement was initialled in Bucharest, pledging co-operation between the two states. If the two could enter the war together, then they ought to be able to ask a higher price for what must prove a most effective military thrust.[61]

Nor did San Giuliano ignore Italian weakness. He listened with interest to British offers to sustain an Italian war effort through a large loan floated on easy terms by Rothschilds. How 'wholly delightful', he said gaily, to be Foreign Minister in wartime when Italy was treated with 'deference from every side'.[62]

There was also the nitty-gritty of the drafting of entry terms on which so much historiography has concentrated. In a series of notes, commencing on 11 August (one day before the Anglo-French declaration of war against Austria), Italy requested the Trentino and Trieste, Istria as far as the River Quarnaro, the Dalmatian islands, sovereignty over Valona, and an admission of commercial and perhaps territorial control over Adalia and Ethiopia. The Dodecanese islands might be handed back one day but .... . Meanwhile, San Giuliano surveyed the front, and saw little reason to believe that an end to the war was imminent. At the moment of his death on 16 October, Italy was committed to no certain policy. She would enter the war on the Entente side 'if and when the occasion arises', if and when her interests were met, if and when she was a certain winner.

But, with San Giuliano's death, Italian diplomacy fell into the inexpert hands of Salandra and Sonnino. There was a chance that Bertolini, a man who would have preserved Giolittian continuity, would become Foreign Minister.[63] Instead, by 5 November, Salandra's choice had fallen on Sonnino who, for the next five years, would solidify his major claims to be Italy's worst-ever Foreign Minister.

Sonnino kept negotiating going with the Triple Entente and, for a time also, in doubtful sincerity, with the Central Powers.[64] By February–March he was engaged in detailed exchanges with London.[65] Most historians agree that his terms were 'stiff',[66] although some patriotic Italian writers believe that he did not ask for enough. By 26 April, in spite of difficulties with the Russians who, in the flush of their military success, strove to defend Slav designs in the Adriatic, the Treaty of London was signed. Italy would denounce the Triple Alliance and soon enter the war. In return she would get the Trentino and Trieste, Istria, much of Dalmatia and its islands, Valona, recognition in the Dodecanese and dangerously vaguely worded compensation in Asia Minor and Africa.

Except perhaps in the last instance, Sonnino had got the detail right enough. But, in his dealings, he had lost sight of all the context painted in with such a fine hand by San Giuliano in the previous year. No mention was heard of an Anglo-French fleet in the Adriatic. Instead Sonnino appeared to regard the Anglo-French attack on the Dardanelles as its equivalent and certainly believed that an Entente naval victory and the end of the war were near.[67] While confusing what had to be done, Sonnino and Salandra recklessly endeavoured to make Italian policy truthful and honest. On 18 October, only two days after the death of San Giuliano and the very day on which De Martino was counselling his chiefs always to remember that Italy must be on the winning side, Salandra uttered the fatal phrase, 'sacro egoismo', in order to define his policy for Italy. In harness with this foolish rectitude, when Italy did enter the conflict, she declared war only on Austria, not daring formally to oppose Germany until August 1916, nor even Turkey until October 1915. Salandra and Sonnino self-righteously maintained, then and later,[68] that they were fighting Italy's war and not that of the Triple Entente. For a weak Great Power, whose relationship with her allies was bound to be difficult, this was the very worst psychological preparation for war diplomacy within an alliance. For Italy to seem to be loyal, willing and equal was more important than any reality.

Nor did Sonnino's errors cease there. He capriciously ignored Romania, despite a further pledge of co-operation in February 1915.

As a result, somewhat to the dismay of optimists in the Entente, Romania decided May 1915 was not the ideal moment for her intervention.[69] Believing that the war was about to end, Sonnino did not even bother to ascertain the detail of loan arrangements by which the Italian effort would be funded. Once Italy was in the war he discovered, to his surprise but to no-one else's, that financial terms were stiffer than he would have hoped.[70] With this catalogue of mistakes and simplicities, the error of loose negotiating about Adalia or Ethiopia was the least of his failings.

What was the reason for this catalogue of misjudgements, which would, in turn, contribute to Italy's many diplomatic troubles from 1915 to 1922? Much of the explanation is personal. Sonnino was inexperienced. Perhaps he knew something about state finance or the complexities of Sicilian land-tenure, but he knew little about international relations. He had not been Foreign Minister before; except in his youth, he had not been a diplomat. Compared with San Giuliano, or with other possible appointments in 1914–15, with Bertolini or Tittoni, Sonnino was an easily gulled novice. It is also generally true that Sonnino, like many of the other critics of the Giolittian system, had a far higher contemporary reputation than he deserved. To criticise is easier than to administer. Moreover, Sonnino's emphasis on 'morality', on 'being straight' while yet continuing to accept and sponsor the myth that Italy was a Great Power, a myth which simply could not be upheld by honesty or straightness, made him peculiarly ill-fitted to be Italian Foreign Minister in wartime. All Sonnino managed to demonstrate was that he (and Salandra) were not intelligent conservatives.

Beyond personalities, there was also another reason why Italian war entry was negotiated so incompetently. Foreign policy had become embroiled with domestic affairs. It was perhaps characteristic of conservatives of the type of Sonnino and Salandra that, for all their proclaimed morality, they trod into the dust one of the most sacred rules of Italian diplomacy – that it should strive for continuity and be above party, that, as Giolitti had put it in 1911: 'foreign policy must not influence in any way, directly or indirectly, internal policy'.[71] Instead, Salandra and Sonnino saw the move into war as the way to checkmate Giolitti. As Salandra had proclaimed, with almost endearing vanity, in August 1914: 'I only had the modest intentions of putting the State back on its feet [after it had been] weakened by ten years of ruinous policies; but now I must enter into history'.[72]

Giolitti himself did something to dig his own grave. Confident in San Giuliano's tenure of the Foreign Ministry, in August 1914 he rejected overtures from his friends in the majority which he had always preserved in Parliament, that he occasion a government crisis and return to office. His thesis was that the moment was not propitious since any change of Ministries would make public many politicians' ideological stances towards the war and therefore, by implication, might illustrate with perilous clarity that the only option for Italy was eventually to join the Entente. The Triple Alliance might be dead but Giolitti was sufficiently patriotic not to want to preside yet over its funeral ceremony.

After San Giuliano died and Sonnino replaced him, Giolitti soon commenced soundings about a possible comeback. When Parliament briefly assembled in early December, he made sensational, and oddly inaccurate, revelations about an incident during the Balkan war known as 'the Austro-Serb war scare'.[73] He thus embarrassed Salandra with the evidence that San Giuliano had not bothered to inform his new Prime Minister about such a serious event. Perhaps Giolitti thought that a mere reminder of his own seniority in foreign affairs would be enough to make Salandra see his patriotic responsibilities, pack up and go home to Apulia. Perhaps he still feared the publicity within Italy and abroad which must occur with the substitution of one Ministry for another. Perhaps he was simply growing old, as his uncharacteristic inaccuracy appeared to imply, and his coolness and sense of logic was evaporating. Whatever the reason, he did not press his advantage in December, nor in February when *La Tribuna* published his advice that *parecchio* ('quite a lot') could be gained from a present deal with Austria, without immediate involvement in the war.[74]

Giolitti's unaccustomed fumbling only encouraged Salandra and Sonnino in their belief that war had converted them into men of destiny. Despite such natural and economic disasters as the Marsica earthquake in January 1915, major flooding in the Tiber valley in February, and the continued severe effects of the 1914 harvest failure, many political currents were running in the interventionists' favour. Educated urban opinion saw, with the melting of the winter snows on the Dolomites and the Julian Alps, the chance to complete the Risorgimento. The foundation of the Banca di Sconto was only one signal of a general drift in Parliament and in the press towards what Salandra loved to call his 'national policy'. Even F. S. Nitti, with his accountant's love for the accurate and unemotional, began to sympathise with Salandra when it became obvious that the war was not over by Christmas.[75] The *parecchio* letter and its mishandling had provided the opportunity for Giolitti to be cast as an outright neutralist, someone who, like the maximalist wing of the socialists, could be alleged to oppose war at any cost.

The showdown came in May 1915 in the so-called 'Radiant May' days. It was a springtime of *bellezza* neither for Giolitti, nor for Salandra and Sonnino. The latter two confronted the dilemma that they still lacked a parliamentary majority, that their recently commissioned prefects' reports only revealed a country opposed to war at the moment,[76] and that their very conservatism made them unhappy about allying too closely with interventionist demonstrators who were noisily filling the *piazze* of Italian cities. Conservatives shivered in apprehension and refused to admit that they tingled with hope when, on 5 May, D'Annunzio shouldered the mantle of Garibaldi. At Quarto near Genoa, in a speech which deliciously parodied the Sermon on the Mount,[77] D'Annunzio swung poetic Italy behind the Treaty of London.

Coinciding with the revelation that Salandra could count on such disgraceful friends, the military situation turned sour. The long prophesied decisive breakthrough at the Dardanelles, where landings had begun on 25 April, did not eventuate. Worse, in Galicia, Austrian forces repelled a Russian attack and started an advance of their own. Italy was pledged to join a losing, not a winning side.

In Rome, Bülow and Erzberger frenziedly pointed this out, and made wide-ranging, but not very concrete, promises about revision to the Austro-Italian frontier. In reply, the Entente increased their generosity to the pro-interventionist cause; in Rome, the wife of the British ambassador poured rose petals from the embassy balcony over pro-war demonstrators.[78]

At the centre of power, there was a vacuum. On 13 May, the Salandra government, faced with its hopeless minority in the Chamber, resigned. But Giolitti, too, hesitated. Not unjustifiably, he feared that the signature of the Treaty of London had irrevocably committed Italian honour and its monarchical institutions. Moreover, he was no knight-errant for the Triple Alliance; if Italy now forsook the Treaty of London, would not all bridges to the Triple Entente be burned? In that case, there would be less reason than ever to put faith in Austrian generosity or German forgiveness. *Parecchio* for the moment would turn into *niente* for ever.

While he vacillated, the demonstrations, especially in Rome, increased in number and violence. D'Annunzio, Mussolini, the syndicalists, the futurists, rhetoricians young and old, revolutionists all, had a field day. The time of old men, of gravity, of seriousness was passing, and the orgy of celebration could be accredited to patriotism. In honourable silence, but also taking the easy way out, Giolitti withdrew from the contest and retired to Piedmont. On 20 May, the Salandra government was reconfirmed: on 22 May Italy mobilised; on 24 May she was at war. G. M. Trevelyan in Cambridge found the most fatuous phrases to celebrate this 'victory': 'Italy's *soul* has conquered her baser part, represented by the political "boss" Giolitti. Mazzini has triumphed over Machiavelli'.[79]

In fact Italy had entered a war with a divided elite and a divided society, at a time when her allies were losing, with an underprepared Army, economy and administration. Objectively speaking, for Italy the Great Power it was a worse moment to choose to join a war than was June 1940. Although at tremendous cost to herself, Italy's war effort would be comparatively modest and, with the defeat at Caporetto, would confirm foreign sneers about her incompetence and make certain that when, as at Versailles or during the Ethiopian war, victims for the altar of 'international morality' were being demanded, then Italy would be the ideal scapegoat. But then, given Mazzini's own twin record of political failure and magniloquence, perhaps Trevelyan did not select such a bad metaphor after all.

In many ways, Italy's deliberate choice for war in 'Radiant May' seems a perfect example of the supremacy of internal concerns in foreign policy decision-making. Pressure of a right-wing revolution from the *piazza*, and the dull determination of Sonnino and Salandra to oust Giolitti and *giolittismo*, combined to decide Italian entry despite the unpropitious international situation. Yet such an analysis is too short-term, and must again be set in the context of all the diplomacy of Liberal Italy.

In his novel, *Malombra*, Antonio Fogazzaro depicts a character who

had a fine contempt for everything French except the wines of Bordeaux and Burgundy. A republican of the old school, he used to say that the French make love to noble ideas, and ruin them and cast them on one side. He detested them as inventors of the formula, *Liberté, egalité, fraternité,* where the second phrase, he would say, lay in wait behind the first to stab it in the dark.[80]

In his vignette, the novelist has underlined the predicament of nineteenth-century liberalism: liberty, yes; democracy, the triumph of the masses, no.

By the middle of the nineteenth century, it was becoming evident to a liberal such as Cavour or to a conservative such as Bismarck that the means by which *liberté* and *egalité* could be kept apart was *fraternité* – nationalism. According to the research of Fritz Fischer, nationalism, imperialism, and an expansionist foreign policy were then utilised, at least in Germany, by the old ruling class and its new allies in order to divert socialism and democracy. For all the lip-service paid to the superior interests of the state, or to the continuity of foreign policy and its high seriousness above party, thus it has been maintained that diplomacy was conditioned and decided by domestic affairs.

What may be true for Imperial Germany, is not true of Liberal Italy. The making of Italian foreign policy lay in the appropriate hands of Prime Minister or Foreign Minister and was not controlled in any direct sense either by a 'military-industrial' complex or by the aggressive rhetoric of the Nationalist Association. Instead, politicians plotted diplomatic advantage, while regretting that Big Business was so underdeveloped and timid, and while complaining that nationalist opinion was so wayward in its analysis of the international situation and of such limited impact at home. Italian foreign policy was conditioned by fear, by some comprehension of the menace of general war: for Turkey or for Greece, Italian statesmen, in cavalier fashion, could predict or foment war; but, with a certain naivety, a certain optimism and a certain conscious self-delusion, 'Italians, born in the twenty year period from 1870 to 1890, did not believe in the possibility of war' between the Great Powers.[81] The 'coming struggle of the nations', the just and necessary 'completing the Risorgimento', were events for which Italy must prepare, but they were also, thankfully, events which lay in a future of unspecified date. No Liberal Italian politician ever sought to embroil the Great Powers in war.

On the other hand, there is much evidence for a greater continuity in the foreign policy of Liberal (and Fascist) Italy than has sometimes been assumed. Periods of restraint and periods of expansion occurred more because of opportunity and the nature of the relationship between the Greater Powers than because of ideology or personality. Continuity was thus accompanied by consensus.

By 1910 ruling-class opinion believed that the new Italy, whose economy was improving and whose political system was functioning with a certain predictability, should adopt a more pushing foreign policy which better fitted a state looking out on to a sea which ought to be known as the 'mare nostrum'. That foreign policy had become of immediate importance again owed something to the enveloping domestic challenge to the Giolittian system. It owed something more to the series of international crises, Algeciras, Bosnia–Herzegovina, Agadir and then the Balkans wars. Agadir apart, the major influence of these crises was not specific but general. After the stimulating experience of the Libyan war, it was plain that the balance of power was so delicate that it allowed Italy major opportunity. The profundity of belief in the 'primacy of external politics' made it unlikely that any Italian leadership would long resist temptation. For, should Italy's policy be too ethical or restrained, then the myth of Italian greatness might be exposed. If it was clear that Italy was not a Great Power, then it might also become evident that Italy was not a united nation, and that 'liberty' had regressed almost as much as it had progressed since the Risorgimento.

In turn, foreign policy decisions, the invasion of Libya and the muddled entry into the First Word War, wrought drastic damage to the always fragile social and economic base of the Liberal system. Diplomatic historians are sometimes written off by our trendier brethren as simpletons or boors who fail to see that all answers lie in society. But, within the complex structures of world capitalism, for Italy, from 1860 to 1945, social crisis came from war, and war from foreign policy. Italy had to endure Fascism very much because the ruling class victorious in the Risorgimento could not conceal or amend their proclamation, and the proclamation of foreigners, that Italy was a Great Power.

Antonio Gramsci, in that same newspaper article in October 1914 when he flirted with Mussolinian inverventionism, remarked on 'the scant interest the broad mass of the people has always manifested in political struggle, and which can therefore be all the more easily won over by someone who knows how to display energy and a clear vision of where they are going'.[82] Gramsci's words can be read as an ironical prediction of Fascism. But there is a deeper irony as well. Despite Fascism and its 'years of consensus', Italy, of all the major European states, was the one in which, until 1945, the 'nationalisation of the masses' proceeded least quickly. That it was so tardy owed much to the social, economic and political nature of underdevelopment. But it also owed much to foreign affairs.

Italy was the state which sought imperial advantage, for 'political' motives, at Massawa, Mogadiscio, Tripoli, Smyrna or Valona and then explained away the dim economic prospects there with rhetoric about wealth making a nation soft. Italy endeavoured to restore a Roman Empire in the Mediterranean, but ignored the fact that her emigrants were building a potential cultural and economic empire in North and South America. A foreign policy which, at its best moments, directed itself only at national defence or the regaining of Trento and Trieste, drifted into a miasma of shoddy imitation or an impossible quest for real prestige. All Italians from 1860 to 1945 had their lives severely affected by the myth that Italy was a Great Power and therefore must needs behave as did the other, Greater, Powers.

Bibliography

The list below contains only the most basic English languages sources. For a much fuller bibliography see my *Italy, the Least of the Great Powers* (Cambridge, 1979) pp. 431–51.

SECONDARY SOURCES

L. ALBERTINI, *The Origins of the War of 1914*, 3 vols (London, 1952–7)

G. ARE, 'Economic Liberalism in Italy: 1845–1915', *Journal of Italian History*, I (1978)

W. C. ASKEW, *Europe and Italy's Acquisition of Libya, 1911–12* (Durham, N. C., 1942)

——, 'The Austro-Italian antagonism, 1896–1914', in L. P. Wallace and W. C. Askew (eds), *Power, Public Opinion and Diplomacy* (Durham, N. C., 1959)

R. J. B. BOSWORTH, *Italy, the Least of the Great Powers: Italian Foreign Policy Before the First World War* (Cambridge, 1979)

B. BOYD CAIROLI, *Italian Repatriation from the United States 1900–1914* (New York, 1973)

L. CAFAGNA, 'The Industrial Revolution in Italy, 1830–1914', in C. M. Cipolla (ed.), *The Fontana Economic History of Europe* (London, 1971)

R. ALBRECHT-CARRIÉ, 'Italian Colonial Policy, 1914–1918', *Journal of Modern History*, 18 (1946)

V. CASTRONOVO, 'The Italian Take-off: a ciritical re-examination of the problem', *Journal of Italian History*, 1 (1978)

S. B. CLOUGH, *The Economic History of Modern Italy* (New York, 1964)

F. J. COPPA, 'Giolitti and the Gentiloni Pact between Myth and Reality', *Catholic Historical Review*, LIII (1967)

——, 'The Italian Tariff and the Conflict between Agriculture and Industry: the commercial policy of Liberal Italy, 1860–1922', *Journal of Economic History*, XXX (1970)

——, Economic and Ethical Liberalism in Conflict: the

extraordinary liberalism of Giovanni Giolitti', *Journal of Modern History*, 42 (1970)

——, *Planning, Protectionism and Politics in Liberal Italy: Economics and Politics in the Giolittian Age* (Washington, 1971)

B. CROCE, *A History of Italy 1871–1915* (Oxford, 1929)

R. S. CUNSOLO, 'Libya, Italian Nationalism and the Revolt against Giolitti', *Journal of Modern History*, 37 (1965)

J. A. DAVIS, (ed.) *Gramsci and Italy's Passive Revolution* (London, 1979)

A. J. DE GRAND, 'The Italian Nationalist Association in the Period of Italian Neutrality August 1914–May 1915', *Journal of Modern History*, 43 (1971)

——, *The Italian Nationalist Association and the Rise of Fascism in Italy* (Lincoln, 1978)

R. DRAKE, *Byzantium for Rome: the politics of nostalgia in Umbertian Italy, 1878–1900* (Chapel Hill, 1980)

R. F. FOERSTER, *The Italian Emigration of Our Times* (Cambridge, Mass., 1919)

A. GERSCHENKRON, *Economic Backwardness in Historical Perspective* (Cambridge, Mass., 1962)

G. GIOLITTI, *Memoirs of My Life* (London, 1923)

J. L. GLANVILLE, *Italy's Relations with England, 1896–1905* (Baltimore, 1934)

W. W. GOTTLIEB, *Studies in Secret Diplomacy during the First World War* (London, 1957)

P. G. HALPERN, *The Mediterranean Naval Situation, 1908–1914* (Cambridge, Mass., 1971)

——, 'The Anglo-French-Italian Naval Convention of 1915', *Historical Journal*, XIII (1970)

R. L. HESS, 'Italy and Africa: Colonial Ambitions in the First World War', *Journal of African History*, IV (1963)

——, *Italian Colonialism in Somalia* (Chicago, 1966)

D. L. HOROWITZ, *The Italian Labor Movement* (Cambridge, Mass., 1963)

R. HOSTETTER, *The Italian Socialist Movement*, vol. I (Princeton, 1958)

——, 'The "Evangelical" Socialism of Camillo Prampolini', *Italian Quarterly*, XVIII (1975)

C. HOWARD, 'The Treaty of London, 1915', *History*, XXV (1941)

H. S. HUGHES, 'The Aftermath of the Risorgimento in Four Successive Interpretations', *American Historical Review*, LXI (1955)

——, *The United States and Italy*, rev. ed. (Cambridge, Mass., 1965)

A. C. JEMOLO, *Church and State in Italy, 1850–1950* (Oxford, 1960)

J. JOLL, 'Marinetti', in *Three Intellectuals in Politics* (London, 1960)
———, *Gramsci* (Glasgow, 1977)

C. J. LOWE, 'Britain and Italian Intervention, 1914–1915', *Historical Journal*, XII (1969)

C. J. LOWE AND F. MARZARI, *Italian Foreign Policy, 1870–1940* (London, 1975)

A. LYTTELTON (ed.), *Italian Fascisms from Pareto to Gentile* (London, 1973)

D. MACK SMITH, *Italy a Modern History*, rev. ed. (Ann Arbor, 1969)

F. MARINETTI, *Selected writings*, ed. R. W. Flint (London 1972)

D. McLEAN, 'British Finance and Foreign Policy in Turkey: the Smyrna-Aidin Railway Settlement, 1913–14', *Historical Journal*, XIX (1976)

M. B. PETROVICH, 'The Italo-Yugoslav Boundary Question, 1914–15', in A. Dallin *et al.* (eds.), *Russian Diplomacy and Eastern Europe 1914–1917* (New York, 1963)

G. PROCACCI, 'The Italian Workers' Movement in the Liberal Era', in R. J. B. Bosworth and G. Cresciani (eds.), *Altro Polo: a Volume of Italian Studies* (Sydney, 1979)

R. PRYCE, 'Italy and the Outbreak of the First World War', *Cambridge Historical Journal*, XI (1954)

W. A. RENZI, 'Italy's Neutrality and Entrance into the Great War: a re-examination', *American Historical Review*, LXXIII (1967–8)
———, 'The Entente and the Vatican During the Period of Italian Neutrality, August 1914–May 1915', *Historical Journal*, XIII (1970)

A. J. RHODES, *The Poet as Superman: a life of Gabriele D'Annunzio* (London, 1959)

D. D. ROBERTS, *The Syndicalist Tradition and Italian Fascism* (Manchester, 1979)

A. SALANDRA, *Italy and the Great War* (London, 1932)

A. W. SALOMONE, *Italy in the Giolittian Era: Italian Democracy in the Making, 1900–14* (Philadelphia, 1960)
——— (ed.), *Italy from the Risorgimento to Fascism* (Garden City, 1970)

B. SCHMITT, 'The Italian Documents for July 1914', *Journal of Modern History*, 37 (1965)

T. R. SYKES, 'Revolutionary Syndicalism in the Italian Labor Movement: the agrarian strikes of 1907–8 in the province of Parma', *International Review of Social History*, XXI (1976)

F. M. TAMAGNA, *Italy's Interests and Policies in the Far East* (New York, 1941)

A. TAMBORRA, 'The Rise of Italian Industry and the Balkans (1900–1914)', *Journal of European Economic History*, 3 (1974)

J. A. THAYER, *Italy and the Great War, Politics and Culture, 1870–1915* (Madison, 1964)

L. A. TILLEY, 'I fatti di maggio: the working class of Milan and the rebellion of 1898', in R. J. Bezucha (ed.), *Modern European Social History* (Lexington, 1972)

G. E. TORREY, 'The Rumanian-Italian Agreement of 23 September 1914', *Slavonic and East European Review*, XLIV (1966)

L. VALIANI, 'Italian-Austro-Hungarian Negotiations, 1914–15', *Journal of Contemporary History*, 1 (1966)

B. VIGEZZI, 'Italian Socialism and the First World War: Mussolini, Lazzari and Turati', *Journal of Italian History*, 2 (1979)

C. WAGSTAFF, 'Dead Men Erect: F. T. Marinetti, *L'alcova d'acciaio*', in H. Klein (ed.), *The First World War in Fiction: a Collection of Essays* (London, 1976)

C. SETON-WATSON, *Italy from Liberalism to Fascism* (London, 1967)

R. A. WEBSTER, *Industrial Imperialism in Italy 1908–1915* (Berkeley, 1975)

J. WHITTAM, *The Politics of the Italian Army* (London, 1977)

——, 'War and Italian Society', in B. Bond and I. Roy (eds), *War and Society* (London, 1975)

——, 'War Aims and Strategy: the Italian Government and High Command 1914–1919', in B. Hunt and A. Preston (eds), *War Aims and Strategic Policy in the Great War 1914–18* (London, 1977)

W. HILTON-YOUNG, *The Italian Left* (London, 1949)

Notes and References

ABBREVIATIONS

AG	Archivio di gabinetto, 1910–14
AP	Asquith papers
AR	Archivio riservato di gabinetto, 1906–10.
BD	*British Documents* (ed. Gooch and Temperley)
BP	Bertie papers
CD	*Atti parlamentari, Camera dei deputati*
CG	Carte Giolitti
CHJ	*Cambridge Historical Journal*
CHR	*Catholic Historical Review*
CM	Carte Martini
CP	Confidential Print
CS	Carte Salandra
DDF	*Documents diplomatiques françaises*
DDI	*Documenti diplomatici italiani*
DGP	*Die Grosse Politik*
ESR	*European Studies Review*
GP	Grey papers
HJ	*Historical Journal*
HP	Hardinge papers
HT	*History Today*
IQ	*Italian Quarterly*
JAH	*Journal of African History*
JCEA	*Journal of Central European Affairs*
JCH	*Journal of Contemporary History*
JEH	*Journal of Economic History*
JIH	*Journal of Italian History*
LP	Lansdowne papers
NA	*Nuova Antologia*
NP	Nicolson papers
NRS	*Nuova Rivista Storica*
P	Archivio politica, Ministero degli affari esteri
PCG	Presidenza del consiglio, gabinetto, atti
RC	*Rivista Coloniale*
RHMC	*Revue d'histoire moderne et contemporaine*
RP	Rodd papers
RSPI	*Rivista di studi politici internazionali*
RSR	*Rassegna Storica del Risorgimento*
RSS	*Rivista Storica del Socialismo*
SC	*Storia Contemporanea*

SEER   *Slavonic and East European Review*
SP   Sonnino papers
SS   *Studi Storici*

PREFACE

1. M. Loh (ed.), *With courage in their cases : the experience of thirty-five Italian immigrant workers and their families in Australia* (Melbourne, 1980) p.80
2. W. D. Borrie, *Immigration : Australia's problems and prospects* (Sydney, 1949) p.88
3. A. Aquarone, in *SC*, II (1980) and R. Romeo in *Il Giornale Nuovo* (13 November 1980).

1. LIBERAL ITALY: MYTHS AND REALITY

1. G. Sabbatucci, 'Il problema dell'irredentismo e le origini del movimento nazionalista in Italia', *SC*, 1 (1970) 486.
2. The other volumes were *Garibaldi's Defence of the Roman Republic* (1907), *Garibaldi and the Thousand* (1909). All were published by Longmans. The third volume in fact came out in October 1911 just as British public opinion was at its most excited about the Libyan War.
3. G. M. Trevelyan, *Garibaldi's Defence of the Roman Republic*, p.11.
4. Ibid., p.x.
5. Ibid., p.16.
6. T. Mann, *Death in Venice* (London, 1932).
7. J. Thies, 'Hitler's European Building Programme', *JCH*, 13 (1978) 420.
8. J. Tilley, *London to Tokyo* (London, n.d.) p.32.
9. B. von Bülow, *Memoirs* (London, 1930–2), vol. 3, p.455.
10. E. Hutton, *The Cities of Umbria* (London, 1905) p.115.
11. For example, see N. Douglas, *Old Calabria* (London, 1915).
12. Quoted in R. Cooper, 'The Image of Italy in English Writing 1815–1915' (unpublished M.A., University of Sydney, 1967) p.57.
13. J. W. Goethe, *Italian Journey (1786–1788)* (Harmondsworth, 1962) pp.42, 129.
14. H. Wickham Steed, *Through Thirty Years 1892–1922* (London, 1924) vol. 1, pp.103–4.
15. Trevelyan, *Garibaldi and the Thousand*, p.41; *Scenes from Italy's War* (London, 1919) p.12. Free with his historical analogies, Trevelyan also (p.14) thought Giolitti's contest with Salandra was rather like that of the Duke of Newcastle against the elder Pitt.
16. F. Fischer, *War of Illusions* (London, 1975) pp.447–8.
17. M. Weber, *The Protestant Ethic and the Spirit of Capitalism* (London, 1930) pp.56–7; cf. pp.77–9.
18. R. Soucy, *Fascism in France: the case of Maurice Barrès* (Berkeley, 1972) p.48.
19. H. Belloc, 'The Three Races', in *Ladies and Gentlemen* (London, 1940).
20. J. Joll, *The Second International* (New York, 1956) p.18.
21. A. J. P. Taylor, *Bismarck, the Man and Statesman* (London, 1965) p.166.
22. J. L. Glanville, *Italy's Relations with England, 1896–1905* (Baltimore, 1934) p.31.
23. A. T. Mahan, *The Influence of Sea Power upon History, 1660–1783* (London, n.d.) p.32.
24. Quoted by C. Seton-Watson, *Italy from Liberalism to Fascism* (London, 1967)

p.327. Seton-Watson notes two other instances in the same period of Bülow using similar metaphors.

25.   BP, FO 800/173, 15 Apr 1905, Bertie to Mallet.
26.   *CD*, XXIII, xiii, p.15357, debate of 7 June 1911.
27.   RP, 8 Sept 1902, Rodd to Cromer.
28.   *The Times*, 21 June 1924.
29.   cf. also the too ready generalisations of E. C. Banfield, *The Moral Basis of a Backward Society* (New York, 1958).
30.   G. Puccini, *Letters* (New York, 1973) p.67.
31.   A. Gramsci, *Letters from Prison* (New York, 1975) p.127.
32.   Sergio Panunzio, cited by D. D. Roberts, *The Syndicalist Tradition and Italian Fascism* (Manchester, 1979) p.81.
33.   O. Bonutto, *A Migrant's Story* (Brisbane, 1963) pp.127–8.
34.   M. A. Jones, *Destination America* (Glasgow, 1976) p.124.
35.   G. Mosca, *The Ruling Class* (New York, 1939) p.11; cf, B. Caizzi, *Nuova antologia della questione meridionale* (Milan, 1962) pp.337–48.
36.   B. Stringher, 'Gli scambi con l'estero e la politica commerciale italiana', in P. Blaserna (ed.), *Cinquanta anni di storia italiana* (Milan, 1911) vol. 3, pp.121–5.
37.   R. Bagot, *My Italian Year* (London, 1911) p.2.
38.   T. De Mauro, *Storia linguistica dell'Italia unita* (Bari, 1963).
39.   S. Brugger, *Australians and Egypt 1914–1919* (Melbourne, 1980) p.36.
40.   D. Mack Smith (ed.), *The Making of Italy, 1796–1870* (New York, 1968) p.2.
41.   Earl of Oxford and Asquith, *Memories and Reflections, 1852–1927* (London, 1928) vol. 2, p.120.
42.   Trevelyan, *Scenes from Italy's War*, p.59.
43.   E. Scarfoglio, *Il popolo dai cinque pasti (brindisi a Mr. Asquith)* (Rome, 1923): pp.60–1 compares British law to that of Genghis Khan.
44.   For example, see F. T. Marinetti, 'The Futurist Manifesto', in A. Lyttelton (ed.), *Italian Fascisms from Pareto to Gentile* (London, 1973) pp.212–14.
45.   For example, see E. Corradini, *Discorsi politici (1902–1925)* (Florence, 1925); *Il nazionalismo italiano* (Milan, 1914); or in Lyttelton, *Italian Fascisms*, pp.135–64.
46.   A. Di San Giuliano, 'L'emigrazione negli Stati Uniti d'America', *NA*, f.805, 1 July 1905; and, more generally, F. Manzotti, *La polemica sull' emigrazione nell' Italia unita* (Milan, 1962).
47.   The classic study in any language has long been R. F. Foerster, *The Italian Emigration of our Times* (Cambridge, Mass., 1919) but now see E. Sori, *L'emigrazione italiana dall' Unità alla seconda guerra mondiale* (Bologna, 1979).
48.   C. Cartiglia, *Rinaldo Rigola e il sindacalismo riformista in Italia* (Milan, 1976) pp.19–24.
49.   M. Abrate, *Ricerche per la storia dell' organizzazione sindacale dell' industria in Italia* (Turin, 1966) p.20.
50.   G. Baglioni, *L'ideologia della borghesia industriale nell' Italia liberale* (Turin, 1974) p.377.
51.   R. C. Fried, *Planning the Eternal City* (New Haven, 1973) p.18.
52.   For an evocation of the atmosphere of Naples see the novel by M. Serao, *The Land of Cockayne*, 2 vols (New York, n.d.).
53.   Fulco di Verdura, *These Happy Summer Days* (London, 1976) p.113.
54.   The standard study of Rome in this period is A. Caracciolo, *Roma capitale* (Rome, 1956).
55.   P. Corti (ed.), *Inchiesta Zanardelli sulla Basilicata* (Turin, 1976) p.xv.
56.   J. Davis, *Land and Family in Pisticci* (London, 1973) p.21.
57.   A. L. Maraspini, *The Study of an Italian Village* (Paris, 1968) pp.12–13.
58.   E. Martinengo Cesaresco, *Cavour* (London, 1898) p.v.

59.   L. Franchetti and S. Sonnino, *Inchiesta in Sicilia* (Florence, 1974) vol. 1, p.41.

60.   G. Candeloro, *Storia dell'Italia moderna*, vol. 7 *la crisi di fine secolo e l'età giolittiana* (Milan, 1974) p.132.

61.   For example, see A. Blok, *The Mafia of a Sicilian Village, 1860–1960* (Oxford, 1974).

62.   N. Malatino (ed.), *1908–1958 cinquant'anni dal terremoto* (Messina, 1958) p.13.

63.   For an account, see R. J. B. Bosworth, 'The Messina Earthquake of 28 December 1908', *ESR*, II (1981) 193.

64.   E. Hobsbawm, *Bandits* (Harmondsworth, 1972).

65.   G. Cingari, *Brigantaggio, proprietari e contadini nel sud (1799–1900)* (Reggio Calabria, 1976) p.209.

66.   Ibid., pp.242–4.

67.   Ibid., pp.237, 246.

68.   P. D'Angiolini, 'L'Italia al termine della crisi agraria della fine del secolo XIX', *NRS*, LIII (1969) 345.

69.   R. Bachi, *L'Italia economica nell'anno 1913* (Città di Castello, 1914).

70.   A. Riosa, *Il sindacalismo rivoluzionario in Italia* (Bari, 1976), p.17.

71.   P. Corner, *Fascism in Ferrara* (London, 1975) pp.16–17; cf. R. Zangheri (ed.), *Lotte agrarie in Italia. La Federazione nazionale dei lavoratori della terra 1901–1926* (Milan, 1960); *Agricoltura e contadini nella storia d'Italia* (Turin, 1977).

72.   Corner, *Fascism in Ferrara*, p.10.

73.   L. Preti, *Le lotte agrarie nella valle padana* (Turin, 1955) pp.218–23.

74.   V. Castronovo, *Economia e società in Piemonte dall'Unità al 1914* (Milan, 1969) pp.106–10.

75.   For a devastating critique, see F. M. Snowden; 'From Sharecropper to Proletarian: the background to Fascism in rural Tuscany', in J. A. Davis (ed.), *Gramsci and Italy's Passive Revolution* (London, 1979).

76.   F. De Felice, *L'agricoltura in terra di Bari dal 1880 al 1914* (Milan, 1971) pp.11–12, 93–6, 109, 122–4.

77.   For example, see Davis, *Land and Family in Pisticci*, pp.74–86.

78.   F. J. Coppa, 'The Italian Tariff and the Conflict between Agriculture and Industry: the commercial policy of Liberal Italy, 1860–1922', *JEH*, XXX (1970) 755–63.

79.   Corti, *Inchiesta Zanardelli*, pp. xxxii–xxxiii.

80.   Franchetti and Sonnino, *Inchiesta in Sicilia*, pp.xii–xiv.

81.   Corti, *Inchiesta Zanardelli*, p.xvi.

82.   Corner, *Fascism in Ferrara*. p.5.

83.   For a review see J. M. Cammett, 'Two Recent Polemics on the Character of the Italian Risorgimento', *Science and Society*, XXVII (1963) 433–57.

84.   R. Romeo, *Risorgimento e capitalismo* (Bari, 1959).

85.   A. Gerschenkron, 'Notes on the Rate of Industrial Growth in Italy, 1881–1913, *JEH*, XV (1955); *Economic Backwardness in Historical Perspective* (Cambridge, Mass., 1962). For an able summary of the current state of the debate, see V. Castronovo, 'The Italian take-off: a critical re-examination of the problem, *JIH*, 1 (1978) 492–510.

86.   L. Cafagna, *The Industrial Revolution in Italy 1830–1914* (Glasgow, 1971) p.48.

87.   R. A. Webster, *Industrial Imperialism in Italy 1908–1915* (Berkeley, 1975).

88.   G. A. Williams, *Proletarian Order: Antonio Gramsci, factory councils and the origins of Italian communism, 1911–1921* (London, 1975) p.14.

89.   V. Castronovo, *Giovanni Agnelli* (Turin, 1977) p.36; M. Sedgwick, *Fiat* (New York, 1974) p.89.

90.   Castronovo, pp.46–7; Abrate, *Ricerche per la storia . . .* , p.110.

91.   Cafagna, *The Industrial Revolution in Italy*, p.28.

92.   Castronovo, *Economia e società in Piemonte*, pp.188–98. The municipality had set up its own hydro-electric station.

93.   A. Papa, *Classe politica e intervento pubblico nell'età giolittiana: la nazionalizzazione delle ferrovie* (Naples, 1973).

94.   For example, see A. Caroleo, *Le banche cattoliche dalla prima guerra mondiale al fascismo* (Milan, 1976).

95.   B. Vigezzi, 'La "classe dirigente" italiana e la prima guerra mondiale', in A. Caracciolo, *Il trauma dell' intervento: 1914–19* (Florence, 1968) p.77.

96.   R. A. Webster, *L'imperialismo industriale italiano, 1908–1915* (Turin, 1974) especially pp.116–241; P. Milza, 'Les rapports economiques franco-italiens en 1914–1915 et leurs incidents politiques', *RHMC*, XIV (1967) 33–8.

97.   Castronovo, *Giovanni Agnelli*, pp.27–32; M. Abrate, *La lotta sindacale nella industrializzazione in Italia, 1906–1926* (Turin, 1967) p.27.

98.   R. Bachi, *L'Italia economica nell'anno 1914* (Città di Castello, 1915).

99.   G. Mori, 'Le guerre parallele. L'industria elettrica in Italia nel periodo della grande guerra (1914–1919), *SS*, XIV (1973) 294.

100.   M. Kent, *Oil and Empire* (London, 1976) pp.202–3.

101.   D. Mack Smith, *Mussolini's Roman Empire* (London, 1970) p.122.

102.   Seton-Watson, *Italy from Liberalism to Fascism*, p.286.

103.   Webster, *Industrial Imperialism in Italy*, pp.49–50.

104.   N. Tranfaglia (ed.), *L'Italia unita nella storiografia del secondo dopoguerra* (Milan, 1980) p.80.

105.   A. A. Kelikian, 'From Liberalism to Corporatism: the province of Brescia during the First World War', in Davis, *Gramsci and Italy's Passive Revolution* p.215.

106.   For very favourable reviews of his career see L. Solari, *Marconi nell'intimità e nel lavoro* (Milan, 1940); and very briefly K. Geddes, *Guglielmo Marconi: 1874–1937* (London, 1974).

107.   Mori, 'Le guerre parallele', pp.303–4.

108.   See, in general review, D. Bertoni Jovine, *La scuola italiana dal 1870 ai nostri giorni* (Cassino, 1958).

109.   G. Barone and A. Petrucci, *Primo: non leggere: biblioteche e pubblica lettura in Italia dal 1861 ai nostri giorni* (Milan, 1976) pp.46, 59, 68.

110.   Corti, *Inchiesta Zanardelli*, p.xlvii.

111.   Franchetti and Sonnino, for example, told of armed guards meeting trains at stations and escorting passengers and property in to Sicilian agro-towns. Franchetti and Sonnino, *Inchiesta in Sicilia*, p.21.

112.   Davis, *Land and Family in Pisticci*, p.21.

113.   Webster, *L'imperialismo industriale italiano*, pp.258–9.

114.   For example, see F. J. Coppa, *Planning, Protectionism and Politics in Liberal Italy* (Washington, 1971) pp.201–2.

115.   Abrate, *Ricerche per la storia* . . . , pp.150–1.

116.   See generally Abrate, *La lotta sindacale*   . . .

117.   Castronovo, *Giovanni Agnelli*, p.51.

118.   Baglioni, *L'ideologia della borghesia industriale*, pp.232–97.

119.   For the continued tradition see M. V. Posner and S. J. Woolf, *Italian Public Enterprise* (London, 1967).

120.   For a detailed study see F. Bonelli, *Lo sviluppo di una grande impresa in Italia: la Terni dal 1884 al 1962* (Turin, 1975).

121.   P, 675/844, 5 Nov 1913, San Giuliano to Joel.

122.   eg. see AG, 2/14, 16 Oct 1910, San Giuliano to diplomatic and consular representatives; 4/30 bis, 11 May 1911, Tedesco to Giolitti.

123.   M. Mureddu, *Il Quirinale del Re* (Milan, 1977) pp.17, 56 says that Victor

Emmanuel was sometimes at his numismatic work by 7.30 a.m. His coin-collection had 22,000 pieces by 1900 and over 100,000 by 1943. His *Corpus Numorum Italicorum* began to be published by 1910. The twentieth volume had appeared by 1943.

124. V. J. Bordeux, *Margherita of Savoy* (London, 1929) p.238.

125. Mureddu, *Il Quirinale del Re*, pp.66–7.

126. AG, 22/184, 15 Sept 1911, San Giuliano to Victor Emmanuel III.

127. S. Scaroni, *Con Vittorio Emanuele III* (Milan, 1954) pp.66, 69. He also opined (p.108) that peasants always said that they were dying of hunger but, in fact, lived well.

128. L. P. Wallace, *Leo XIII and the Rise of Socialism* (Durham, N.C., 1966) p.332.

129. W. A. Renzi, 'The Entente and the Vatican during the period of Italian Neutrality, August 1914–May 1915', *HJ*, XIII (1970) 491–508.

130. H. Ullrich, *Le elezioni del 1913 a Roma* (Milan, 1972) p.11.

131. G. De Rosa, *Il movimento cattolico in Italia* (Bari, 1970) p.174.

132. A. Sapelli, *Memorie d'Africa* (Bologna, 1935) p.75.

133. L. Ganapini, *Il nazionalismo cattolico* (Bari, 1970) p.154.

134. *CD*, XXIII, viii, p.9779, debate of 5 July 1910.

135. R. A. Webster, *Christian Democracy in Italy 1860–1960* (London, 1961) p.22; G. De Rosa, *Il movimento cattolico in Italia* pp.313, 318.

136. F. J. Coppa, 'Giolitti and the Gentiloni Pact between Myth and Reality', *CHR*, LIII (1969) 217–28.

137. G. Salvemini quoted in A. W. Salomone (ed.), *Italy from the Risorgimento to Fascism* (New York, 1970) p.487.

138. P. Togliatti, *Lectures on Fascism* (London, 1976) p.31.

139. L. Peano, *Ricordi della guerra dei trent'anni* (Florence, 1948) p.4; P. Villari, 'Dove andiamo?', *NA*, f.535 (1893) 7–8.

140. T. Antongini, *D'Annunzio* (London, 1938) p.388.

141. L. Barzini, *Peking to Paris* (London, 1972) pp.137–8.

142. For a most able sociological analysis see P. Farneti, *Sistema politico e società civile* (Turin, 1971).

143. R. Collino Pansa, *Marcello Soleri* (Cernusco sul Naviglio, 1948) pp.2–43.

144. For his own account see N. Nasi, *Memorie* (Rome, 1943).

145. M. Vaina, *Popolarismo e nasismo in Sicilia* (Florence, 1911) p.169; V. Mantegazza, *Note e ricordi* (Milan, 1910) p.96.

146. See generally G. Neppi Modona, *Sciopero, potere politico e magistratura, 1870–1922* (Bari, 1969).

2. THE MAKING OF FOREIGN POLICY

1. For example, J. M. K. Vyvyan, 'The Approach of the War of 1914', *New Cambridge Modern History* (Cambridge, 1960) vol. 12.

2. A. J. P. Taylor, *The Struggle for Mastery in Europe 1848–1918* (Oxford, 1971) p.xxiii, fn.4; S. B. Fay, *The Origins of the World War* (New York, 1929) vol.1, p.81; K. Zilliacus, *The Mirror of the Past* (London, 1944) p.79.

3. N. Kogan, *The Politics of Italian Foreign Policy* (London, 1963).

4. For example, the work in English of René Albrecht-Carrié, notably his *Italy at the Paris Peace Conference* (Hamden, Conn., 1966).

5. A. J. P. Taylor, 'Accident Prone or What Happened Next', *JMH*, 49 (1977) 5–6.

6. A. F. Pribram, *Austria-Hungary and Great Britain, 1908–1914* (London, 1951) pp.156–7; *The Secret Treaties of Austria-Hungary, 1879–1914* (London, 1920–1) vol. 1, p.12.

7.   For this whole question see, for example, J. A. Moses, *The Politics of Illusion* (St Lucia, 1975); F. Fischer, *World Power or Decline* (London, 1975).

8.   R. Romeo, *L'Italia unita e la prima guerra mondiale* (Bari, 1978) p.157.

9.   D. Mack Smith, *Victor Emanuel, Cavour and the Risorgimento* (London, 1971) p.ix. Cf. Croce's endorsement of the Libyan war: B. Croce, *Storia d'Italia dal 1971 al 1915* (Bari, 1967) p.247; *A History of Italy 1871–1915* (Oxford, 1929) p.261.

10.   For example, M. Toscano, *The Origins of the Pact of Steel* (Baltimore, 1967).

11.   M. Toscano, *Storia diplomatica della questione dell'Alto Adige* (Bari, 1967). Also available in English as *Alto Adige, South Tyrol: Italy's frontier with the German World* (Baltimore, 1967).

12.   M. Toscano, *Il Patto di Londra* (Bologna, 1934); *Gli accordi di San Giovanni di Moriana* (Milan, 1936); cf. 'Le ignorate conseguenze diplomatiche della tentata aggressione abissina', *Rassegna Italiana*, Mar 1940.

13.   For example, see P. Pastorelli, *L'Albania nella politica estera italiana 1914–1920* (Naples, 1970); G. Spadolini 'Ricordo di Mario Toscano (con una nota bio-bibliografica)' *NA*. f.504 (Oct 1968) 158–66.

14.   F. Chabod, *Storia della politica estera italiana dal 1870 al 1896* (Bari, 1965) p.7.

15.   L. Salvatorelli, *La Triplice Alleanza* (Rome, 1939).

16.   L. Albertini, *The Origins of the War of 1914* (London, 1952–7) vol. 2, pp.245, 252–3, 322.

17.   V. Castronovo, *La stampa italiana dall'Unità al fascismo* (Bari, 1973) pp.337–9.

18.   For further details on Albertini, see A. Albertini, *Venti anni di vita politica* (Bologna, 1950–1); *Epistolario 1911–1926* (Milan, 1926); A. Albertini, *Vita di Luigi Albertini* (Rome, 1945); G. Licata, *Storia del Corriere della Sera* (Milan, 1976).

19.   As usual political control was easier in the south. In 1905, 47 per cent of papers were published in the north, 31 per cent in the centre, 21 per cent in the south. Castronovo, *La stampa italiana* ... , p.161.

20.   Albertini, *Venti anni di vita politica*, vol. I, part I, pp.209–11.

21.   See the famous objection to this thesis by the editor of the rival *La Stampa* (that is the paper of Turin against Albertini in Milan). A. Frassati, *Giolitti* (Florence, 1959); cf. L. Frassati, *Un uomo, un giornale*, 2 vols (Rome, 1978).

22.   G. Carocci, 'Appunti sull'imperialismo fascista negli anni '20', *SS*, VIII (1967) 115.

23.   For the best recent summaries for these states see V. R. Berghahn, *Germany and the Approach of War in 1914* (London, 1973); Z. S. Steiner, *Britain and the Origins of the First World War* (London, 1977).

24.   J. Joll, *1914: the Unspoken Assumptions* (London, 1968). Also available in H. W. Koch (ed.), *The Origins of the First World War* (London, 1977).

25.   G. Limo, *La guerra del 190* ... (La Spezia, 1899). See generally I. F. Clarke, *Voices Prophesying War 1763–1984* (London, 1970).

26.   In English see the collection in Lyttelton, *Italian Fascisms*.

27.   A. J. P. Taylor, *Politics in Wartime and Other Essays* (London, 1964) p.66.

28.   F. Cataluccio, *La politica estera di E. Visconti Venosta* (Florence, 1940) p.25. Cataluccio, the biographer of Visconti Venosta and San Giuliano, is another diplomatic historian whose career flowered under Fascism and survived happily into the Republic.

29.   V. Mantegazza, *L'altra sponda* (Milan, 1906) p.33.

30.   R. Marvasi, *Così parlò Fabroni* (Rome, 1914).

31.   Mantegazza said it was because the King and Tittoni shared a passionate interest in automobiles. Mantegazza, *L'altra sponda*, p.40.

32.   G. Spadolini, *Giolitti e i cattolici* (Florence, 1960) pp.38–87.

33.   D. Varè, *Laughing Diplomat* (London, 1938) p.61.

34.   For further information on San Giuliano see R. J. B. Bosworth, *Italy the Least of the Great Powers* (Cambridge, 1979) *passim*.

35. See S. Sonnino, *Scritti e discorsi extraparlamentari* (Bari, 1972) vol. 2, pp.1177–211.

36. Mantegazza, *L'altra sponda*, p.26.

37. For example, note the almost total omission of comment on foreign affairs: *Dalle carte di Giovanni Giolitti: quarant' anni di politica italiana*, vol. 2, *Dieci anni al potere*, ed. G. Carocci (Milan, 1962).

38. See L. V. Ferraris, 'L'amministrazione centrale del Ministero degli Esteri italiano nel suo sviluppo storico (1848–1954)', *RSPI*, XXI (1954) 426–62, 605–63.

39. Mantegazza, *L'altra sponda*, pp.56–64.

40. V. Mantegazza, *La Turchia liberale e le questioni balcaniche* (Milan, 1908) p.xxxix–xl; M. E. Durham, *Twenty Years of Balkan Tangle* (London, n.d.) p.43.

41. L. Aldrovandi Marescotti, *Guerra diplomatica* (Milan, 1936) p.20.

42. Mantegazza, *La Turchia liberale e le questioni balcaniche*, pp.xvii, xxi.

43. R. Guariglia, *Primi passi in diplomazia* (Naples, 1972) p.10.

44. F. Loverci, 'Il primo ambasciatore italiano a Washington: Saverio Fava', *Clio*, XIII (1977) 239–76; 'Justus', *V. Macchi di Cellere all'ambasciata di Washington* (Florence, 1920). See also L. Villari, *Gli Stati Uniti d'America e l'emigrazione italiana* (Milan, 1912).

45. R. Trevelyan, *Princes under the Volcano* (New York, 1943) p.312.

46. E. Serra, *Camille Barrère e l'intesa italo-francese* (Milan, 1950).

47. R. J. B. Bosworth, 'Sir Rennell Rodd e l'Italia', *NRS*, LIV (1970) 432.

48. For a brief summary in English see J. Whittam, *The Politics of the Italian Army* (London, 1977) and in Italian, E. Forcella (ed.), *Il potere militare in Italia* (Bari, 1971). Note especially the article by G. Rochat.

49. G. Rochat and G. Massobrio, *Breve storia dell'esercito italiano dal 1861 al 1943* (Turin, 1978) p.100.

50. Italian military historians dispute the significance of the figures. See G. Rochat, 'L'esercito italiano nell' estate 1914', *NRS*, XLV (1961); G. Restifo, 'L'esercito italiano alla vigilia della grande guerra', *SS*, XI (1970); M. Mazzetti, 'Spese militari italiane e preparazione nel 1914', *Clio*, VIII (1972).

51. G. Bompiani and C. Prepositi, *Le ali della guerra* (Milan, 1931) pp.17–19, 21, 155–7.

52. R. Bachi, *L'Italia economica nell'anno 1913* (Città di Castello, 1914) p.215.

53. Forcella *Il potere militare in Italia*, p.54.

54. E. De Bono, *La guerra come e dove l'ho vista e combattuta io* (Milan, 1935) p.26.

55. Sapelli, *Memorie d'Africa*, p.1. For a less starry-eyed version, see E. De Rossi, *La vita di un ufficiale italiano sino alla guerra* (Milan, 1927).

56. For example, M. Mazzetti, *L'esercito italiano nella triplice alleanza* (Naples, 1974) p.341; L. Cadorna, *Altre pagine sulla grande guerra* (Milan, 1925) p.21.

57. Forcella *Il potere militare in Italia*, p.53.

58. E. Lussu, *Sardinian Brigade* (New York, 1970) pp.216–18.

59. E. De Bono, *Nell'esercito nostro prima della guerra* (Milan, 1931) p.135.

60. Forcella *Il potere militare in Italia*, p.55.

61. A. A. Mola, *Storia della Massoneria italiana dall'Unità alla Repubblica* (Milan, 1976) pp.285–312.

62. Mazzetti, *L'esercito italiano nella triplice alleanza*, p.274.

63. Ibid., pp.288, 342–3.

64. M. Gabriele, *Le convenzioni navali della Triplice* (Rome, 1969) pp.394–5.

65. C. Manfroni, *I nostri alleati navali* (Milan, 1927) p.14.

66. Mazzetti, *L'esercito italiano nella triplice alleanza*, p.396.

67. G. Rochat, 'La preparazione dell'esercito italiano nell'inverno 1914–15 in relazione alle informazioni disponibili sulla guerra disposizione', *Risorgimento*, XIII (1961) 10–32.

68. P. Audenino, *Cinquant'anni di stampa operaia dall'Unità alla guerra di Libia* (Lodi,

1976) p.249. *La soffitta* was first published in Rome on May Day 1911.
69. Castronovo, *La stampa italiana* . . . , pp.163–4.
70. Ibid., pp.199–202.
71. Licata, *Storia del Corriere della Sera*, pp.49–50.
72. L. Barzini, *Peking to Paris: a journey across two continents in 1907* (London, 1972).
73. L. Tosi, 'Giuseppe Antonio Borgese e la prima guerra mondiale (1914–1918)', *S.C.*, 4 (1973) 290–2.
74. AG, 19/116, 17 Feb 1914, De Martino memorandum.
75. R. Mussolini, *The Real Mussolini* (Farnborough, 1973) p.66.
76. T. Zeldin, *France 1848–1945* (Oxford, 1973–4) vol. 2, p.139.
77. E. Mercadante (ed.), *Il terremoto di Messina* (Rome, 1962) p.18.
78. T. Tittoni, *Sei anni di politica estera, 1903–9* (Rome, 1912) p.5.

3. ITALY AMONG THE POWERS, 1900–11

1. RP, 8 Sept 1902, Rodd to Cromer.
2. S. F. Romano, *Storia dei fasci siciliani* (Bari, 1959); F. Renda, *I fasci siciliani 1892–1894* (Turin, 1977).
3. U. Levra, *Il colpo di stato della borghesia* (Milan, 1975) p.84.
4. Ibid., pp.339–40.
5. Ibid., p.137.
6. CM, 13, 24 Dec 1899, San Giuliano to Martini.
7. Lady G. Cecil, *Life of Robert, Marquess of Salisbury* (London, 1932) vol. 4, pp.404–5.
8. For an account in English see the still useful G. F. H. Berkeley, *The Campaign of Adowa and the Rise of Menelik* (London, 1902; rev. ed., 1935).
9. P. G. Halpern, *The Mediterranean Naval Situation 1908–1914* (Cambridge, Mass., 1971) pp.187–8.
10. Levra, *Il colpo di stato della borghesia*, pp.40–1.
11. *Saturday Review* quoted by Glanville, *Italy's Relations with England*, p.33.
12. A. Aquarone, 'La politica coloniale italiana dopo Adua: Ferdinando Martini Governatore in Eritrea', *RSR* LXII (1975) 449–83.
13. T. Hohler, *Diplomatic Petrel* (London, 1942) p.59.
14. C. G. Segrè, *Fourth Shore* (Chicago, 1974) p.14.
15. F. Martini, *Lettere, 1860–1928* (Milan, 1934) pp.368–9.
16. H. G. Marcus, *The Life and Times of Menelik II* (Oxford, 1975).
17. LP, FO 800/132, 26 May 1903, Bertie to Lansdowne; /133, 27 Dec 1903, Bertie to Lansdowne.
18. In English see R. L. Hess, *Italian Colonialism in Somalia* (Chicago, 1966); cf. F. Grassi, *Le origini dell'imperialismo italiano: il caso Somalo 1896–1915* (Lecce, 1980).
19. A. Del Boca, *Gli italiani in Africa orientale* (Bari, 1976) p.783.
20. See R. L. Hess, 'The "Mad Mullah" and Northern Somalia', *JAH*, 5 (1964) 415–33.
21. See G. De Martino, *La Somalia nostra* (Bergamo, 1913) for an account of his stewardship.
22. Del Boca, *Gli italiani in Africa orientale*, p.828.
23. FO 371/1/42039, 13 Dec 1906, Grey to Bertie.
24. Pribram, *The Secret Treaties of Austria–Hungary*, vol. 1, pp.64–9.
25. For background see R. Ciasca, *Storia coloniale dell'Italia contemporanea* (Milan, 1938); E. Michel, *Esuli italiani in Tunisia (1815–1861)* (Milan, 1941). It is worth recalling that the mother of Ahmad, the enlightened Bey of Tunis who tried to modernise his country from 1837 to 1855, was a Sardinian peasant girl kidnapped by

Tunisian pirates in 1798. L. C. Brown, *The Tunisia of Ahmad Bey* (Princeton, 1974) p.3.

26. Its loss was constantly bewailed by Italian politicians. For example, Francesco Guicciardini, an ex-Foreign Minister, in a speech in December 1911, cited the loss of Bizerta (and Malta) as 'two arrows affixed into the heart' of Italy. F. Guicciardini, *Cento giorni alla Consulta* (Florence, 1943) p.14.

27. Foerster, *The Italian Emigration of our Times*, pp.215–16.

28. For example, see the Italian 'Additional Declaration' of 22 May 1882 pledging that the Triple Alliance would be in no case 'directed against England', Pribram, *The Secret Treaties of Austria–Hungary*, vol. 1 pp.68–9.

29. Ibid., pp.94–7.

30. In English see H. N. Gay (ed.), *Italy's Great War and her National Aspirations* (Milan, 1917).

31. D. L. Rusinow, *Italy's Austrian Heritage* (Oxford, 1969) p.26.

32. For a popular account in English of his story see A. Alexander, *The Hanging of William Oberdank* (London, 1977).

33. For a modern anthropological study of the area, drawing a number of interesting distinctions between the Italian and German zones, see J. W. Cole and E. R. Wolf, *The Hidden Frontier: ecology and ethnicity in an Alpine valley* (New York, 1974).

34. The great Triestine novelist, 'Italo Svevo', is a fine example of the complex of nationality in his city. He had at least Jewish, German, Magyar and Italian blood, and his very pseudonym means the 'Italo-Swabian' or Italo-German. For an introduction to his life and works, see P. N. Furbank, *Italo Svevo* (London, 1966).

35. R. Grew, *A Sterner Plan for Italian Unity* (Princeton, 1963) p.157.

36. G. Salvemini, *La politica estera italiana dal 1871 al 1915,* ed. A. Torre (Milan, 1970) p.345.

37. R. Monteleone, 'Iniziative e convegni socialisti italo-austriaci per la pace nel decennio prebellico', *RSS*, x (1967) 1–42.

38. B. Vigezzi, 'La neutralità italiana del luglio-agosto 1914 e il problema dell'Austria-Ungheria', *Clio*, I (1965) 84.

39. A. Vivante, *Irredentismo Adriatico* (Florence, 1912) p.1.

40. M. Alberti, *L'irredentismo senza romanticismi* (Como, 1936) p.35. For a general English summary see W. C. Askew, 'The Austro-Italian Antagonism 1896–1914', in L. P. Wallace and W. C. Askew (eds), *Power, Public Opinion and Diplomacy. Essays in Honour of Eber Malcolm Carroll* (Durham, N.C., 1959). pp.172–221.

41. F. Martini, *Diario 1914–1918*, ed. G. De Rosa (Milan, 1966).

42. F. Papafava, *Dieci anni di vita italiana (1899–1909)* (Bari, 1913) vol. 2, p.757.

43. For a summary of Austrian policies see F. R. Bridge, *From Sadowa to Sarajevo* (London, 1972).

44. N. Stone, 'Conrad von Hötzendorf, Chief of Staff in the Austro-Hungarian Army', *HT*, XIII (1963) 483.

45. R. Bachi, *L'Italia economica nell'anno 1913* (Città di Castello, 1914) p.37. The figures were (in thousands of lire):

	Imports		Exports	
	1912	1913	1912	1913
Austria–Hungary	294,479	264,120	219,191	218,839
France	289,591	280,875	222,570	230,880

46. For an English summary see Halpern *The Mediterranean Naval Situation*, pp.150–279.

47. CS, 2/16, 30 July 1914, Thaon di Revel to Salandra enclosing copy of 25 July 1913 report by Leonardi Cattolica.

48. Pribram, *The Secret Treaties of Austria-Hungary*, vol. 1, pp.150–63.

49. Ibid., pp.164–73.

50. Ibid., pp.196–201.

51. Ibid., pp.220–33.

52. Ibid., pp.232–5.

53. G. Zucconi, 'La politica italiana nel processo di riavvicinamento franco-italiano (1896–1902)', *RSPI*, XXVI (1959) 243–62; S. Romano, 'Il riavvicinamento italo-francese del 1900–1902: diplomazia e modelli di svilluppo', SC, 9 (1978). Romano gives a sane review of the huge study by P. Milza, 'Les origines du rapprochement franco-italien de 1900–1902', University of Paris thesis, 1977.

54. For French policy see C. M. Andrew, *Théophile Delcassé and the Making of the Entente Cordiale 1898–1905* (London, 1908) especially pp.82–3, 138–45.

55. He also had declared in 1899, 'For Tripoli even I would put a match to the powder barrel'. H. Wickham Steed, *Through Thirty Years* (London, 1924) vol. I, p.150.

56. E. Decleva, *Da Adua a Sarajevo* (Bari, 1971) p.112.

57. Ibid., pp.146–8.

58. Glanville, *Italy's Relations with England*, p.98.

59. BD, I, 361, 12 Mar 1902, Currie to Lansdowne. For a detailed Italian assessment which much over-emphasises the real significance of the exchange see E. Serra, *L'Intesa Mediterranea del 1902: una fase risolutiva nei rapporti italo-inglesi* (Milan, 1957).

60. Prinetti had promised: 'Italy on her part has not entered, and will not enter, into arrangements with other Powers in regard to this or other portions of the coast of the Mediterranean of a nature inimical to British interests'. *BD*, I, 360, 7 Mar 1902, Lansdowne to Currie; CP, 8181/150, 15 Mar 1902, Lansdowne to Lascelles; cf. also the diary of the British Chargé (and later ambassador) Sir James Rennell Rodd. RP, Diary, 27 Mar 1902, complained that Prinetti's exercise had aimed at putting Britain 'in the wrong'. 'This is Italian policy and it has succeeded'. Prinetti had his agreement 'for what it is worth'.

61. Serra, *Camille Barrère e l'intesa italo-francese*, pp.197–8.

62. C. J. Lowe, *Salisbury and the Mediterranean, 1886–1896* (London, 1965) pp.71–2.

63. *DDF*, 2 s, ii, 30 June 1902, Barrère to Delcassé. For an analysis of the treatying, Serra, *Camille Barrère e l'intesa italo-francese*, pp.101–65.

64. C. Masi, 'La preparazione dell'impresa libica', in T. Sillani (ed.), *La Libia in venti anni di occupazione* (Rome, 1932) p.18.

65. Decleva, *Da Adua a Sarajevo*, p.159.

66. O. Malagodi, *Conversazioni della guerra, 1914–1919* (Milan, 1960) vol. 1, p.20.

67. Decleva, *Da Adua a Sarajevo*, p.283.

68. HP, 17, 28 Oct 1909, Hardinge to Bax-Ironside; cf. C. Hardinge, *Old Diplomacy* (London, 1947) p.179.

69. For the standard account see E. N. Anderson, *The First Moroccan Crisis, 1904–1906* (Chicago, 1930).

70. CP, 8737/32, 14 Nov 1905, Egerton to Lansdowne.

71. CP, 8737/35, 24 Nov 1905, Egerton to Lansdowne; cf. DDF, 2s, ix i 236, 20 Feb 1906, Barrère to Rouvier.

72. J. Laroche, *Quinze ans a Rome avec Camille Barrère (1898–1913)* (Paris, 1948) p.197. By Jan 1908 Tittoni asked the Foreign Office to replace Egerton since 'any worthwhile relationship with this English ambassador is impossible for me'. AR, 2/103, 28 Jan 1908, Tittoni to San Giuliano.

73. FO 371/171/1655, 9 Jan 1906, Egerton to Grey.

74. S. Sonnino, *Discorsi parlamentari* (Rome, 1925) vol. 3, pp.194–5.

75. P, 209/24, 23 Feb 1906, Visconti Venosta to Guicciardini.

76. NP, FO 800/336, 26 Feb 1906, Nicolson to Grey.

77. L. Albertini, *The Origins of the War of 1914* (London, 1952–7), vol. I, p.163.

78. Anderson, *The First Moroccan Crisis*, pp.398–402.

79.   *BD*, III, 11, 20 Apr 1906, Lascelles to Grey.

80.   For example, 'XXX' 'La ripresa della Triplice e la giovane diplomazia italianà, *NA*, f.836, 16 Oct 1906, pp.666–74; Papafava, *Dieci anni di vita italiana* vol. 2, p.741.

81.   For the standard account see B. E. Schmitt, *The annexation of Bosnia 1908–9* (Cambridge, 1937).

82.   AR, 1/38, 18 Feb 1908, Tittoni to Giolitti.

83.   AR, 2/86, 12 Oct 1908, Tittoni to San Giuliano.

84.   FO 371/551/35042, 5 Oct 1908, Egerton to Grey; cf. 554/36754, 22 Oct 1908, Egerton to Grey, which earned another derisive minute: 'The Italian decision to hold a conference somewhat resembles the Servian decision to go to war.'

85.   AR, 2/101, 20 Apr 1908, Tittoni to Giolitti.

86.   N. Stone, 'Moltke–Conrad: Relations between the Austro-Hungarian and German General Staffs 1909–14', *HJ*, IX (1966) 207.

87.   AR, 2/91, 20 Dec 1908, Avarna to Tittoni.

88.   Brusati papers, 10, VI.4.36, 30 Oct 1910, Spingardi to Tedesco.

89.   HP, 16, 26 Jan 1909, Rodd to Hardinge. These ideas had been expressed by Pietro Lanza di Scalea, Under-secretary for Foreign Affairs and a great landowner in Western Sicily.

90.   Albertini, *The Origins of the War of 1914*, vol. I, pp.306–17.

91.   Fay, *The Origins of the World War*, vol. I, p.408.

92.   RP, 9 Feb 1909, Rodd to Hardinge.

93.   Decleva, *Da Adua a Sarajevo*, pp.347–8.

94.   For example, article by L. Luzzatti, *Corriere della Sera*, 1 Jan 1909.

95.   A. Aquarone, 'Politica estera e organizzazione del consenso nell'età giolittiana: il Congresso dell'Asmara e la fondazione dell'Istituto Coloniale Italiano', *SC*, 8 (1977).

96.   CM, Oct 1905, Martini report.

97.   *RC*, I, II, III, May 1906; Sept–Dec, 1906; Jan–June 1907. Cf. the account by the journal's first director, R. Paoli, *Nella colonia Eritrea* (Milan, 1908).

98.   *RC*, III, Jan–June 1907, account of the ICI meeting of 28 Apr 1907. For a brief and eulogistic history see M. Pierotti, *L'Istituto Coloniale Italiano, sue origini, suo sviluppo* (Rome, 1922).

99.   Abrate, *Ricerche per la storia* . . . , p.53; *La lotta sindacale* . . . , pp.41,49.

100.   *RC*, VI, Jan–June 1909; 'XXX', La federazione dell' italianità, *NA*, f.885, 1 Nov 1908.

101.   AR, 1/64, 2 Nov 1908, Tittoni to San Giuliano.

102.   Pribram, *The Secret Treaties of Austria-Hungary*, vol. I, pp.240–3.

103.   F. Stieve, *Isvolsky and the World War* (London, 1906) p.79.

104.   For example, F. S. Nitti, *Peaceless Europe* (London, 1922) pp.82–3.

105.   Malagodi, *Conversazioni della guerra*, vol. I, p.86.

106.   The Italian case thus provides another upside-down version, for example of A. J. Mayer's views about the reality behind the Versailles peacemaking. See A. J. Mayer, *Politics and Diplomacy of Peacemaking* (London, 1968); *Wilson versus Lenin* (New Haven, 1959).

107.   R. Mori, 'La penetrazione pacifica italiana in Libia dal 1907 al 1911', *RSPI*, XXIV (1957) 102–18.

108.   *CD*, XXIII, ix, pp.10079–89, 10164–6, 10170–80.

109.   AR, 5/180, 3 Apr 1910, San Giuliano to Pansa.

110.   P, 128/17, 2 Dec 1910, San Giuliano to Mayor.

111.   Decleva, *Da Adua a Sarajevo*, p.399.

112.   P. Foscari, *Per l'Italia più grande* (Rome, 1928) p.96. For Italian public opinion see F. Malgeri, *La guerra libica, (1911–1912)* (Rome, 1970); P. Maltese, *La*

terra premessa (Milan, 1960).

113. G. Volpe, *L'impresa di Tripoli* (Rome, 1946) p.44.

114. R. J. B. Bosworth, 'The Opening of the Victor Emmanuel Monument', *IQ*, XVIII (1975) 78–87.

115. For example, P, 128/17, 7 Dec 1910, San Giuliano to Mayor.

116. *CD*, XXIII, xiii, pp.15348–56.

117. For his account see G. De Martino, 'Ricordi di carriera: la mia missione a Costantinopoli per la guerra di Libia', *Rassegna di politica internazionale*, IV (1937).

118. C. Galli. *Diarii e lettere* (Florence, 1951) pp.45–6.

119. For example, *Dalle carte di Giovanni Giolitti: quarant'anni di politica italiana*, vol. 3, ed. C. Pavone (Milan, 1962) pp.52–60.

120. C. De Biase, *L'Aquila d'oro: storia dello Stato Maggiore Italiano (1861–1945)* (Milan, 1970) p.228. For Moneta see his *Le guerre, le insurrezioni e la pace nel secolo decimonono*, 2 vols (Milan, 1905).

121. For socialism and the war see M. Degl'Innocenti, *Il socialismo italiano e la guerra di Libia* (Rome, 1976).

122. Malgeri, *La guerra libica*, pp.127–8.

123. P, 13/1/1, 16, 19 Sept 1911, De Martino to San Giuliano.

124. For the standard account of the Second Moroccan crisis, see I. C. Barlow, *The Agadir Crisis* (Durham, N.C., 1940).

125. FO 371/1250/29707, 28 July 1911, Grey to Rodd; cf. *Dalle carte di Giovanni Giolitti*, vol. 3, pp.52–6.

126. CG, 22/59, C/2, 13 Sept 1911, San Giuliano memorandum.

127. Malgeri, *La guerra libica*, p.139.

128. W. C. Askew, *Europe and Italy's Acquisition of Libya, 1911–12* (Durham, N.C., 1942) p.52.

129. Malgeri, *La guerra libica*, pp.155–60.

130. R. Michels, *L'imperialismo italiano: studi politico-demografici* (Milan, 1914) p.138; cf. his *Political Parties* (New York, 1962).

4. THE ITALIAN PEOPLE AND FOREIGN POLICY

1. E. Vercesi, *Il Vaticano, l'Italia e la guerra* (Milan, 1925) pp.262–9.

2. E. J. Leed, *No Man's Land* (Cambridge, 1979) p.50.

3. In English, a new but limited study is available, A. J. De Grand, *The Italian Nationalist Association and the Rise of Fascism in Italy* (Lincoln, 1978).

4. L. Federzoni, *Paradossi di ieri* (Milan, 1926) pp.11–12.

5. A. J. De Grand, 'The Italian Nationalist Association in the period of Italian Neutrality August 1914–May 1915', *JMH*, 43 (1971) 407.

6. F. Gaeta (ed.), *La stampa nazionalista* (Rocca San Casciano, 1965) p.7.

7. R. Molinelli, 'Per una storia del nazionalismo italiano', *RSR*, L (1963) 400.

8. M. Isnenghi, *Il mito della grande guerra*, (Bari, 1973) p.88.

9. G. Carocci, *Giolitti e l'età giolittiana* (Turin, 1961) p.152.

10. In N. Tranfaglia (ed.), *L'Italia unita nella storiografia del secondo dopoguerra* (Milan, 1980); cf. the chapters of Asor Rosa who does begin the attempt and Furio Diaz who does not.

11. In L. De Maria, *Marinetti e il futurismo* (Milan, 1977) p.323.

12. F. Tamagna, *Italy's Interests and Policies in the Far East* (New York, 1941) p.5.

13. E. Dobie, *Malta's Road to Independence* (Norman, Oklahoma, 1967) pp.60–72.

14. U. Alfassio Grimaldi, *Il re'buono'* (Milan, 1970) p.89.

15. L. Ganapini, *Il nazionalismo cattolico* (Bari, 1970) pp.172–3.

16. B. Lai, *Finanze e finanzieri vaticani fra l'ottocento e il novecento da Pio IX a Benedetto XV: atti e documenti* (Milan, 1979) p.163.

17. B. Lai, *Finanze e finanzien tra l'oltocento e il novecento da Pio IX a Benedetto XV* (Milan 1979) pp.284–8.

18. Ibid., p.237.

19. L. Bissolati, *La politica estera dell'Italia dal 1897 al 1920* (Milan, 1923) p.20.

20. Degl'Innocenti, *Il socialismo italiano e la guerra di Libia*, p.297.

21. For a staunch statement of this purity see L. Valiani, *Il partito socialista italiano nel periodo della neutralità 1914–1915* (rev. ed. Milan, 1977).

22. E.g. for background in English see R. Hostetter, *The Italian socialist movement*, (Princeton, 1958) vol. 1; 'The "evangelical" socialism of Camillo Prampolini', *IQ*, XVIII (1975).

23. A. Kuliscioff, *Lettere d'amore a Andrea Costa 1880–1909* (Milan, 1976) p.325.

24. Levra, *Il colpo di stato della borghesia*, p.192.

25. G. Arfé, *Storia del socialismo italiano (1892–1926)* (Turin, 1965) p.35.

26. In English see e.g. G. Procacci, 'The Italian Worker's Movement in the Liberal Era', in R. J. B Bosworth and G. Cresciani (eds), *Altro polo, a volume of Italian studies* (Sydney, 1979) pp.53–70.

27. Levra, *Il colpo di stato della borghesia*, p.43.

28. S. Merli, 'La classe operaia di fabbrica verso la fine del secolo XIX', in G. Mori (ed.), *L'industrializzazione in Italia, 1861–1900* (Bologna, 1977) p.101.

29. M. Marmo, *Il proletariato industriale a Napoli in età liberale (1880–1914)* (Naples, 1978) p.27.

30. Ibid., p.484.

31. F. Squarzina, 'Proprietà e organizzazione del lavoro nelle zolfare siciliane', in Mori *L'industrializzazione in Italia*, p.292.

32. E. Sereni, *Il capitalismo nelle campagne (1860–1900)* (rev. edn Turin, 1968) p.167.

33. A. Leonetti, *Da Andria contadina a Torino operaia* (Urbino, 1974) p.10. Sereni, *Il capitalismo nelle campagne* p.172 ironically compared peasant housing on aristocratic estates around Rome to that of Ethiopian tribesmen.

34. Leonetti, *Da Andria contadina a Torino operaia*, p.28.

35. E. Ragionieri, *Un comune socialista: Sesto Fiorentino* (Rome, 1976) p.37.

36. Ibid., p.107.

37. Ibid., p.145.

38. See record O. Profazio (ed.), *L'Altra Spolete* (Turin, 1975).

39. C. E. Schorske, *German Social Democracy 1905–1917* (New York, 1972) p.77.

40. O. Jászi, *The Dissolution of the Habsburg Monarchy* (Chicago, 1966) pp.181–2.

41. See generally G. Cresciani, *Fascismo, antifascismo e gli italiani in Australia, 1922–1945* (Rome, 1979).

42. Farneti, *Sistema politico e società civile* pp.237–8, 328–9.

43. A. Davidson, *Antonio Gramsci: towards an intellectual biography* (London, 1977) pp.1, 22.

44. Cited Bosworth, 'The Messina earthquake of 28 December 1908', p.199. Cf. F. Grassi, *Il tramonto dell'età giolittiana nel Salento* (Bari, 1973) p.251.

45. Grassi, *Il tramonto dell'età giolittiana nel Salento*, p.9.

46. A. Labriola, *La guerra di Libia e l'opinione socialista* (Naples, 1912) pp.8, 25.

47. Roberts, *The Syndicalist Tradition and Italian Fascism*, p.80.

48. Ibid., p.103.

49. F. Turati, 'Militaristi senza saperlo', *Critica Sociale*, XIX (1 May 1909) pp.129–31.

50. Cf. M. Giovi, 'La politica militare ed estera italiana', *Critica Sociale*, XIX (16 July–1 Aug 1909) 223–6.

51. Rochat and Massobrio, *Breve storia dell' esercito italiano*, pp.134–5; cf. E. Santarelli, *Fascismo e neofascismo* (Rome, 1974) p.57.

52. B. Vigezzi, *Giolitti e Turati: un incontro mancato* (Milan, 1926) vol. I, p.461.

53. E. Amendola Kühn, *Vita con Giovanni Amendola* (Florence, 1960) pp.295–7, 300–2.

54. B. Vigezzi, 'Politica estera e opinione pubblica in Italia dal 1870 al 1945', *NRS*, LXIII (1979) 553. Vigezzi draws attention to the book by P. Arcari, *La coscienza nazionale in Italia* (Milan, 1911) where much similar evidence can be found.

55. A. Bordiga, *Scritti scelti* (Milan, 1975) p.60. Earlier Bordiga (p.57) had been 'against all wars, in defence of the proletariat which in a [war] has everything to lose, nothing to gain, nothing to save'.

56. B. Vigezzi, 'Italian Socialism and the First World War: Mussolini, Lazzari and Turati', *JIH*, 2 (1979) 241. Cf. C. Pinzani, 'I socialisti italiani e francesi nel periodo della neutralità italiana', *SS*, XV (1974) 364–99.

57. Bordiga, *Scritti scelti*, pp.55–6.

58. B. Vigezzi, 'Italian Socialism and the First World War', p.241.

59. See F. Molfese, *Storia del brigantaggio dopo l'Unità* (Milan, 1964).

60. A. Bravo, 'Donne contadine e prima guerra mondiale', *Società e Storia*, III (1980) 850.

61. N. Tranfaglia, 'Politica e Magistratura nell'Italia liberale', *Studi Storici*, XI 3 (1970) 525.

62. Rochat and Massobrio, *Breve storia dell'esercito italiano*, pp.131-2.

63. G. Amendola, *Un isola* (Milan, 1980) p.131.

64. G. Sabbatucci, *I combattenti nel primo dopoguerra* (Bari, 1974) pp.3–5.

65. See, now available in English, G. Ledda, *Padre padrone* (London, 1979).

66. E. Lussu, *Il cinghiale del diavolo* (Turin, 1976) p.13.

67. F. S. Nitti, *Scritti politici*, vol. 3, Part ii (Bari, 1966) p.383.

68. Manzotti, *La polemica sull'emigrazione nell'Italia unita*, pp. 170–1.

69. Papafava, *Dieci anni di vita italiana*, vol. 1, p.29.

70. E. Corradini, *Il Nazionalismo italiano* (Milan, 1914) pp.53–4, 58–9.

71. F. Coletti, 'Dell'emigrazione italiana', in Blaserna, *Cinquanta anni di storia italiana*, vol. 3, p.81.

72. L. Avagliano (ed.), *L'emigrazione italiana: testi e documenti* (Naples, 1976) p.8.

73. B. Boyd Cairoli, *Italian Repatriation from the United States* (New York, 1973) p.v.

74. Ibid., p.56.

75. G. Cresciani, 'Italian Immigrants in Australia, 1900–22', *Labor History*, 42 (1982).

76. Amendola, *Un isola*, p.231.

77. Jones, *Destination America*, p.131.

78. For Italy's tardy diplomatic reaction see Loverci, 'Il primo ambasciatore italiano a Washington', pp.254–7.

79. T. Vertone, 'Antecedents et causes des evenements d'Aigues-Mortes', in Avagliano, *L'emigrazione italiana*, p.258; J-B, Duroselle and E. Serra (eds), *L'emigrazione italiana in Francia prima del 1914* (Milan, 1978) pp.107-37.

80. Viz. the sarcasm of Villari, *Gli Stati Uniti d'America e l'emigrazione italiana*, p.282; R. Murri, 'Impressioni d'America', *NA*, f.985, 1 Jan 1913, p.86.

81. P. Levi, *Missione nell'Africa settentrionale, giugno–luglio 1908* (Rome, 1908) pp.167–9.

82. Roberts, *The Syndicalist Tradition and Italian Fascism*, p.108.

83. R. Murri, 'Gl'Italiani nell'America latina-impressioni di viaggio', *NA*, f.991, 1 Apr 1913, p.437.

84. G. M. Cherchi, *Togliatti a Sassari 1908–1911* (Rome, 1972) pp.46,127.

5. ITALY AND THE LAST YEARS OF PEACE, 1911–14

1.   Stieve, *Isvolsky and the World War*, p.37.
2.   P, 132/17, 26 Nov 1911, Nobili to San Giuliano.
3.   R. G. Vansittart, *The Mist Procession* (London, 1958) p.100.
4.   For a general review of Italy's position in Turkey see R. J. B. Bosworth, 'Italy and the End of the Ottoman Empire', in M. Kent (ed.), *The Great Powers and the Dissolution of the Ottoman Empire* (forthcoming).
5.   R. Esher, *Journal and Letters* (London, 1934–8) vol. 2, p.94.
6.   C. F. Abbott, *The Holy War in Tripoli* (London, 1912) p.115.
7.   CG, 20/47, 8 Oct 1911, San Giuliano to Giolitti.
8.   For a review of the incident see E. C. Thaden. 'Charykov and Russian Foreign Policy at Constantinople', *JCEA*, XVI (1956–7) 25–44
9.   For a review of the affair and the general state of Franco-Italian relations see Decleva, *Da Adua a Sarajevo*.
10. For the incident, see R. J. B. Bosworth, 'Britain and Italy's Acquisition of the Dodecanese, 1912–1915', *HJ*, XIII (1970).
11. CG, 22/59 C/5, 29 June 1912, Pollio pro-memoria.
12. For an example, see Bosworth, 'The Messina Earthquake of 28 December 1908'.
13. See A. Theodoli, *A cavallo di due secoli* (Rome, 1950) pp.59–67.
14. For an introductory biography see S. Romano, *Giuseppe Volpi* (Milan, 1979).
15. G. Ciano, *Ciano's Diary, 1937–1938* ed. A. Mayor (London, 1952) p.129.
16. CG, 18/43/9 13 May 1912, Giolitti to Volpi.
17. Albertini, *Epistolario, 1911–1926*, vol. 1, pp.139–40.
18. Senate, XIII, xiii, debate of 26 Nov 1912.
19. Romano, *Giuseppe Volpi*, p.48.
20. Seton-Watson, *Italy from Liberalism to Fascism*, p.391, fn. 2.
21. E. Grey, *Twenty-five Years, 1892–1916* (London, 1925) vol. 1, p.263.
22. Nitti, *Peaceless Europe*, vol. 3, p.386; S. Sonnino, *Discorsi parlamentari*, vol. 3, p.429; F. Guicciardini, 'Serbia e Grecia in Albania', *NA*, f.984, 16 Dec 1912, p.652.
23. E.g. C. Zoli, *La guerra turco-bulgara* (Milan, 1913) p.13.
24. AG, 28/364, 15 Apr 1913, Giolitti to San Giuliano.
25. R. Graziani, *Ho difeso la patria* (Cernusco sul Naviglio, 1948) p.14.
26. A. Del Boca, *Gli italiani in Africa orientale: dall'unità alla marcia su Roma* (Bari, 1976) pp.757–8.
27. AG, 4/30 bis, 29 July 1911, Torretta memorandum.
28. G. Piazza, *Alla corte di Menelik: lettere dall'Etiopia* (Ancona, 1912) p.140.
29. P, 754/1145, 18 Jan 1914, Ministry of Colonies to San Giuliano.
30. CS, 8/63, 11 June 1914, San Giuliano to Salandra.
31. T. Tittoni, *Italy's Foreign and Colonial Policy*, ed. B. Quaranta di San Severino (London, 1915) p.114.
32. AG, 13/81, 17 Dec 1913, San Giuliano to Giolitti.
33. Corradini, *Discorsi politici (1902–1924)* pp.170, 176.
34. *DGP*, 37, ii, 15053, 8 July 1913, Jagow to Flotow.
35. AG, 17/106, 11 Jan 1914, San Giuliano to his major ambassadors.
36. D. McLean, 'British Finance and Foreign Policy in Turkey: the Smyrna-Aidin railway settlement 1913–14', *HJ*, XIX (1976) p.527.
37. Romano, *Giuseppe Volpi*, p.58.
38. The best introduction to Albania in this period remains S. Skendi, *The Albanian National Awakening 1878–1912* (Princeton, 1969).
39. E.g. A. I. Sulliotti, *In Albania: sei mesi di regno da Guglielmo di Wied a Essad Pascià*

(Milan, 1914) p.149.

40. Guicciardini thought that it really should be regarded as 'an Italian port'. F. Guicciardini, 'Impressioni d'Albania', *NA*, f.708, 16 June 1901, p.27.

41. E. Maserati, 'L'Albania nella politica estera italiana degli anni 1896–1901', *Clio*, XIII (1977) 75–6.

42. Martini, *Diario*, p.90.

43. HP, 93, 25 Feb 1914, Hardinge to Nicolson.

44. A. Torre, 'Italia e Albania durante le guerre balcaniche', *Rivista d'Albania*, f.II–III–IV (1940) 175.

45. Sulliotti, *In Albania*, p.69.

46. Maserati, 'L'Albania nella politica estera italiana', p.64.

47. AG, 15/94 bis, 4 Apr 1913, San Giuliano to Giolitti; 19/117 bis, 30 Apr 1914, De Martino pro-memoria.

48. PCG, 9/2, 11 Oct 1913, San Giuliano to Giolitti.

49. CM, 13, 20 May 1914, Scarfoglio to Martini.

50. For narrative of one splendid example see R. J. B. Bosworth, 'The Albanian forests of Signor Giacomo Vismara: a case study of Italian economic imperialism during the Foreign Ministry of Antonino Di San Giuliano', *HJ*, XVIII (1975) 571–86.

51. Mantegazza, *L'altra sponda*, p.308.

52. P, 675/844, 3 Aug 1913, P. Levi memorandum; *DGP*, 36, ii, 14432, 4 Apr 1914, Flotow to Bethmann Hollweg.

53. AG, 27/314, 6 Apr 1913, Giolitti to San Giuliano.

54. M. Mazzetti, 'L'Italia e la crisi albanese del marzo-maggio 1913', *SC*, iv (1973) 247–8, 251–3.

55. CS, 2/16, 27 Mar 1914, Thaon di Revel to Salandra.

56. For a narrative see G. Andrè, *L'Italia e il Mediterraneo alla vigilia della prima guerra mondiale* (Milan, 1967) vol. 1.

57. F. Fischer, *War of Illusions* (London, 1975) p.407.

58. See San Giuliano's famous despatch, *DDI*, 4 s, xii, 225, 14 July 1914, San Giuliano to Bollati.

6. ITALY AND THE GREAT WAR

1. Albertini, *The Origins of the War of 1914*, vol. 3, pp.328–31.

2. R. Pryce, 'Italy and the Outbreak of the First World War', *CHJ*, XI (1954) 224.

3. K. H. Jarausch, *The Enigmatic Chancellor: Bethmann Hollweg and the hubris of Imperial Germany* (New Haven, 1973) pp.160–1. In Budapest, Tisza was for a time alarmed by the prospect of a war against Serbia, but he expressed more concern about finding Romania on the other side than about Italy. N. Stone, 'Hungary and the Crisis of July 1914', *JCH*, 1 (1966) 163–5, 168.

4. For a much detailed analysis of these months see Bosworth, *Italy, the Least of the Great Powers*, pp.377–417.

5. Martini, *Diario*, p.185.

6. B. Vigezzi, *Da Giolitti a Salandra* (Florence, 1969) p.84.

7. Malagodi, *Conversazioni della guerra 1914–1919*, vol. 1, p.27.

8. Martini, *Diario*, pp.16–31, 53–4, 126; Albertini, *Epistolario*, vol. 1, pp.256–8.

9. S. Scaroni, *Con Vittorio Emanuele III*, p.27; N. Bolla, *Il segreto di due re* (Milan, 1951) p.197.

10. CS, 2/16, 1 Aug 1914, Thaon di Revel to Salandra.

11. L. Cadorna, *Lettere famigliari*, ed. R. Cadorna (Milan, 1967) p.102.

12. A. Salandra, *Italy and the Great War* (London, 1932); Martini, *Diario*, p.320.

13. Marcus, *The Life and Times of Menelik II*, pp.265–6.

14. Rochat and Massobrio, *Breve storia dell'esercito italiano*, pp.158–9.

15. Martini, *Diario*, pp.399–400; on 4 May he added that folly was succeeding folly there and that the situation was very grave.

16. J. Whittam, 'War and Italian society 1914–1916', in B. Bond and I. Roy (eds), *War and Society* (London, 1975) p.153.

17. E.g. the usually Italophile British military attaché, Delmé-Radcliffe, warned against expecting too much. NP, F0 800/377, 29 Mar 1915, Nicolson to Grey.

18. P. Pieri, *L'Italia nella prima guerra mondiale (1915–1918)* (Turin, 1965) p.67.

19. A. Salandra, *La neutralità italiana (1914): ricordi e pensieri* (Milan, 1928) p.348.

20. B. Vigezzi, 'Le "radiose giornate" del maggio 1915 nei rapporti dei prefetti', *NRS*, XLIV (1960) 110.

21. The Naval leadership preserved its ancient suspicions of France (and Greece), but, dependent as it was on British coal, did not demur from the Army's view that Italy could only join the Entente side. See e.g. SP, 51:3, Dec 1914, Thaon di Revel to Sonnino; Martini, *Diario*, p.21.

22. B. Vigezzi, 'L'imperialismo e il suo ruolo nella storia italiana del primo '900', *SC*, II (1980) 52–4.

23. Mori, 'Le guerre parallele, p.316.

24. E. Conti, *Dal taccuino di un borghese* (Cremona, 1946) p.100.

25. Castronovo, *Giovanni Agnelli*, pp.58–9.

26. Abrate, *Ricerche per la storia . . .* , pp.151–2, 154.

27. Sori, *L'emigrazione italiana . . .* , pp.401–2.

28. E.g. E. M. Gray *The Bloodless War* (New York, 1916) pp.56–7.

29. See Vigezzi, *Da Giolitti a Salandra*, pp.203–62.

30. Gray, *The Bloodless War*, pp.167–8 described this pioneer of Italian imperialism as 'the wrecker of the Treaty of Ouchy . . . the man who ought to be regarded in Italy as an undesirable alien'.

31. Abrate, *La lotta sindacale . . .* , pp.153–4, 160–3.

32. M. Degl'Innocenti, *Storia della cooperazione in Italia* (Rome, 1977) pp.303–5.

33. 28 Jan 1915, Albertini to De Roberto in Albertini, *Epistolario*, vol. 1, no. 277.

34. See generally B. Vigezzi, 'L'opinione pubblica italiana e la Francia nell'estate 1914', *NRS*, LIX (1975).

35. Isnenghi, *Il mito della grande guerra*, p.86.

36. Ibid., p.97.

37. A. J. Rhodes, *The Poet as Superman* (London, 1959) p.140.

38. J. Joll, *Intellectuals in Politics: three biographical essays* (London, 1960) p.162.

39. The most extraordinary example always remains A. J. Gregor, *Italian Fascism and Developmental Dictatorship* (Princeton, 1979).

40. Cited by R. N. Stromberg. 'The Intellectuals and the Coming of War in 1914', *JES*, 3 (1973) 111.

41. G. M. Trevelyan, *Scenes from Italy's War* (London, 1919) p.1.

42. E.g. see Leed, *No Man's Land*, R. Wohl, *The Generation of 1914* (London, 1980).

43. Vigezzi, *Da Giolitti a Salandra*, p.58.

44. E.g. Grey minute on FO 371/2375/14043, 5 Feb 1915, Rodd to Grey.

45. E.g. final examples in Malagodi, *Conversazioni della guerra*, vol. 1, pp.22–4.

46. N. Stone, *The Eastern Front 1914–1917* (London, 1975) p.127.

47. Taylor, *The First World War*, p.90.

48. E.g. FO 371/2375/7338, 14 Jan 1915, Rodd to Grey; 32154, 13 Mar 1915, Rodd to Grey.

49. E.g. FO 371/2508/46726, 19 Apr 1915, Grey to Nicolson appealing to Sazonov that the 'moral effect' of Italian entry would be very great; GP, FO 800/108, 26 Apr 1915, Lansdowne to Grey, in which Lansdowne recalled also how justified

Salisbury had been in labelling the Italians as 'sturdy beggars'.

50.   H. H. Asquith, *Memories and Reflections 1852-1927* (London, 1928) vol. 2, p.72. Grey had just advised Asquith that: 'the Italians . . . are slightly contracting the orifice of their gullet' (p.69); cf. Sir Thomas Bertie in Paris who pronounced: 'Italy has irrevocably undertaken to confirm her charms on her suitors, but it is still like Romeo and Juliet with, however, no *precise* answer to "à quelle heure, en quel lieu".' *The Diary of Lord Bertie of Thame*, ed. Lady A. Gordon Lennox (London, 1924) vol. 1, p.161. Bertie and Grey's metaphors are characteristic and illuminating.

51.   HP, 93, 25 May 1915, Hardinge to Nicolson. Hardinge predicted that, militarily, Italy would not 'be of much assistance since the Austrian frontier is so very strongly fortified that the Austrians will be able to hold the Italian armies with a comparatively small force'.

52.   Vercesi, *Il Vaticano, l'Italia e la guerra*, p.19.

53.   For the detail see A. Monticone, *La Germania e la neutralità italiana: 1914-1915* (Bologna, 1971).

54.   Ibid., p.85. Cf. also Rodd's clear-sighted appraisal that for all Bülow's desire to turn up trumps, he could not do more than prolong Italian neutrality. FO 371/2009/82546, 5 Dec 1914, Rodd to Grey.

55.   See G. E. Silberstein, *The Troubled Alliance: German Austrian Relations 1914 to 1917* (Lexington, Kentucky, 1970).

56.   E.g. FO 371/2374/4032, 11 Jan 1915, Buchanan to Grey in which Sazonov expressed his fear that 'Italy aims at taking Austria's place in the Balkans and at forming a Block of Balkan States in an anti-Slav sense'.

57.   Serra, *Camille Barrère e l'intesa italo-francese*, pp. 297-336.

58.   The most famous recipient of their money being Mussolini. See W. A. Renzi, 'Mussolini's Sources of Financial Support, 1914-1915', *History*, 56 (1971).

59.   E.g. *DDI*, 5s, 201, 11 Aug 1914, San Giuliano to Imperiali.

60.   Ibid., 726, 17 Sept 1914, San Giuliano to Imperiali.

61.   See G. E. Torrey, 'The Rumanian-Italian Agreement of 23 September 1914', *SEER*, XLIV (1966).

62.   Malagodi, *Conversazioni della guerra*, vol. 1, p.22.

63.   P. Bertolini, 'Diario (agosto 1914-maggio 1915)', *NA*, f.1221, 1 Feb 1923, pp.214-9, gives examples of his line of 'neutralism until absolutely necessary'; V. E. Orlando, *Memorie 1915-1919*, ed. R. Mosca (Milan, 1960) p.28.

64.   See L. Valiani, 'Italian-Austro-Hungarian negotiations, 1914-1915', *JCH*, 1 (1966) for details.

65.   The list of terms was formally conveyed to London on 4 March. FO 371/2507/28275, 4 Mar 1915, Imperiali to Grey.

66.   E.g. Seton-Watson, *Italy from Liberalism to Fascism*, p.430.

67.   It is notable that when the Dardanelles expedition was under discussion in London, Grey did raise the countering prospect of action in the Adriatic. Little interest was displayed on the effect this might have on Italy, and Churchill's confidence and rhetoric carried the day for action more in keeping with an imperial policy.

68.   E.g. FO 371/2379/171650, 15 Nov 1915, Beaumont to Grey reporting sadly that Sonnino was still anxious to delay a declaration of war against Germany. Salandra had already bewailed the way in which the Entente interpreted the letter of agreements, SP, 52, 5 July 1915, Salandra to Imperiali. It is significant that in explaining the need for an Italian alliance in March 1915, Asquith said to King George V that the Italians must 'agree to bring all their forces into common stock against all our enemies (including Germany)', AP, vol. 8, 23 Mar 1915, Asquith to King George V.

69.   G. E. Torrey, 'Rumania and the Belligerents 1914-1916', *JCH*, 1 (1966)

pp.180–3. De Martino had also anxiously suggested the preservation of the wire to Bucharest. SP, 47, 1, 27 Jan 1915, De Martino to Sonnino.

70. E.g. FO 371/2379/136788, 15 Sept 1915, Delmé-Radcliffe to D.M.O. reporting that Italy needed at once to double her current loan in order to make her army effective.

71. G. Giolitti, *Discorsi extraparlamentari* (Turin, 1952) p.262.

72. A. Solmi, 'Carteggio tra Salandra e Sonnino nella prima fase della neutralità italiana', *NA*, f.1510, 16 Feb 1935, p.487.

73. See C. De Biase, *La rivelazione di Giolitti del dicembre 1914* (Modena, 1960).

74. For a (hostile) analysis in English of this stage of the negotiations, see W. W. Gottlieb, *Studies in Secret Diplomacy During the First World War* (London, 1957).

75. A. Monticone, *Nitti e la Grande Guerra* (Milan, 1961) pp.7–14.

76. See B. Vigezzi, 'Le radiose giornate del maggio 1915 nei rapporti dei prefetti', *NRS*, 43–4 (1959–60).

77. Rhodes, *The Poet as Superman*, p.147.

78. J. R. Rodd, *Social and Diplomatic Memories 1902–1919* (London, 1925) vol. 3, p.253.

79. Trevelyan papers, Trinity College Library, Cambridge, AD MS C/44/102, 21 May 1915, G. M. Trevelyan to H. Jackson (Regius Professor of Greek).

80. A. Fogazzaro, *Malombra*, trans. T. Fisher (London, 1896).

81. C. Sforza, *L'Italia dal 1914 al 1944* (Milan, 1944) p.13.

82. A. Gramsci, *Selections from Political Writings (1910–1920)*, ed. Q. Hoare (London, 1977) pp.6–9.

Index

Galli, Carlo   72.
Garibaldi, Giuseppe   2–3, 34,
  42, 58, 84, 88, 92, 97, 113,
  128, 137.
Garroni, Camillo   40, 72, 105.
Geiss, Imanuel   32.
Genoa   19, 40, 106, 137.
Gente Del Mare   19.
Gentiloni Pact   23.
Geographical Society   48.
Germany   9, 12, 30–2, 60, 77,
  87–8, 139. Algeciras   65. Asia
  Minor   111–2. Attitude to
  Italy   2–3. Balkan wars   108,
  117–8. Commerce   14–9.
  Intervento   124–6, 128, 130–2,
  134, 137. Italian attitude
  to   8, 23, 40, 49, 68, 92–3.
  July crisis and   32, 78, 121–4.
  Libyan war   73, 99–100, 102,
  104. Military policy   42, 45,
  52, 66, 118–9. Triple
  Alliance   54–8, 60, 62, 69,
  118–20.
Gerschenkron, Alexander   15.
Ginori Ceramic Works   86–7.
Giolitti, Giovanni
  Algeciras   63, 65. Army   41–
  2, 44–5. Asia Minor   40, 117.
  Balkan wars   109, 111–2, 117.
  Giolittian 'system'   10, 14–5,
  18, 22–7, 32–4, 37, 40, 44, 47,
  67, 80, 82, 84, 86, 90, 107,
  138, 140. *Intervento*   36, 46,
  49, 70, 123, 125–6, 131, 133,
  135–8. July crisis   31, 37,
  122–3. Libyan war   1, 45, 70,
  72–6, 101–7. Prime
  Minister   1, 13, 16, 18–9, 23–
  7, 29, 31–3, 36–7, 46–7, 52,
  89, 91, 94, 97, 106.
  Prinetti   61.
Giornale D'Italia   47.
Gramsci, Antonio   5, 14, 49, 81,
  84, 89, 128, 140.
Grandi, Domenico   44.
Great Britain   8–10, 12, 15,
  36–7, 77, 87–8, 95.

Algeciras   63, 65. Asia
Minor   112. Attitude to
Italy   2–7, 39–40, 67. Balkan
wars   ,108, 115. Bosnia-
Herzegovina   65–6, 68–9.
Commerce with,   17, 55, 126.
Ethiopia   53–4. *Intervento*
123, 127, 132–4, 137. Italian
attitude to   23–4, 32, 68, 93,
123. July crisis,   119. Libyan
war   73–4, 100–1. Military
policy   8, 51–2.
Rapprochement with
Italy   60–2.
Greece   10, 109, 112, 114–5,
  117, 130, 139.
Grey, Edward   74, 108, 129,
  132.
Guicciardini, Francesco   63,
  70–2, 108, 116.

Hague Peace Conference   22.
Hardinge, Charles   62.
Hindenburg, Paul von   41.
Hobsbawn, Eric   12.
Hohenlohe Decrees   119.

Ibrahim Pasha   70–1.
L'Idea Nazionale   71, 78, 109.
Ilva   17.
Imbriani-Poerio, Matteo   42, 56.
Imola   84.
Imperial, Guglielmo   38, 60,
  108, 114, 132.
Industrialisation of Italy   8,
  15–8, 40, 84.
Irredentism   35, 56–7.
Istituto Coloniale Italiano   48,
  68, 70–1, 109.
Istituto per gli studi di politica
  internazionale   31.
Istria   125, 133–4.
Izvolsky, Alexander
  Petrovich   65–6, 69, 99.

Joel, Otto   16, 126.
Joll, James   32–3.

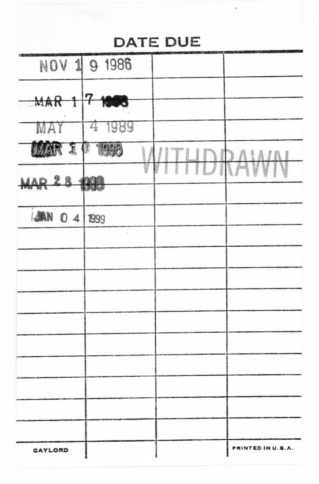